TRAPPED IN PARADISE

Catholic Nuns in the South Pacific 1940 – 1943

A Journal Written by Sister Hedda Jaeger, CSJ, RN
Territory of New Guinea

With a Sequel Written by Father Joseph Lamarre, S.M.

Editors:

Eileen McNerney, CSJ
Maureen McNerney Habel

DOCKSIDE SAILING PRESS®

Newport Beach, California

Newport Beach, California
www.docksidesailingpress.com
2

This book is dedicated to Catholic nuns throughout the world who have put their own lives at risk to relieve the sufferings of others

෩ ෩ ෩

Sister Eileen McKenney, csj

CONTENTS

INTRODUCTION

*T*his journal, written by Sister Hedda Jaeger in the first years of World War II, sat in the archives of the Sisters of St. Joseph of Orange for quite a long time.[1] It wasn't hidden under lock and key, it's just that no one seemed particularly interested in what happened so many years ago. When I asked one of the oldest sisters in our congregation why she thought these valuable and historic words were all but buried in dusty old files, she responded, "I think that everyone was just tired of the war when it was over. People just wanted to move forward at that time and put the past behind." Another sister added, "Well, as Catholic nuns in a congregation of equals, no one of us is supposed to stand out as having any more recognition than the next one. We all knew about their rescue and their pictures had been in the paper. When they returned during the war, it wasn't like us to make a fuss over those four sisters for very long."

December 7, 2016, marked the 75th anniversary of the bombing of Pearl Harbor. In declaring war on Japan on that day in 1941, President Franklin Roosevelt proclaimed that, "This day will live in infamy." Two thousand four hundred and three people were killed that day, the majority being U.S. Navy personnel. Their average age was 23. The entry of the United States into the war created a profound impact throughout the world and altered the outcome of the war.

In this journal, Sister Hedda tells in a simple and straightforward way, the unanticipated impact that the war had on Buka—a seemingly insignificant island in the North Solomons. What neither the Australian government, who had jurisdiction for the North

Solomons, nor the Marists, [2] a congregation of Catholic priests who had served there for decades, could have known in early December 1941, was that Japan wanted control of Buka Island, and they wanted it fast. Less than 200 miles from Rabaul, a recent Japanese takeover, the Japanese wanted to use relatively flat Buka as an airbase to conquer the string of islands in the South Pacific. Because of this, Japan wanted to rid Buka of anyone who was not indigenous to the island—that included plantation owners, Chinese storekeepers and missionaries.

The four Sisters of St. Joseph on Buka were newcomers to Catholic missionary work in the South Pacific. They had been invited by Marist Missionaries (Society of Mary),[3] to join them in their work of evangelization—principally through educating the young and providing critical healthcare services to the natives who had long suffered from debilitating tropical diseases.

Late in 1940, after three months of ocean travel and in response to the invitation of the Marists, the four Sisters of St. Joseph arrived at Hanahan mission station on Buka Island. They didn't know the language—chiefly pidgin—or the customs and culture of the people who had lived on that island for many generations. With optimism born of their faith, the sisters rolled up their sleeves, and with the support of the pastor of the Hanahan mission station, Joseph Lamarre, SM, they made their way forward one step at a time.

After Pearl Harbor, when Japan began the swift, strong moves of invasion and conquest, all territory within its wake began to tremble in expectation and fear. In March 1942, when the Japanese began to make moves on Buka, the sisters, still newcomers to missionary life, were far more vulnerable than they knew. The Marist priests were aware of this, worried about them, and when trouble ensued, sheltered them as best they could behind enemy lines.

Trapped in Paradise is more than a story of war, crisis and rescue. It is the story of stalwart women and men, who long before having put their lives in God's hands, now trusted that this same provident God would use them for good whatever the circumstances.

The pages found in *Trapped in Paradise* were not written as Sister Hedda's personal diary. The words that she wrote reflected the common experience of her sister-companions. Piece by piece, the journal was sent as a quarterly report back to the Superior General of the Sisters of St. Joseph of Orange, Mother Louis Bachand. After the bombing of Pearl Harbor, when correspondence was no longer possible, Sister Hedda kept on writing.

Trapped in Paradise first tells the story of the wondrous and exciting journey that these sisters took through Hawaii, Samoa, Fiji and New Zealand. It tells of their exploration of Australia while impatiently waiting for a ship to take them northward. Ultimately, it is a first person account, not only of their travels, but of their sometimes uncomfortable efforts to embrace a culture not their own, and the perils of hiding and surviving while waiting for an unlikely rescue in the midst of a vicious war.

Father Joseph Lamarre, SM, pastor in Hanahan on Buka, was not so lucky as the sisters. In his companion piece, *War Comes to Buka*, he lets the reader see war through his eyes—the story of his imprisonment and survival. Through his own internment, Father Lamarre gives us a graphic picture of what the four Sisters of St. Joseph might have endured had they been imprisoned.

Ultimately, not only did Father Lamarre and the sisters survive their ordeals, but when the war ended, with incredible generosity, they all returned to Buka to pick up the work that they had left behind.

Altogether, the Sisters of St. Joseph of Orange spent nearly 50 years on Buka and the neighboring islands of Bougainville and Nissan. When in 1991, due to a long civil war in the northern province of Papua New Guinea, the sisters could no longer enter and exit that province freely or safely, they were compelled to leave. In God's name, the Marist Missionaries, both men and women; local diocesan clergy, the Sisters of Nazareth, a congregation of local Bougainvillian women; and trained lay church workers continue to help and to heal in this remote and beautiful corner of the world.

Eileen McNerney, CSJ
Orange, California
2016

SETTING THE SCENE

August 4, 1943
Eveche, New Caledonia

Dear Mother Louis:

Friday, I was allowed to leave the hospital here after an operation and the extraction of teeth. The doctor decided I needed new "uppers" to regain my health. Personally, I think that my trouble has been "Japanitis"; it is about the best slimming method current. Give my best to Sisters Isabelle, Hedda, Celestine and Irene. I am indeed happy to learn of their safe arrival. They just got out in time. Life from then on was more of a hop, skip and jump than ever, as the Japanese poured thousands onto the islands. Things became very hot. The Japs sent the word, "Come in, or pay for it, as we are going to sweep the island." The natives arranged for my hide-out in a most inaccessible place. They brought food, and water was on the spot.

When I finally escaped, I arrived here in a state of collapse, and as the natives would say in pidgin, "bone-nothing." It's a sad story. All priests, brothers and sisters south of Asitavi are now prisoners in Kieta. Most mission stations are in ruins. The story ends with 33 evacuated, 39 prisoners. I feel that I did my best, although the thought of prisoners, especially the sisters, nearly breaks me up. I shall always be grateful to the Sisters of St. Joseph for their fine spirit during a period of trial that I hope we shall never experience again. Kindly thank each one of them for me. At times, I am afraid that I gave external signs of caving in under pressure; ask them to forget that and be ready to cooperate anew for the re-building of the Mission from the ground up when circumstances permit.

Respectfully in Jesus, Mary and Joseph,

*Wade, S.M.

PS. Important: Please do not announce the reception of this letter to any reporter. The Japanese might resent it and be severe with the prisoners.

*Note: Bishop Thomas Wade, S.M. was appointed the first bishop of the Vicariate of the North Solomon Islands in 1930.

*Our first thought was
to catch a glimpse of the Solomon Islands.
Such a picture as greeted our eyes
is beyond description.
The early rays of the morning sun
covered the islands with a golden glow,
and the graceful, towering coconut palms
turned them into a fairyland.*

Sister Hedda Jaeger

THE SISTERS' JOURNAL

*T*he war in the South Pacific was far from over, when in the summer of 1943, Bishop Thomas Wade, SM, penned his letter to Mother Louis Bachand in Orange, California. What he did not know at that time, was that by the end of the war in August 1945, of those he presumed to be prisoners—6 priests, 4 brothers and 2 sisters would be dead.

In the fall of 1940, it was a far different world in the minds and hearts of the Sisters of St. Joseph of Orange and the Marist Congregation who had invited the zealous sisters to join them in their missionary work. The Marists were experienced Catholic missionaries, having served on numerous islands in the South Pacific since the last decade of the 19*th* Century. The Marists understood the culture, language and challenges of the indigenous people of this remote area. The Sisters of St. Joseph were newcomers in every way. They arrived in the North Solomon Islands a year and a day before the bombing of Pearl Harbor. The sisters stepped into an unfamiliar world, and as teachers and nurses, they began to make their way in a new culture.

The story that follows is the story of their journey, an account written faithfully and sent regularly to Reverend Mother Louis Bachand, their Superior General in Orange, California. Through their journal, we become witnesses to their lives—the wonder of a larger world, the strangeness of an unfamiliar culture and the horror of a war they could not have imagined. No one had warned them of an impending war. Only Sister Irene Alton had received a caution from her brother-in-law in the summer of 1940, shortly before she left for Buka. "He asked me," 'Why are you going way down there? Don't you know we're going to have a war with Japan?' "I didn't believe him," she said, and buried the thought deeply within her.

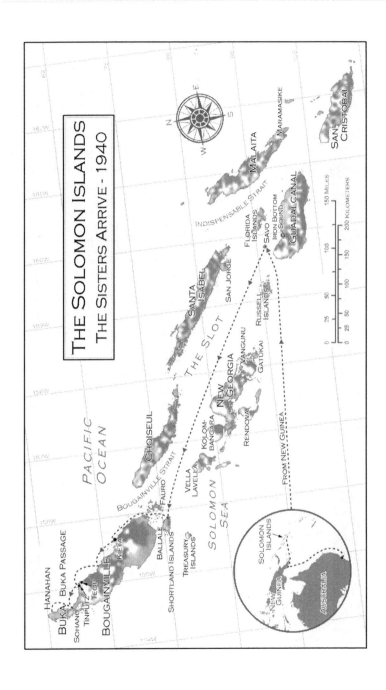

CHAPTER 1

So Much Joy Fills Our Hearts

September 18, 1940

*O*n September 18, 1940, four Sisters of Saint Joseph, under the guidance of Mother Francis Lirette, sailed from Wilmington, California, on the SS *Mariposa* to begin the journey to our foreign mission in the Solomon Islands. The group included: Mother Francis Lirette; Sister Isabelle Aubin, the superior of the new mission; Sister Irene Alton, R.N.; Sister Celestine Belanger; and Sister Hedda Jaeger, R.N.—two were teachers and two were nurses.

Previous to the departure, representatives from the different local convents met at the Motherhouse in Orange to spend a few days with the new missionaries. At 3:00 P.M., on September 18th, Right Reverend Monsignor John J. Cawley, Vicar General, gave Benediction of the Most Blessed Sacrament and his farewell message. After an exchange of farewells on the patio of the Motherhouse, cars drew up to the side entrance, and Reverend Mother Louis Bachand and about 30 sisters accompanied the new missionaries to the boat. Promptly at 10:00 P.M., the ship slowly moved out into the deep, and we saw our beloved sisters gradually fade from our sight.

In our cabins many tokens of good will awaited us—telegrams, boxes of candy, roses and *bon voyage* messages.

September 19, 1940

A calm sea, a beautiful day and we are five very happy sisters. So much joy fills our hearts to know that we are really on our way to the new mission. Mother Francis is a real mother to us all and has taken care of all the details of travel such as assignment of places in the dining hall, deck chairs and so on. Two of us are seasick, but one doesn't dare to smile for one's own turn may be next.

September 20, 1940

*T*he day began with Holy Mass at 7:30 A.M. What a privilege to assist at Mass in mid-ocean. The sea was very calm and smooth; there was little motion on the boat. The priest on board is on his way to Honolulu to begin work for a seminary for native boys. He is from Washington, D.C., and belongs to the Sacred Heart order. Today, Sister Isabelle came down to breakfast with us. Sister Irene and Sister Celestine had breakfast in the cabin. Sister Celestine has been quite ill with *le mal de mer* that is not checked by any of the remedies we brought with us. Mother Francis and Sister Isabelle are strolling around the ship somewhere, probably comparing their watches with various clocks to find out just why they were a half hour late. We set our time pieces back a half hour every night on the way to Honolulu. At 4:00 P.M., we are well enough to be together for tea and a concert in the social room.

September 21, 1940

*A*nother beautiful day began with Holy Mass. All of the Marist sisters were present as well as our entire group. We do not have a chapel on the boat, so a temporary altar is set up in the cabin lounge and chairs arranged for us. It is so nice to have everyone well again! Sister Celestine is a full-fledged sailor. She has been out for a constitutional on deck and just about robbed the writing room of all of its postcards and is now keeping the typewriter humming along. We are due in Honolulu Monday morning, and everyone wants to send a picture of the boat to the folks back on the farm. Sister Celestine, have you an extra card?

September 22, 1940

*W*e began this beautiful Sunday at sea with Holy Mass. Quite a number of passengers attended, as well as many of the ship's officers. All of the sisters except one Marist sister were present; she is still seasick. It makes us realize our complete helplessness and the greatness and the majesty of God. Our little bark is tossed from side to side, and one thinks of Saint Peter's words to our Lord as he slept on their little fishing boat. During the Mass, a collection was taken up for the "Apostleship of the Sea," a fund used to provide aid to seafaring men in different parts of the world. Truly, our Mother the Church does not forget any of her children. We passed a merchant ship at sea about 9:00 A.M. The air is becoming warmer, and we have all the ventilators on, as well as doors open. Mother Francis stays right close to the pitcher of ice water.

September 23, 1940

*E*veryone was up bright and early for Mass at 6:30 A.M., as we expect to dock at Honolulu at 9:00 A.M. However, we were delayed, and it was about 12:00 P.M. when we landed. Our friends were there to meet us. The Sisters of Saint Joseph of Carondelet and Wava Morris, one of Sister Isabelle's former music pupils, took us for a sightseeing tour around the island. The day was clear and not too warm with a delightful breeze from the sea. The seven Marist sisters came with us, so there were three cars full. *Everything is interesting*!

As we were docking at the pier, we were intrigued

with the many perfumes coming from the multi-colored leis that everyone seemed to be wearing. Dignified old gentlemen and plump bejeweled dowagers wore as many as ten leis of different flowers. As each passenger came down the gangplank, a lei was placed around their necks. The perfume was exquisite. Mine happened to be white ginger flowers. What a cosmopolitan center that dock was! It was fascinating. We stood and watched Japanese, Chinese, Hawaiians, and dark-skinned mixed races mingling with American and European travelers. Crossing the street from the wharves, we entered a little park where native women were at work making leis. The lawn was so green, and the palm trees looked more tropical than ours at home. One of our party spied a coconut palm just loaded with large nuts. We caught her sleeve just in time to prevent her scaling the tree to get a nut.

The main part of Honolulu is just like any street in downtown Los Angeles, except for Asian faces. All of the automobiles from Model T's to the very latest models were driven by almond-eyed chauffeurs. Those who live there can distinguish at a glance the race, or combinations of races, to which an individual belongs. The young woman who was our driver and hostess was a charming, well-educated, perfectly poised native Hawaiian with a mixture of Chinese. Her father is a Congregational minister, and she is a talented musician and teacher in an exclusive school in Honolulu. Her conversation was delightful, and she seemed to know just what would be most interesting to hear. She drove a shiny, black new Packard, and nonchalantly piloted us around some of the steepest precipices. One cannot describe the natural beauty of the vegetation and the winding roads that lead up to the mountains—flowers of every shape and hue, magnificent trees and vines, and sparkling little streams that trickle down the mountainside and fill the reservoir that supplies the city with water. The scenic route took us up into the heights. We could overlook miles of sugarcane and pineapple plantations. Everything is green, and the breeze is so cool at this elevation. As we stopped, we noticed swarms of bees flying and walking over the windows of our car. We were a bit apprehensive, but they appeared to be cold or stunned by the wind, and no one was stung.

Back down to the city again, we visited Waikiki beach. It is three or four miles long and fully deserves its famed reputation. The Royal Hawaiian Hotel is built near to the water's edge, and hundreds of visitors bask in the sunshine on that inviting white sand. An artificial barrier has been constructed some distance out in the ocean as a protection for swimmers. The water is very clear and so blue! Tiny children seem to be enjoying the shallow places as much as the grown-ups.

At 4:30 P.M., we were back with our cousins of Carondelet. Our gracious hostess, Mother Virginia, had a delicious luncheon prepared for us. Three of the sisters returned with us to the boat, and Wava Morris bought us each a lei of carnations. About 6:00 P.M., our boat slowly moved out into the water to the strains of *Aloha.*

September 24, 1940

"*D*oes anyone know what time it is?" This from Sister Irene long after the rest of us had completed a half-day's work. Out in this big ocean our clocks are changed so many times, usually an hour each night. So many hours have already been dropped into this Pacific Ocean, that we aren't sure whether it is today or tomorrow.

This morning we gathered all the sisters from other congregations, and Mother Francis took movies of us with our leis from Honolulu.

A little girl nicknamed "Pickles" is on her way to Sydney with her mother, Mrs. Rosing. Pickles is seven years old, swims every day, and has taken quite a fancy to us. She asks so many questions about our rosaries and crucifixes. Mrs. Rosing is an Australian and often comes to sit with us on deck. We sit there for hours watching the pageant of clouds. Sister Irene says, "There isn't any end to all this water." The sea is so calm; the waves aren't an eighth as big as those at

Seal Beach. We are having a breeze all along—the trade winds. They tell us we shall have this breeze all the way to Sydney. We expect to cross the equator Thursday, and Mr. Ryan, the Deck Steward, says to be on our guard, so we'll be sure to feel the bump.

September 25, 1940

Now that our clocks are regulated for a few hours, we can sit down to enjoy the tropics. Everyone is perspiring, including Mother Francis. She came in a short time ago with such a pathetic plea for assistance to rip out her inside sleeves that we didn't have the heart even to hesitate. Those helpful trade winds cool one side while you perspire on the other. We have an air-conditioned dining room, and it is like going into an icebox three times a day. It is a well-filled icebox, and the management is not making a profit on us. Our appetites are good except for Sister Isabelle's. She has trouble with her menus. She orders all those new-fangled things, then waits breathlessly to see whether the steward uncovers fish or fowl. Usually, Mother Francis has to come to her rescue.

We take daily walks around the deck and sit to read or say our prayers. We miss having a chapel with the Blessed Sacrament, and the days are not the same without Mass and Communion. We have been on the steamer a week today, and it seems like a dream we are so far from Orange. How good our dear Lord has been to choose us to make Him known and loved in a land so far away! It is a most consoling thought to know we have "left home and loved ones as well as our homeland" that we may honor Him and help our neighbor. We hope we will be worthy of His love and of our dear community's expectations.

September 26, 1940

We were awake at dawn to watch the sunrise over the blue Pacific. There was the most gorgeous display of colors, and we said our morning prayers as the first golden rays tinted the surface of the waters. This is the big day in the trip. We are to cross the equator at 1:30 P.M. There is to be a ceremony of initiation, and we are anxious to watch the other passengers take part in it.

We did have the ceremony and received a diploma embellished in gold and blue. King Neptune is riding in full regalia and appears to be chauffeured by one of the Pacific's fastest sharks.

September 27, 1940
On this date, Japan joins Italy and Germany, forming the "Axis" coalition, thus broadening the scope of the Second World War.

The days are much too short, and morning is here before yesterday is finished. We are all writing letters again so the stamp collectors at home will have some from Samoa. We have just learned that the mail is not picked up until the return of the SS *Mariposa* from Sydney, so we decided to send our mail from Fiji so that it may be picked up by a British steamer.

We learned that we are floating on water three miles deep. All of the officers and men wear white suits. We noticed the change into white shortly before reaching Honolulu.

At 3:30 P.M., we had a fire drill. When the alarm sounds, each passenger proceeds as quickly as possible to the deck to which his stateroom number assigns him. When all are assembled, instructions are given through a loud speaker, and officers stand near the railing ready to help each passenger into the lifeboat. The names are called out, and each one is checked off the list as he answers.

Tomorrow we arrive at Pago Pago. Four of us are ready to take the scenic ride by trolley to the mountains.

We even have a jug of ice water and a sandwich ready, for they say it is a three-hour ride to the mountains, and to take heavy clothes for it is cold up there. We tourists can't afford to miss anything. Tomorrow, we'll tell you about it.

September 28, 1940

Just where should one begin to tell about Samoa? We saw the islands in the distance at 11:00 A.M., and all of us came on deck to watch the ship slowly move into the large horseshoe shaped harbor. We were surrounded on all sides by a palm-fringed shoreline. The native villages as well as government buildings stand 200 to 300 yards from the water's edge. Behind these and rising half a mile into the clouds are mountains covered with every kind of tree and vine. The town follows the circle of the bay in which our steamer was anchored. Since it cannot dock at the water's edge, passengers take taxi-boats about a quarter of a mile in to land. These boats are driven by native policemen wearing a costume consisting of a red pulou or hat and a lava-lava. This garment is a two-yard strip of cotton material that they wrap around the waist, giving it a twist so that the two ends meet at one hip. It covers the person about to the ankle. Huge bare feet complete the picture. It looked strange to see these big natives mingling with smartly dressed officers and bejeweled ladies in the foyer of the ship as we waited for our turn in the water taxi.

The Marist Sisters met us, and we were helped into the motorboat from the steamer, no small feat in itself, by a burly, brown policeman. In a few minutes we were in town, and Mother Jeanne D'Arc made arrangements for our transportation to their convent. And there's where the fun begins. Eighteen sisters climbed into this vehicle, which was a combination of a Mack Truck and the Toonerville Trolley, the former supplying only the noise. Painted on each side of this sight-seeing bus was the name "Hurricane." Its pilot was an extra-large brown Samoan in native costume, all smiles. I think he enjoyed the trip as much as we did. Finally, we were all inside, and each one grasped her cincture and rosary and sat in wide-eyed wonderment at seeing how the other half of the world lives. Our four-wheeled conveyance was thrown into gear with a thunderous roar, and we were off! We tore around the turn on an unpaved road at the terrific speed of ten miles an hour. Children, chickens, cats, in fact everything living, scrambled for safety as the siren warned them of approaching danger. We sped over rocks, down big and little dips and skimmed on two wheels around curves so close to the water that one's act of contrition was interwoven with peals of laughter. We came to an abrupt stop 15 minutes later in front of the convent, and the "Hurricane," by some mechanical miracle, managed to turn on the narrow road for its return to the village.

The convent of the Marist sisters is right at the foot of one of those straight-up-and-down, mile-high mountains. The beautiful old church has the most picturesque setting. It is surrounded by tropical vegetation and is only a short distance from the water. We were very happy to visit Our Lord in the chapel. We visited the Marist priests who are stationed there and the sisters' school for the Samoans. The schoolroom was decorated with garlands of flowers in our honor, and the girls sat on the floor and sang native songs. The melodies are all very plaintive. The girls have most harmonious voices and accompany themselves by gentle hand clapping and movements of the head. They wear flowers in their hair and leis around their necks. The girls ranged in age from 9 to 18 years. They were all quite pretty with their dark brown skins, beautiful dark brown eyes and jet-black hair worn in a knot at the back of the neck. Next in entertainment was the native dance, and how we enjoyed the simplicity, beauty and perfect coordination of all the movements. They are grace itself. The dance is performed very slowly in imitation of wind, waves and fans floating in the breeze, as well as varied interpretations of their work. They love to sing and dance, and little tots of all ages could execute those complicated movements of hands and feet.

We visited the sisters' residence that is mostly screened-in porches. The refectory overlooked the bay on the south and the tropical garden on the north. The garden contains bananas, coconuts, pineapples, etc. Here grows a tree that produces tapioca or starch. The roots are pounded and soaked in water and the residue collected and dried. We were much puzzled by the word "copra" in relation to coconut and its various uses. It was explained that over-ripe coconuts are not used for food but are opened and the meaty part lifted out of its thick, brown shell and dried. This copra contains the coconut oil. Large soap companies purchase it and send it to the refineries to remove the oil. The natives pack these nutmeats in sacks and load them on the steamer. Oleomargarine is made from this oil, but now the big European markets are closed on account of the war. One of the SS *Mariposa* officers told us that Tahiti has tons of copra stored in sheds awaiting shipment, and that its reduction in sales has been a real hardship for the people of the islands.

At 4:30 P.M., after a refreshing lunch consisting of homemade lemonade, cookies and other dainties, as well as a sample of breadfruit, coconut milk and green coconut, we were ready to come back to the ship. The "Hurricane" steamed into view promptly at 5:00 PM, and in a few minutes we were back in the village of Pago Pago. In the center of the town is a small round park where all the natives sit on the grass mats and sell their wares. They do very beautiful woodcarving and basket weaving, and sit there in a squatting position for hours. They appeared to be in family groups and ranged in age from one day old to 90 years. Each group specialized in one thing, such as shell collections, grass skirts, fancy mats, wicker sewing baskets, and shell beads. There is no high-powered salesmanship. They just sit there and look at you in a pleading sort of way with the result that Mother Francis mounted the stately SS *Mariposa's* gangplank with a gorgeous grass skirt over her arm. We were all keeping our distance, hoping she wouldn't ask us to carry it. In a few minutes more, we were bidding farewell to the most enchanting fairyland we have yet visited.

September 30, 1940

This is two days in one. Yesterday was Saturday, and today is Monday. During the night we passed the International Date Line. The ocean has been quite choppy since morning.

We had the experience of a tropical storm about 11:00 A.M. One feels very helpless when the water is a deep blue and covered with whitecaps. The boat rolls from side to side, and the whistle is sounded every half minute while going through fog and heavy rain. Subdued excitement is easily detected in the sharp orders given by ship officers. Passengers are warned to stay away from the open deck. After a heavy downpour, the sky cleared and we smiled merrily on our way. About 11:50 A.M., we passed Tin Can Island, a lonely looking spot way out here in the ocean. It is covered with tall coconut palms and other trees that we could not distinguish. It was given this name because of the inaccessibility for landing. The mail is placed in a metal can and tossed overboard at the nearest point to the island, where it is rescued by the native boatmen and brought ashore. At one time stamp collectors reaped a fortune from this island's stamps. The SS *Mariposa* used to stop here but has discontinued it, as much mail was lost in the attempt to land it. We learned that two Marist sisters lived here. Some time ago one died on the island, and the other sister had to live alone with a native woman for eight months before another sister could be sent to join her.

October 1, 1940

*T*he islands of Fiji came into sight about 8:30 A.M., and we were all on deck to watch the ship glide through the coral reefs into the harbor. These reefs are just below the surface, and the breakers roll up on them in great foamy crests. You cannot see the coral from the ship—only the waves breaking on what appears to be these little patches of water. The coral is marked by buoys for the safe passage of the ships. We noticed that all the coral is white when taken from the water, but the natives dye it all colors and sell it to the tourists. As we drew near the dock, we saw our first Fijians. They are large in stature, have an almost black skin, deep set black eyes, large flat noses, and thick lips. The native police, dressed in white knee-length shirts with pointed scallops and blue serge capes with red trimming, stood at the foot of the gang-plank as we descended. They carefully examined our passports and quite authoritatively motioned to us to pass on. A drizzling rain greeted us, and we went into a shed-like building that serves as a general storage and warehouse. One sight caused a smile—huge boxes marked *Kellogg's Corn Flakes* carried by be-turbaned Hindus and large barefoot Fijians.

Because we are in a war zone no visitors were permitted near the boat. We saw the Marist habit quite a distance from us, on the other side of an eight-foot barbed wire fence. Suva is a very clean city and surprisingly up to date, with large schools, apartment buildings, warehouses, and packinghouses. Drugstores sell everything from goldfish to dog collars.

We walked back to the place where the Marist sisters were waiting. The four sisters who were assigned to their mission here were with us. Mother Mary Agnes, who has charge of all the Marist houses in Fiji, greeted us. What a precious soul she is! She has been a missionary for 50 years—26 of those have been spent at the leper colony. She is 72 years old, and her brown, wrinkled, weather-beaten hands tell a story that can be written only in heaven. Her whole face lit up with the sweetest smile as she gave instructions in native tongue to the Fijian chauffeur. It seems everyone knows her. As a group collected around her, she conversed as freely with them as we did among ourselves. We learned that they were inquiring about their relatives who are under her care at the leper colony.

Finally, we were all seated in the automobile driven by an Anglicized Hindu. Hindus form a third of the population at Suva. They are small-boned, fine-featured, courteous, and somewhat shrewd and sophisticated. The Hindu women retain their native costume which usually is of fine, lacy material draped around them in such a manner as to cover them from neck to ankles, and it seems to be all in one piece. As for the men's draperies, none of us could figure out how two or three twists could fashion a pair of trousers.

Our car, a good American Dodge with the steering

wheel on the right-hand side, rolled up the left-hand side of the street and kept going through traffic. It is bewildering to see everything going just the opposite to our rules at home. There were many American cars on the streets, as well as a great many of those little Austins that were popular with us a few years ago. The streets are wide, and tropical trees and flowers are carefully trimmed. Metal containers are placed at intervals on the streets with the invitation, "Be Tidy." One does not see matches or cigarette stubs lying on the sidewalk.

A ten-minute ride brought us to the convent of the Sisters of Saint Joseph of Cluny where we were given a most cordial welcome. Mother Ursula, who is superior there, had been 32 years in India. We had lunch, dinner, and lunch again with them. They are such a happy group, and we enjoyed their English accents and broad Irish brogues. How good it is, when so far from home, to meet our Sisters in Christ who would gladly do as much for us as for their own. No one knows what it means until she climbs the steps of a strange convent in a distant land and is met at the entrance with a welcome such as we received! There have been so many Good Samaritans at every crossroad, and Our Lord has written in letters of gold their deeds of kindness to us.

At 11:00 A.M., Mother Mary Agnes led the way to the bishop's residence that is about five blocks up a straight and slippery hill. Bear in mind that it rained about every half hour during the day, and we watched the clouds and started our climb between showers. Bishop Nicholas, a venerable old man of 80 years, met us on the veranda and brought us into the reception room. There were 15 of us. We visited for a few minutes only, received his blessing, and started home to the convent. The houses we visited were large frame buildings with high ceilings and large rooms. There were straight-backed chairs and old-fashioned electric lights hanging from the center of the ceilings. The damp air and the drizzling rain gave it all a cheerless effect. At the same time our clothes were dripping with perspiration. One does not feel warm. We had on our heavy black habits.

They have a very nice school for both resident and day

pupils. Most of the children were white. There are 18 sisters at that mission, most of them teaching at the native school which is two or three blocks away. The church is really a beautiful stone structure, and how glad we pilgrims were to visit our Lord after such a long absence. We said our prayers, made the Way of the Cross and inwardly rejoiced in the presence of Him in the tabernacle. The main altar was decorated with tropical ferns and flowers. Of course, Saint Therese of Lisieux is there in all her loveliness. Her statue is beautiful and seemed to smile so sweetly at us. It is surrounded by tiny electric lights set in rose buds, producing a most pleasing effect. Roses and ferns were placed in every available spot at her feet. She greets us from every church and chapel in these missionary islands, and somehow, it is helpful to see her.

Time for departure came much too soon. We decided to walk to the boat and see as much of the town as we could. We passed large storehouses filled with copra, and we were glad to leave it behind as it has a very sweet sickening odor. As we neared the boat, the usual number of hucksters sat upon the ground near the sidewalk with their wares. Most interesting of all were the shells—gorgeous specimens of all sizes, the most exquisitely beautiful creations you ever looked at. Some of them were quite large and from deep water. They tell us there is a shell resembling a clam that is three to five feet in diameter. We saw some smaller in size that we thought would make good washbasins for our medical center. So it is not to be wondered at that three minutes before the boat was to sail, Mother Francis was still admiring those shells.

We sailed at 5:00 P.M., and as we stood on deck watching the ship wind its way among the coral, a rainbow of the most dazzling brilliance held us spellbound. A shower of rain soon brought us back to earth a bit disillusioned for even rainbows in the South Seas are contradictory.

October 2, 1940

*W*e were so accustomed to life on this boat that we'll be lost when we get back on land. It is two weeks tonight since we left you all, and it seems like years. We are on the way to New Zealand, and the weather is much cooler. All of the ship's officers are back to blue uniforms again. The sea is choppy, and the boat rolls considerably. The sky is overcast, though we have not had any rain.

This morning our good friend, Mr. Casey, the Head Steward, took us all through the ship's galley. It is about twice the size of the main kitchen at Saint Joseph Hospital. There are separate sections for washing silver, glassware and china. The stove is electric and stands in the center of the kitchen, thus allowing ten men to cook on either side. Some were preparing the roasts, others fish, soup, vegetables, and so on. It is the busiest place at 11:00 A.M. you ever saw.

October 3, 1940   Feast of Saint Therese of Lisieux[4]

*A*rough sea kept some of us awake a good part of the night. Our boat seemed to be tossed about like a leaf in the breeze, though it was not due to a storm, just a strong head wind. Enormous swells top the boat from 10 to 15 feet. Occasionally, an extra dip makes one reach down under the bed to make certain the life preserver is just where you felt it last. Dawn more than compensated with its azure and gold loveliness. We put our shipmates through a severe test of good sportsmanship by waking them to enjoy a sunrise. They rose magnificently to the occasion and half unconsciously climbed up to look out of the porthole. Earlier, a star of exceptional beauty with long silver rays glistened from its background of velvety blue. It is three times larger than any we have ever seen.

We are in cooler waters now, and everyone is shivering. Sister Celestine broke the late morning stillness by shuffling through the contents of her suitcase. She seemed to think she had some red flannels down in the bottom. Sister Hedda doesn't tell anything on herself. Let me tell you that she spent part of the forenoon wrapped in a green woolen blanket, and even put the rug close to the door so she wouldn't feel a draft. She was just wishing to be back in Fiji.

October 4, 1940

*I*t might be spring for New Zealanders, but it's mighty cold to Californians. We wrapped up in our heaviest wraps and braved a chilling N'Wester to go out on deck and watch the ship into port. The day was overcast, and the sea was rough, but our hearts were gay and we were very anxious to see this—shall we call it Utopia? Everyone speaks so highly of New Zealand. The climate is boasted about as much as our own.

The city of Auckland has a population of approximately 150,000. It is built over a large area made up of 28 extinct volcanoes. It is quite as hilly as San Francisco, and as you go down the main street you can easily imagine you are on Market Street.

Before we landed, the mayor of the city came on board to greet his niece who was *en route* to Sydney. By a strange coincidence, she happened to be Mrs. Rosing with her daughter, "Pickles." They were sitting near us when the mayor came in, and he turned to us and asked if we were through passengers to Sydney. We told him that we were but were planning to go ashore and visit Auckland while our boat was in dock. Upon learning that we were total strangers, he gallantly offered his chauffeur and car for the afternoon. You can well imagine our joy and gratitude. He took us around the city past public buildings of interest, by schools with boys in uniform playing cricket, through parks, up steep hills, and along beautiful shore-line drives. We stopped at Saint Benedict School and met more Sisters of Saint Joseph not even distantly related to us. They wear a brown habit with white flexiline guimpes like ours but with an additional standing collar, very uncomfortable looking. The material in their habits is brown alpaca that looks very neat. Nearly all of the sisters have a marked Irish brogue, twinkling blue eyes and a welcoming smile. We stayed a few minutes and then continued to Sacred Heart College, conducted by Sisters of Mercy. It is a beautifully arranged group of buildings, and the grounds are large with little gravel pathways to each building.

We next went to the top of an extinct volcano to get a magnificent view of the city and miles of surrounding country. The houses in Auckland are rather small and usually only two stories and built of wood. They have frequent earthquakes here, and that explains the type of building. The roofs are corrugated iron, some green, but most are red. Really you would think you were in one of our California cities, except that the grass is greener. We are forgetting that October is spring. The flowers are in profusion and simply beautiful. Words cannot paint their actual beauty, and they grow wild in every corner. Quite close to the city there are pastures with cattle and sheep grazing. There are the woolliest little lambs and English sheep dogs standing guard. The countryside is so picturesque, particularly at this time of the year. Back in the city we passed all kinds of American cars— Pontiacs, Fords, Plymouths, and others. We seemed to be the center of attention in the mayor's car. People looked at the license plate and then gave a puzzled glance at the occupants. Our kind chauffeur let us out at Saint Patrick's Cathedral where we were happy to visit our dear Lord again.

October 5, 1940

We were all up bright and early and were the first ones down the gangplank at 7:00 A.M. We were all so happy to be able to hear Mass again. The cathedral, in spite of its size, gave the friendliest welcome. One feels so much at home. The altars are strictly liturgical, and a relief from the gaudy flower draped altars of the islands. The interior decorations are deep red and gold and everything throughout seems to be so restful and in such good taste. One could spend a whole day there without a rosary or meditation book. After Mass, a kind old gentleman came up to our pew and gave Sister Celestine a box full of rosaries, saying that he had been told we were going to the Solomons and wanted to make a small offering. He is having a Mass offered for us tomorrow morning. So you see how kind everyone is to us when we are so far from home.

After Mass, the Marist Missionary Sisters sent a taxi for us so we could have breakfast over at their convent. They are a different order from the Marists who are traveling with us. Their habit is dark blue serge with a white cape, and a silver cross is suspended from the neck by a white woolen cord. Their habit is one of the prettiest we have seen, and most of the sisters are rosy cheeked and Irish. Father Redahan, our Chaplain at Orange, has a sister in this community; he showed us her picture before we left. They were very hospitable and served us a delicious breakfast of ham and eggs and tea. A short distance away is the convent of the Sisters of Compassion, founded in New Zealand about 20 years ago. They have homes for unwed mothers, and take care of children until they are adopted or the mother makes arrangements to care for the baby herself. We went through the home which was a new stucco building all on one floor. They have eight mothers and thirty-three babies. Their work is all charity, and two sisters go out begging every day. They really seem to be appreciated, for everyone helps them.

After visiting was over, our cars called to take us back to the boat. All of the sisters were safely tucked in, leaving the remaining car, a tiny Austin, for your journalist, who took a couple of gulps and folded her knees under her chin for a ride down the steepest hill in Auckland. The others were waiting at the gangplank. Sister Isabelle's lips were blue with cold, and she went around wondering why a ship of this size didn't have steam heat. It does have plenty of green woolen blankets. After we were out of the harbor, the only way to keep our teeth from chattering was to climb under four blankets in the cabin. It is now 8:00 P.M., and we are well out on the Tasman Sea on the last lap of our journey. We are all prepared for a rough trip; the boat is rolling from side to side. Good News! There are three priests aboard, so we shall have Mass tomorrow. Since they are experienced seamen, having come from Europe through the Panama Canal, they are all able to be up.

We forgot to mention that everyone we met in Auckland seemed to know Father McHardy and his book,

Blazing the Trail.[5] He is a native of Auckland, and has a brother, a priest, who lives there. The Sisters of Compassion took care of him in his last illness, and we met a sister who went to school with him. She has some pictures of him after his death, taken in his vestments. His illness was prolonged, and he showed remarkable patience and fortitude through it all.

We are a little uneasy tonight, as the steward has made the rounds of the ship and closed all the portholes. He says there's a possibility of a storm.

October 7, 1940

The printing department accuses me of being too talkative, but we maintain that the folks at home like details. It will be short today, but wait till we reach Sydney!

This forenoon the boat was forced to stop for a few minutes, and we were told a whale got too close to the ship's propeller and was severely injured. It was necessary to change the position of the ship before proceeding. That is a good fish story, to say the least.

October 8, 1940

So this is Sydney! The entrance to the harbor is magnificent. Great precipices of stone form the shoreline, and the city is built on sloping hills, giving a wide panorama of this large metropolis. Our boat was met in the bay by government officials and health inspectors, and we were all carefully catalogued. Everyone was courteous and kind and our first impression of Australia was decidedly favorable. It is so interesting to come into the docks and watch the ship make all the arrangements for our landing and then to wait in the large terminal building while each passenger goes through custom inspections. In about two and a half hours we were ready to leave, and we all came to Villa Maria. Mother Mary Rose was not able to come to the wharf but met us just outside of the gate and accompanied us home in the taxi. We came through the city out to this suburb, a distance of seven miles. We saw a part of the manufacturing section and the large warehouses. The city looks very much like San Francisco with its tall buildings, though we have not seen its main streets or the shopping districts. Our drive seemed all too short, but it gave us some idea of the vegetation and the climate. It was delightfully warm, and the sunshine made us feel as though we were still in California. It is springtime here; the birds are working overtime at nest building, and green leaves are coming out on all the trees. We saw some of the grandparents of our California trees: eucalyptus, pepper, star pine, and camphor trees. There are many types of palms similar to ours. The temperature is just about the same as Los Angeles.

We arrived at the Marist convent at noon, and how happy we were to resume community life after three weeks at sea. We visited the chapel and told our Lord how thankful we were to have arrived safely, this far, on the way to our mission. We soon learned that our boat, the SS *Malaita*, had gone to the Solomon Islands a few days before our arrival, and it would be five weeks before it would return to repeat this same voyage. Meanwhile, we would wait in Sydney.

We have our meals with the sisters, and the two Irish sisters have quite a time making signs and understanding pidgin French. We expect to start French lessons as soon as Sister Isabelle finds time. Nearly all the sisters speak French, and it is the common language among themselves. In mid-afternoon, Father Bergeron, the Provincial of the Marist Fathers, came to visit us, and told us some interesting news. We are going to be missioned at Hanahan, Buka, north of Bougainville Island instead of Nila. In the evening, an officer from the police department came to check on our whereabouts, and look over our legal documents. He went away apparently satisfied that we were associating with the right people.

October 9, 1940

*I*t was tempting for us younger members to get up before dawn and explore the new country, but Mother Francis forestalled that possibility. We began the day with Mass at 6:00 A.M., and after prayers were finished, we were free to admire all the natural beauty that surrounds us. We are separated from the parish church by a high fence that surrounds the whole property. Nearby, the Marist priests have their Provincial House while on the far side of the church is the pastor's residence. He is also a Marist, but belonging to the Australian Province. The sisters here take care of the parish church and launder all the linens. The whole compound forms a square of ground covering from 10 to 12 acres. The sisters' quarters are all fenced in. There is a nice green lawn with little pathways leading through the flower garden and benches under the large shady poplar trees where one may sit and read near the statue of Our Lady of Lourdes. Many birds come near and look at us while collecting straws for nests. There are starlings by the dozens and strangest of all an Australian kookaburra, commonly known as the "laughing jackass." This bird cries like a baby. He is quite large and comical to look at—guess he thought we were, too, the way he stared at us. On the way a reptilian monster, all of 12 inches long, stopped to survey these strange Americans. Violent protests burst forth at the offer to catch this lizard, and bring him home for a pet.

One thing we noticed here and in New Zealand is the total lack of screens on the windows and doors. Everything is wide open, and we think a manufacture of that article could do wonders to hamper those little winged insects. No one pays the slightest attention to their size or number.

October 12, 1940 Columbus Day

*I*t was decided the night before that we visit the zoo before the weather became too warm. Bright and early this morning seven of us started out with a suitcase full of refreshments. The ride downtown on the tram was quite exciting as it gave us an opportunity to observe the people as well as the buildings we passed. These trams are streetcars to us, and the passengers sit in double rows facing each other. The conductor walks along on a little platform on the outside and collects the fares. It was an hour's ride through the industrial center and over the bridges and through the main street to the ferry. We noticed that all the factories and other commercial buildings burned coal so that part of the city was a bit sooty. Coal is mined in the Blue Mountains, and many railroad cars, full to the brim, stood on the tracks. Many of the buildings are made of stone and some of brick. One sees ledges of stone everywhere, as it's a natural as well as a cheap building material. They do not have earthquakes here, so these buildings will last forever. The newer residences are little California bungalows, and others are old-fashioned two and three story structures with little balconies of wrought iron on nearly every one. Going through the town we saw many wool packinghouses, as Australia produces the finest wool in the world. It is a great sheep raising country. Then, too, the Australian people use a lot of mutton. Some of the meat markets have window decorations that would put *Sees' Candy* displays to shame. The different cuts of meat are folded and decorated with curled papers in fancy style. We did not stop in the main business section, as we are planning a shopping day for next week. So we'll tell you all about it then. Coming to the ferry building we got our transportation across the bay to the zoo.

The zoo is built on a hill, and the animal cages are made out of the natural rock formation with the addition of cement. One follows a winding road around the hill and visits each section along the way. It is quite large, and the animals are about the same as any zoological collection with the exception of those most common to Australia. Instead of one or two kangaroos, there were several pens full of different species. The enclosures for the koala bears were the center of much interest. We went inside close to the trees where they were being fed. They are the size of a full-grown rabbit, grey in color with funny little black half-closed eyes. Really, you have never seen such lovable little animals. The keeper had cut the branches of their favorite tree and placed it in a detachable receptacle in a convenient place for them to sit and eat. They balance themselves on their haunches and pay no attention to the admiring public. We patted them on their furry little backs, so we'd have something to tell the folks back home. We held as many as four at a time, and they clung to our habits in a helpless baby-like fashion. These bears are quite harmless and never drink water. We took several snapshots of ourselves holding a number of these little bears. A few years ago they were killed in large numbers for their fur; but recently, the Australian government has taken the matter in hand, and no one can have one even for a pet. They are kept in special parks and are a source of much interest to tourists.

We then visited the birds, monkeys, and our future housemates—the lizards and reptiles. Some of the green reptiles were wound around the trees in such a manner that they could easily pass for foliage. The most interesting of all was the aquarium, and our guide had to drag us one at a time away from those fascinating tanks. They have a splendid assortment of all the colored tropical fish. In the center, heavily guarded with irons, was a shark pool where we saw our first sharks. There were two large ones in the tank—most graceful and perfectly poised creatures one could look at. They seemed to glide through the water without the least effort, and yet, they were at least 12 feet long and weighed well over 100 pounds. They are a deep grey color and cannot be distinguished in the water unless they are near the surface, or the sunrays are directly on them. In the pool with them were tiger sharks and huge turtles, as well as a great many fish of all sizes. We came home about 6:00 P.M.

October 18, 1940 Feast of St. Teresa of Avila

*L*ast night, the Marist sisters and their guests attended a lecture and slides at the parish hall. It was on the Solomon Islands and very interesting. Father Lebel, who is at the monastery making his second novitiate, spoke of his work as well as giving a general outline of the accomplishments of the missionaries in the Solomons. The Marist Fathers have houses in nearly all the South Sea islands, and one cannot imagine how much territory that includes. There are dozens of little islands that make up the Fiji group and the same with New Caledonia, New Hebrides, and Samoa. The missionaries travel around the islands in small boats. In many places the jungle grows right down to the water's edge, making it necessary to go by boat even for a short distance.

The Marist Sisters have been in missionary work over 50 years and are able to turn a hand at almost anything. Father mentioned one sister who had cultivated one of the best coconut plantations in that section. One has to learn to be self-sufficient and know how to use the things obtainable on the island. Each mission has a garden and all kinds of poultry. We will give you firsthand information about those things when we arrive at Hanahan.

October 28, 1940

During the last two weeks we have been gathering information about tropical diseases from the different secular nurses who have spent some time in the Solomon Islands. We also visited one of Sydney's largest hospitals and had a long visit with the sisters in charge. The novitiate is near the hospital building, and they had 90 novices. Everyone enters training after her first vows, [6] so their whole community from the Mother General down, are graduate nurses. They do hospital work only and feel that everyone should understand hospital problems. All the nursing is done exclusively by the sisters, and ward maids are employed to do the cleaning and general work. The congregation is the Little Company of Mary.

The hospital was large and the rooms light and airy. Here again, there was not a screen on any of the windows except in the surgery. The beds were painted pale blue and some of the wards had from 10 to 15 patients. Two rows of beds faced one another and white curtains hung between for screens. What was most interesting was to see "Made in U.S.A." on a large number of the equipment. Some of the larger concerns have branch offices in Australia.

The sisters were very kind to us, and as we were leaving, they gave us a five-pound note worth $25.00 for our mission. About three blocks from Villa Maria stands the Marist Brothers' College. They have five schools in Sydney, and the one we visited had 450 students. The grounds were very large with ample space for sports of all kinds. Of course, cricket is the national game with tennis taking second place.

A venerable old Marist brother took us through from the ground floor up to the tower where we had a splendid view of the city. The buildings were made of stone with large classrooms on both sides of a wide hall. It was in 1872 that the Marist Brothers came to Sydney and built their first little school, and it has been enlarged several times since. A beautiful new chapel was completed just a few months ago, and the very nicest thing about it was that it is light enough to read a book anywhere. Nearly all the private chapels we have seen are so dark that one could scarcely see the altar without all the electric lights being turned on.

The Sunday before our visit to the College, in the company of three Marist sisters, we attended a procession. There is a beautiful grotto of our Lady of Lourdes a short distance from the College, and we had the honor of walking with the Australian Sisters of St. Joseph behind the Blessed Sacrament. The procession was led by little flower girls dressed in pale yellow voile. Behind these were different groups representing the sodalities. Then came the choir of about 80 Marist brothers who sang beautifully. The melodies were all different from those at home so we were unable to join in on a single note. We felt quite foreign for a few minutes. After the procession, all the sisters were invited for tea at the College. The Australians are skilled in the art of fancy pastries and little cakes for tea . . . delicious, too!

Another interesting afternoon was spent visiting the Grail Ladies. This is an organization that originated in

Holland, and it is made up of young Catholic women who wish to lead a more Catholic life. Each parish has its group, and it is the Central House that we have visited. These young women go through a novitiate before being admitted into the working groups. They wear a very neat little uniform. Each parish chooses its color combination. They are youthful shades and very attractive. Within the organization certain members are chosen for choir work, dramatics, arts and crafts, and sewing, as well as all sorts of hobbies that could interest a young girl. The two young ladies who received us were charming, well-educated and very versatile conversationalists. They had spent several years in the work in England, France, Holland, and Germany—though as one expressed it, "We were kicked out of the latter, but not until after we had planted many seeds."

Most interesting of all was a tour around the house. A tour is the only way to describe it, as it is an extensive house that used to be a Jesuit novitiate, but for some reason, they moved to a more secluded part of the city. The location is ideal for the convenience of the Grail Ladies and what a grand time 70 girls must have in that big house. The bishop arranged for the use of it as their headquarters, and they have fixed up the interior with a new coat of varnish and white-washed the walls and ceiling. Bright colored drapes, rugs, and wicker furniture give a very home-like appearance.

We must tell you something about Sydney, as it has been necessary for the sisters to go downtown to make a few purchases before leaving for the islands. The sewing machine has been running at top speed turning out mosquito nets for our beds at Hanahan as well as two complete sets of white habits to wear on the boat from Brisbane to Kieta. Our trunks remain in storage at the pier, so we are unable to get any of our white clothes for the rest of this warm trip.

The stores are very much like those in Los Angeles, and the goods are imported from England and America. From what we can observe, there is comparatively little manufacturing done here.

Our shopping expeditions provide the clerks and

ourselves with considerable merriment. First of all, the shilling and the pence have to be converted into dollars and cents so we will have some idea of the value of an article. At this particular time, everything is greatly increased in price so it makes it necessary to count pennies carefully. We help Mother Francis count them by carrying a pencil and scratch paper.

The downtown streets are wide, and traffic does not travel at high speed. During the rush hours an officer stands in the center and directs pedestrians and vehicles. You grab your life in both hands and make for the other side. Due to the opposite traffic rules, it is quite confusing when crossing, as automobiles are driven on the opposite side from that in America. We have had a couple of close calls and stepped back on the curb with fluttering hearts. We do not see as many women driving cars nor smoking in public. The styles in clothes are very modest and that dreadful habit of wearing slacks has not been accepted in Australia. Life moves at a much slower pace, and people do not seem so high strung and nervous.

There are some beautiful churches in Sydney. St. Patrick's is right in the business district. They have Perpetual Adoration there in memory of the first Mass said in Australia. Before the consecrated host could be consumed, the priest was *forced* to leave. For two years, the few faithful took turns in guarding the Blessed Sacrament in a small cottage until a priest was sent to them. The little shelf on which the host rested is carefully preserved in a glass enclosure at the foot of a side altar. The little cottage that was our Lord's first Australian home is now beside St. Patrick's Church in a convent garden. With such a history, it is not surprising to hear St. Patrick spoken of in a tone of deepest affection, and the constant stream of adorers verify their love and appreciation.

Across from Hyde Park in downtown Sydney, stands St. Mary's Cathedral. It is a very large stone structure—so large, in fact, that we had to hang on to one another's sleeve to prevent our being lost. There were at least ten altars, and all were very beautiful. The statue of St. Therese, the Little Flower, has a very beautiful and prominent altar, and as usual, is well decorated with flowers. She holds an important place in every chapel or convent we have visited since leaving home. About a third of the population is Catholic, and they seem to be very devout.

November 15, 1940

*T*his afternoon, we left Villa Maria convent to begin the last half of the journey to the North Solomon Islands. We were accompanied to our boat, the SS *Malaita,* by our kind hostess, Reverend Mother Mary Rose, Reverend Father Schwehr, and several priests from the Marist Provincial House. Two Marist sisters and a Marist priest joined us on board and are traveling with us to the Solomons. We will first be sailing up the northern coast of Australia, making three stops along the way before heading north into the islands.

Needless to say, this second departure carried with it a small "splinter from the cross," which seems to be a part of all farewells. I think we were silent because of that little lump in our throats, but fortunately we were not permitted the luxury of solitude and an over-sized hankie. Once on board, we were busy finding our berths and arranging our baggage. Three occupy one cabin, so the seventh sister shared a cabin with two charming young women . . . much to their consternation and the sister's enjoyment.

We sailed shortly after 11:00 P.M. As soon as we were out of the harbor, going northward, we struck a severe gale. Our little steamer was tossed about like a cork. By morning everyone was seasick except Mother Francis and Sister Hedda, though the latter was beginning to turn a little pale. We were not able to have Mass as Father Lebel thought it unsafe with the ship listing from side to side. The waves were tremendous and the water a deep blue. It was really a beautiful sight, those mountainous waves swirling upward and breaking in white foam over the prow of the ship. It is really surprising that our little boat is able to stand such terrific force without breaking into pieces. However, it did plenty of creaking, and dishes and other breakables would crash to the floor with a thunderous roar. Early one morning we were awakened by an avalanche of dishes and we assure you, it was the most paralyzing thing we have ever experienced, but it didn't have a lasting effect once we realized it was only broken crockery. This is a British ship, and you know many things could happen, for they are at war.

All day Saturday, Sister Isabelle, Sister Irene, and Sister Celestine were confined to bed; no one could pick up enough courage to face the dining room. Those who were still up and about offered varied suggestions for a cure as well as generous sympathy all wrapped up in smiles. (This is what aggravates you the most when you feel so seasick.) The one who laughed the loudest and the longest (Sister Hedda, in case you make a mistake) surely paid for it in gold coin with compound interest. She was so sick she couldn't raise her head above the railing of her berth, and every time the gong for meals sounded, she would reel into paroxysms of acute agony. Everyone seems to think it is a great joke, and it really is when it is the other fellow. So far, Mother Francis is the best sailor, but just wait until we climb inside of that little mission boat . . . perhaps our score will be even.

November 17, 1940

Your correspondent is too seasick to care what is happening.

CHAPTER 2

Our Pathway Seems Strewn
with Special Favors

November 18, 1940

*M*orning dawned, and the sea was calm, so we had our first Mass. We are so fortunate to have Father Lebel on board so we will have daily Mass and Communion. Our pathway seems to be strewn with special favors. It was a happy reunion as we were all well enough to assist at Mass. Father Lebel arranged the little altar on a small table in the lounge, and there were seven sisters and one other passenger. Owing to the size of the ship, the quarters are rather crowded. The men working around the decks often pass through this lounge to go out to the bridge, so there are frequent distractions. This ship's cat joined the congregation and sat right in the middle of the floor behind Father and carefully washed its face. Usually this Maltese sits at the foot of the stairs in the dining room with all her dignity and watches each passenger. During the course of the meal, she is given a special serving of fish, so you see we travel in real family style.

After breakfast, we went out on deck to see the ship enter Brisbane Harbor. We had a splendid view from the bridge, and it is a most unusual entrance from the ocean into the Brisbane channel and then into the river. The channel is about 30 miles long leading into the river which is about a half mile wide and deep enough for ships of all sizes. Brisbane has a population of 378,000. Many of the buildings are of brick and stone and much more up-to-date than Sydney. We visited the hospital of the Sisters of Mercy and had lunch there. The hospital is one of the finest we have seen in Australia. The compound included several buildings in which different departments are maintained. The surgery was very well equipped with excellent northern exposures and modern surgical lights. The autoclaves were very large, the newest built-in-the-wall type, and it actually gave us a thrill to see "Made in Brisbane" on the fixtures. They do a great deal of manufacturing here, and it seems to be a very progressive city.

The climate in Brisbane is semi-tropical, reaching 117 degrees, but it is rather dry and no great discomfort is felt. The weather was perfect, and the brilliant sunshine brought out the beauty of all the flowering shrubs. One avenue of particular interest was lined with many varieties of hibiscus. They were trimmed like standard roses and covered with brilliant flowers. A poinciana tree spreads out like an umbrella and has scarlet flowers. Most of those trees have seedpods several inches long, quite like the karob tree near the Motherhouse. Even though we were in a strange city, it was a temptation to pick a few ripe pods and send them home.

In the afternoon we visited the cathedral, said our prayers, and made our three wishes.[7] It is such a joy to visit our Lord in this distant land and find Him there to greet us in the same way as in our little chapel at home.

November 19, 1940

The day began with Holy Mass at 6:30 A.M. We were glad to have it at an earlier hour before the other passengers begin roaming around the deck. The ocean was like a mirror, and one could scarcely notice the motion of the ship, such a vast difference from those first days out. The weather is slightly warmer, but a cool breeze keeps the cabins comfortable. We are nearing the city of Townsville, though our ship travels very slowly, so we may not reach it for several hours yet. The sky is cloudless, and the sun is very bright. We have been watching schools of fish from time to time on the starboard side. There is very little space for walking around this little boat.

Many things strike us as being very funny. For example, in the dining room, there is such a marked difference in the way food is served. Our steward is tall and very thin with a certain nervous hastiness in his movements. When he handles a liquid it makes us apprehensive as he nears the table. This particular morning there were prunes on the menu, and as we came downstairs into the dining room, we beheld this shaky waiter balancing two large size bread plates on which five prunes were being transported. The ship was rocking from side to side, and the prune juice threatened to slip over that shallow edge at any moment.

Then, too, there is an Australian way of handling a fork and knife that we are trying to master. The food is placed or loaded on the back of the fork with the knife and then carried in the same position to one's mouth. The trick lies in getting it to stay on the back of the fork. We have fun with those trifles, and no one knows what we're laughing about.

November 20, 1940

*W*e are slowly traveling into warmer waters, and many of the passengers are putting on tropical clothing. The women wear very light dresses, and the men wear knee pants and short-sleeve shirts. They look very strange and very undressed. Having seen them in Suva, we are getting somewhat accustomed to it. We expect to put on our white "Made in Sydney" habits very shortly. We all started taking quinine (5 grains) the day after sailing. It is taken at night with the evening meal, and in that way, one is at rest during the short period when the drug produces a nervous upset feeling. It causes some digestive disturbances, but we hope to overcome that in a couple of weeks.

This has been a perfect day. After prayers and breakfast, we went up on the deck and read the greater part of the morning. A couple of large sharks played in the water to entertain the passengers, and a strange bird sat upon the mast of the ship and serenaded us with a weird Australian melody. We are about 30 miles from the coast, and land is visible from time to time. About 10:00 P.M., the ship's officers had target practice and almost spilled us out of our deck chairs.

An interesting thing came to our attention last evening. While walking on the deck and watching the waves, we saw little flashes of light similar to fireflies. It was described in Father McHardy's book, and we remembered it was phosphorus. At times the light was as vivid as that produced by an ordinary match. As the ship passes through the water, dozens of these little glowing lights are seen, last for a few seconds and then disappear. Of course, you know the ship travels in complete darkness—not a light anywhere on deck. The windows in our cabin are protected by sliding shutters.

In this part of the world the heavens are unusually beautiful at night. Billions of the most gorgeous stars of that deep crystal-like blueness are seen. We stand spellbound as we look at this mysterious universe that surrounds us. If earth is so much beauty, how beyond comprehension heaven must be!

November 21, 1940 Thanksgiving Day

*T*oday, we are celebrating our national holiday very quietly. One sister suggested visiting the lower regions of the ship and capturing one of the pedigreed fowl that was placed in the hold at Brisbane. We seem to be the only Americans on board. Nearly all the passengers are returning to their island homes after vacationing in Australia. Some are mining people from the gold fields of New Guinea, and others are traders and government employees. All eight missionaries on this boat are enjoying the trip to the fullest. Father Lebel is an American who has been in Australia at the Provincial House for the last six months. He has been in the islands nine years and seems very anxious to return to his mission. Fortunately, he has a keen sense of humor and enjoys little jokes with us. He sits at our table in the dining room and chuckles over many of our questions about the islands. We suspect we are catalogued as "babes in the woods." An incident pertaining to our baggage gave us all a good laugh. The day of our departure, a perturbed official notified the Marist procurator that our baggage was far in excess of the 350 pounds allowed on each ticket. To settle the problem without additional expense, the procurator, Father Nicholas, assigned the task to Father Lebel. To the great surprise of everyone, he succeeded in smoothing the ruffled feelings and convincing the shipping department that a few tons of excess baggage was a mere trifle. So we sailed out of Sydney Harbor with five tons and a large debt of gratitude to Father Lebel.

We are passing in and out among a long chain of islands. Some of them are covered with shrubs and once in a while one without the sign of any vegetation whatever. We are inside of the Great Barrier Reef, and the mainland can be seen in the distance. The water is the loveliest shade of azure blue. Little ripples cause it to sparkle in the sunshine as though it was beset with precious jewels. White sea birds skim lazily over the surface. Occasionally, we pass an island where the government has a station, and it is quite a thrilling sight to see the flag hoisted to salute us and slowly lowered as we pass from view. Somehow, flags have a way of touching a sensitive spot when one is far from home. Even a battered tug would receive a royal welcome if the "stars and stripes" were floating above.

November 22, 1940

*A*t 3:30 A.M., we arrived at Townsville, and the workmen began to move planks and make preparations for unloading the cargo. It is always exciting to reach a new port. Daylight was all too slow in coming. After Mass and breakfast, we were ready to visit the new city. Townsville has a population of 23,000 and is chiefly a city of exports. The surrounding country is rich in minerals and tropical fruits. Incidentally, it is about the hottest place at 9:30 A.M. in which one could hope to live and move and still have their bearings. We are nonchalantly informed that the temperature seldom goes above 125 degrees. That alone was enough to undermine one's courage. Nevertheless, our curiosity was aroused, and we five little sisters, dressed in black, ventured out in the blazing, blistering heat. Once in town, some of the sisters almost decided to leave us and go home. Their minds were changed when they spied a large brick church on the top of a hill at least five blocks away. Suggestions were offered that we pay our Lord a visit and at least tell Him what we thought of His choice of a hilltop home. Perspiring with every step, we finally arrived at the church, and with a sigh of relief, entered. We were ready to genuflect and kneel, but suddenly we felt kind of a strange feeling when we noticed there was no sanctuary lamp. We were in an Anglican church. We could hardly believe our eyes, as the statues of all the saints were gazing upon us from everywhere. We hurriedly left, hoping no one had seen us.

Some distance from there, we asked directions, and we were shown a nice new brick building with two spires about six blocks to the north and on the top of another hill. We were already at melting point! We made the trip as a pilgrimage amid much laughter and promises to give up all religion if that proved not to be a Catholic church. It was a beautiful new cathedral, and we were so happy to spend a little time before the Blessed Sacrament. Later, the pastor took us to visit the school of the Sisters of Mercy. We had tea and a pleasant visit. Then Father brought us to the boat with his brand new

Chevrolet. On our way we saw a very new and beautiful shrub just covered with drooping clusters of yellow blossoms—one of the most exquisitely beautiful things one could ever look at. Do you know what it was? A cascara tree!

November 23, 1940

Today our ship dropped anchor in the picturesque harbor of Cairns. We were out on deck to watch the ship slowly wind its way through the blue green waters to the docks. A refreshing breeze was blowing, and just a short distance to the south a sailboat in its newest white regalia was speeding on its way. It is a beautiful thing to look at with the morning sun, bringing all of its stateliness against a distant background of mountains.

We were ready to go ashore by 9:00 A.M., and fortunately, it was much cooler than yesterday. Drifting white clouds protected us from the strong sunrays, and we did not have any hills to climb. This is our last Australian port so we all had a letter for our mothers and our first thought was the post office. The city has a population of about 30,000, and it is about 17 degrees below the equator. All kinds of tropical trees and shrubs grow here in abundance. Really, it is impressive! Australia is all a wonderful country. It seems to have everything and within a comparatively short distance. Here we are in the tropics, and at Melbourne they produce everything requiring a cold climate.

After a brief walk around *Woolworth's* department store, we completed our purchase of one four pence article and then turned our footsteps towards the church. As usual there was an imposing Anglican Church just across the street, but some little girls saw us going that way and directed us to the right one. We said our prayers and the Stations of the Cross. One of the Sisters of Mercy from the nearby school invited us to visit them. We had a cup of tea, and the local bishop came to visit. We spent a pleasant two hours. We are acquiring such poise from all this traveling that we can meet apostolic delegates and bishops without batting an eyelash.

How many times at Orange we have tried to crawl under a leaf to escape meeting one!

November 24, 1940

*T*oday, we are crossing from the mainland to New Guinea, and it's warm! This last trip has been filled to the brim with a great peace, and even we have been captivated by the charm of the ocean's grandeur. One can readily understand what an attraction the sea has for many who make seafaring their life's work. It brings one so close to God. How much He, too, loved the sea and used it to bring home that greatest truth—trust.

November 25, 1940

*M*r. Gulliver didn't have any more fun on his travels than we Sisters of Saint Joseph are having on ours. After 40 winks of sleep, we awakened to find ourselves in another fairyland. You know, this small boat with its strange cargo on board—chickens, sheep, goats, and two cats—make it all seem like a storybook. To add to that, we passed Thursday Island where Robinson Crusoe gathered all his material to entertain us in childhood. Is it any wonder we can hardly believe our eyes as we look at all these foreign people and places? It is late afternoon and we have spent the day in Port Moresby, New Guinea.

We arrived at Port Moresby about 11:00 A.M., and as is our custom, our first visit was to the nearest church. You'll never know how wonderful it is to visit Our Lord in the midst of all His strange children. It makes one feel so very unimportant as one looks about and sees the work accomplished by these priests and sisters who have spent the best part of their lives in missionary work. The Sacred Heart Fathers have a mission here, and four Sacred Heart Sisters are in charge of the school. They teach part of the day and then visit the sick natives in the villages. We visited them, and it so happened that it was their day for conference by one of the Fathers, so we were given the privilege of hearing it also. His topic was on Divine Love that he presented very simply as our only help in fulfilling our daily duties in the work. We are all impressed with the holiness of these priests.

This little corner of the world has about 300 white families, nearly all of whom are government employees. It is an important seaport, but those treacherous coral reefs practically surround the northern entrance. In the distance, the skeleton of an American oil-tanker is to be seen. It has been there 18 years on the reef, and they have used tons of explosives in attempts to blast the reef and dispose of the wreckage, but it remains securely wedged in the corals. We are told that the coral grows slowly and steadily, and that in time it would grow up, in and around the whole of the ship. Nothing was said about its being haunted, but, to look at the spectral form, one could easily imagine goblins beginning their mischievous work at sundown.

November 26, 1940

*T*his is our second day at Port Moresby. We were up bright and early, went ashore for two Masses and then had breakfast with the sisters at the nearby convent. They were so hospitable, and went to considerable trouble preparing tropical dishes to tempt our appetites. It is strange, but one seems to lose all interest in food in this climate, though everyone mentions the importance of eating anyway, so we do. We all tried our first mangoes today, and what fun it was. They are large and green and so juicy. Paper napkins are out of the question in this part of the world, and we missed them at every drop of fruit juice. However, we did manage to eat the mangoes, and Mother Francis had the best time removing the skin and getting a firm grip on the juicy pulp inside. After we all had our try-out, one of the sisters gently took hold of one, and, to our surprise manipulated it so gracefully that she didn't drop a bit of juice on the table, while in our case, one of the sisters had to get a wash bowl and towel. Otherwise we wouldn't have been fit to appear in public. We enjoyed ourselves immensely.

Immediately after breakfast, the pastor called to take us for a ride around the island. We were not prepared for the car that drove up for us, but he sat there laughing and daring us. We entered into the game and hurriedly climbed over his box of tools and away we went. The rest of the party rode in state in the big sedan. Our car held all the qualities of the Samoan van, the "Hurricane," only it rattled in more places. It had a top and a creaky door to hang onto as we sped around the curves, but to compensate for outward appearance, its lack of side curtains provided us with a better view and a cool breeze. Mother Francis and Sister Hedda sat in the back, and Sister Isabelle sat in front hanging on a piece of what used to be the door. We rode 12 miles over the picturesque country to a native school. It was early morning, and the distant mountains were partly hidden among the most gorgeous, powdery white clouds interspersed with heavenly shades of blue. Some of these mountains are from 10,000 to 12,000 feet in height, and the shadows of the early morning covered them with a blue haze. To pause on an elevation and absorb such magnificence was a privilege.

We arrived at the school, and to our surprise, found 38 native boys of all ages, who spoke excellent English. Sister Isabelle told them who we were and a little about our country. They knew their geography well and followed our course on a large map. They were bright youngsters, and were so pleased to display their talents to a group of sisters. They sang beautifully, and their voices blended harmoniously. We wish you could share our feelings as all those little, black upturned faces sang our beloved hymn, *Panis Angelicus*.

One of the younger boys was seriously ill with pneumonia, and our two nurses were given their first opportunity to render professional service by giving the child a cool sponge bath and telling the sisters how to care for him.

About 4:00 P.M., we returned to the village, and after tea with the Sacred Heart sisters, we said our prayers in the chapel before returning to the steamer.

November 27, 1940

*W*e assisted at Mass at 6:30 A.M. at the church and then had breakfast with the sisters at the convent. We then visited the native hospital that is maintained by the government. There are about 200 patients and the buildings are on 15-foot piles right on the beach over the shallow water. Some of the half-caste natives are trained in Sydney as medical assistants. We talked with one who gives intravenous medications and treats tropical ulcers as well as assisting at operations. Many of the natives have tuberculosis (T.B.), and they are isolated as are those with leprosy. The government supplies all the medications and other necessities for the upkeep of the hospital. This part of New Guinea has been settled by Europeans for over 75 years and all the natives speak good English. They are accustomed to tourists and quickly recognized us. One came with a string of fish and tried to sell them for a shilling each. Those fish are unusual in color. Some are bright blue, others, coral and green, and others speckled like ordinary mackerel. The natives spear them and carry them on a pole with a string through the gills.

November 28, 1940

*W*hen daylight came, we found ourselves nearing the island of Samarai. We traveled in and around a group of beautiful islands with sandy beaches and native huts along the shoreline. As we came through a narrow passage, a signal was given, and all the little native children scampered up the bank to their homes. It was about 11:00 A.M. when we docked. Within a few minutes, the natives were on board preparing to unload the cargo. They do all of the work around the docks, and operate the electrical derricks that remove the cargo from the hold. One big, burly fellow stands in a prominent place on a barrel of kerosene, and directs operations. All they wear is a lava-lava and a brilliant hibiscus in their hair. They do very well, but here's hoping our precious boxes of medical supplies are not dropped from the same height. Usually they work until late at night if there is much cargo, and the passengers get very little sleep if the cabin is on the wharf side. The natives yell to one another when giving orders to steady a loaded derrick as it descends.

After lunch, we all went ashore for a walk around the island. Samarai is on the extreme tip of New Guinea and is very small; in fact, we walked around it in three quarters of an hour, and at that, walking very slowly. We examined all the trees and flowers along the way. The rainfall is abundant, so everything is green and fresh looking. In these warm climates, there are colored shrubs called crotons. They grow eight to ten feet high and have multicolored foliage. On a single bush. you find green, red, yellow, orange and variegated leaves. On our walk this afternoon, we saw the loveliest shades of hibiscus in the most fragile and lacy designs. They are twice the size of those at home and of more vivid hues. One cannot blame the natives for tucking one or two of them behind their ears.

This small island is a government station, and to look at the native dwellings, one can easily recognize a foreign influence; nevertheless, the natives do look a bit wild with tattooing all over their faces and bodies, wearing only grass skirts. We tourists approached a group and addressed them in imitation pidgin. To our embarrassment, the young women looked up and answered in perfect English.

November 29, 1940

*T*oday we are sailing along the Pacific toward the South Solomon Islands. We expect to arrive next Friday, December sixth, unless a rough sea slows us up. We have spent a quiet day on board. It is getting quite warm; consequently, we spent most of the day on deck.

November 30, 1940

*W*e feel so grateful for the privilege of daily Mass way out here in mid-ocean. It is hard to believe that Christmas is so near, as we are having such warm weather and are surrounded with tropical vegetation. At Samarai, we saw a couple of stubby little poinsettias stretching their partly reddened leaves up to the sunlight. We stopped to look at them for only a second as they carried our thoughts back to those magnificent ones that will decorate the midnight altar at the Motherhouse. We often think and talk about you at home and wonder what you are doing at that particular time. One thing we wish we could share with you is a view of that heavenly constellation, the Southern Cross. It appears in the heavens toward the southwest. There are four bright stars, a faint little flickering one in the center; the star at the foot of the cross is very close to the horizon. The last few nights have been cloudy, causing us to forego our usual salutation.

We are anxiously waiting for the full moon, that we may feast our eyes on that much-talked-about moonlight on the South Seas. It does not seem possible that those coconut palms could be more beautiful than in midday, but we shall see. Perhaps the effect will start us all writing poetry. Don't worry, though, for Father Lebel assures us that we won't have time to breathe when we reach our mission.

Left to right: Sisters Irene, Celestine, Hedda, Mother Francis, and Sister Isabelle

Less than a half-mile separates Buka from Bougainville

A Sing-Sing on Buka

Multi-tasking on Buka

Buka Belles peroxide their hair for beauty and to control lice

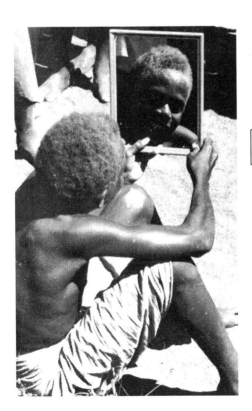

Look at me!

Women carrying food and
supplies from the bush

Inside a native house on Bougainville

A family group on
Bougainville - 1940

CHAPTER 3

The Loveliness of the Tropics

December 1, 1940

*W*e were awakened early by the ship's signal as we entered the harbor of Tagula. Our first thought was to catch a glimpse of the Solomon Islands. Such a picture as greeted our eyes is beyond description. The early rays of the morning sun covered the islands with a golden glow, and the graceful, towering coconut palms turned them into a fairyland. We couldn't dress fast enough to get out on the deck for a complete view. There was great excitement along the shore, as the arrival of the SS *Malaita* every six weeks is a real event in the lives of the white population as well as the natives. After the formalities of passports, we were ready to go ashore to Mass. Father Wall, the Marist who is stationed here, met us with his motor launch and took us to land.

As soon as we arrived at the church, Mass was begun. What a flood of thoughts and sentiments of gratitude filled our hearts as we assisted at our first Mass in the Solomon Islands. The church is very tiny and poor, made of rough boards and having only the barest necessities.

This group of islands is called the South Solomon

Islands, and the district officer has his residence here. There are many well-built homes here and on the nearby islands. Most of them are constructed on cement blocks two or three feet high to escape the excessive moisture from so much rain, and it is cooler, too. We noticed black boys working in the houses and yards. The native women take care of little white children.

After breakfast, we went ashore for a little walk of inspection. An umbrella certainly is a necessity, for the sun beats down unmercifully on one's head. As we walked along the shore we saw little striped and colored fish everywhere, the water was so clear. We asked the natives to get us some coconuts. My, they were good. The young ones are full of milk and so refreshing. To climb the trees, the natives make little notches in the trunks to give them a footing and up they go. They cling to the tree and loosen the nut with one heel.

December 2, 1940

Early this morning the SS *Malaita* moved to another island, a distance of a few miles. We spent most of the forenoon on the deck, and the captain invited us for a tour around the ship, telling us all about how the ship is steered. The chart room is very interesting. It is puzzling to see how ships can be safely guided through these many islands to avoid the coral reefs. Where it is very dangerous they travel only during the day, as it is nerve racking to steer a ship by charts at night. The depth of the water is carefully recorded. Some of the reefs are below the surface, and others are easily seen.

This has been a comparatively cool day. We went ashore and examined . . . well, just about everything. We found a shady pathway covered with vines bearing many different colored flowers. Finally, we found a nice cool place with a long bench. We decided to rest a few minutes. Soon an elderly woman came out to greet us and invited us to tea that we gratefully accepted. She was a delightful person, an Australian who has lived here 17 years. Tea was brought out by a native, and we sat in comfortable wicker chairs listening to her tell about the islands. A pet chicken came and hopped around until she fed him some crumbs, and that attracted a beautiful gray dove who was jealously watching from a branch nearby. A bit of coaxing brought him to share the goodies. We spent such an enjoyable hour under those immense trees, which spread their branches over the whole house and yard. One cannot describe the loveliness of the tropics. There is a profound stillness, yet all the while one is conscious of different forms of life. When we were ready to return to the ship, we found it had moved and was anchored out in the bay obliging us to ride out in a motor launch. This time it was a case of balancing on two feet or sitting on a dirty bench. We stood. It was a ten-minute ride and we were proud to be able to stand while the boat sped through the water.

We changed into white today, which is a great relief. We are wearing the gowns we made in Sydney, as the linen ones are in the hold, stored below 101 cases.

During our walk today we noticed little holes just everywhere in the ground, and we could not figure out what lived in them. Occasionally, we noticed a quick movement, but our inexperienced eyes weren't fast enough to see what it was. Finally, a fellow passenger came along and told us they were land crabs. From then on we walked quietly and slowly, and sure enough, from every hole a crab was peering at us. They vary in size. The largest we saw today was about the size of one's fist. There is another small crab that lives along the water's edge and occupies a shell that has been vacated by its former occupant. As this little hermit crab increases in size, it moves into another stolen shell. We picked up a small one and whistled at it. Each time it climbed part way out, then we gave it a piece of sugar and it took it in one of its claws and began chewing on it.

December 3, 1940

*W*e missionaries are celebrating the feast of Saint Francis Xavier while our ship is anchored out in the bay. We have moved near another island to unload cargo. Islands of all sizes literally dot the sea. Nearly all of them are hilly and covered with trees and vines. Here and there a couple of lone coconut palms stand silhouetted against the skyline. Today, it has been cloudy, and while it rained on one mountain, the sun was shining on the others. Many coconut plantations can be seen from here. Some of them are very clean and orderly, while others are full of undergrowth. The caretakers wait hopefully for a market for their copra. Some experiments are being made to distill the oil for use in diesel engines until the European market for margarine reopens. Some of these islands look very lonely, and we felt sorry for a planter and his wife who left the ship today after a vacation in Sydney.

All along the water's edge are native huts built like those shown in Father McHardy's book. The villagers from the bush, as well as those along the shore, construct their huts from leaves of the pandanus tree. These villagers fear one another, yet they meet at intervals to exchange foodstuffs. The "salt water boys," as they are called, catch fish, crabs and other delicacies, and in return obtain bananas, taro and other tropical foods. Woe betide the fisherman's wife if she short changes the bushman's wife. A war ensues.

Many of the natives are on board traveling from port to port to unload cargo. Whenever they see one of us they say, *"Me Catholic; give me medal."* As a result, these mendicant souls have been begging medals from all of us. We have to sleep with our rosaries under our pillows so the medals won't be removed. And string! Dear me, even our shoelaces aren't safe. Mother Francis cut down the cabin's clothesline and divided it up this morning.

Our boat passed through a tropical downpour that lasted about five minutes. Everything was drenched. The natives stretched a piece of canvas across the place where they stay and are huddled under it. It reminds one of the days of slavery to see them carry heavy boxes on bare shoulders, but they seem happy and stay with the boat. Goodness knows how they get back home. There must be about two-dozen on the fore of the ship. They bring their own taro, but the crew gives them rice besides. We are warned to watch our cabins and keep them closed, as they take anything they can lay their hands on, and will pitch overboard anything that is not useful to them. Their thick, bushy, black hair is kept two or three inches long to serve them as a convenient depository for pencils, combs, flowers, coins and sundry small articles.

December 4, 1940

During the night, the SS *Malaita* moved to another island, and before sunrise we were surprised to see something equal to Alice's Wonderland. It was a small island covered with cultivated coconut palms 25 feet high, and of all growing things, they excel in symmetry and grace. The long, smooth trunk often shapes itself in a curve, while the fronds give the impression of dancing in the breeze. If inanimate things could express moods, one would say that these palms respond to every atmospheric change. They dance in the sunshine and huddle together in silence when it rains. They are melancholy when dark clouds hang heavy overhead.

During Mass, our boat raised anchor and moved several miles to another port of call where we stayed some time to pick up copra. On the plantations, the ripe coconut meats are removed from the shells and thoroughly dried. Then they are broken into small bits and put into gunnysacks ready for shipment. Each sack is labeled with the name of the company and of the island from which it comes. Copra has a peculiar, penetrating, sickening odor. It is important that it be well dried; otherwise, it becomes overheated and spontaneous combustion takes place.

Before lunch today, one of the planters and his wife came on board to greet us. They had heard some time ago that we were coming, and were anxious to welcome us to the Solomons. They were sorry the SS *Malaita* had not come earlier to give them the opportunity to hear Mass. It has been six months since a priest had traveled through.

December 5, 1940

*T*oday, we have been moving about from place to place picking up copra. We are all nauseated from the sickening odor. This ship has not been able to dock at the wharves due to the shallowness of the water, so the motor launch takes two boats tied one behind the other to bring the copra to the SS *Malaita* from the packinghouses. We started for a visit on shore about 10:00 A.M., but a heavy rain fell as we were ready to step into the launch. Soon the sun came out again and we made a successful attempt. We were looking for the post office and stopped at a store on the way. Imagine our exclamations as we saw on the shelves some good old *Heinz's Baked Beans, S & W Products* and *Hills Brothers' Coffee.* This store carries everything from a pin on up. There were iron kettles and saucepans and a long glass case filled with fancy perfumes and talcum powders, including *Coty's* and *Djer Kis.* Two native boys were leaning over that counter as if they would absorb its alluring fragrance through the glass.

From there we started again for the post office, but Mother Francis saw a shell, so we were temporarily sidetracked to acquire two priceless treasures in three tones of pink. We almost stepped into a mud hole while watching two brilliant green lizards chase one another up a pandanus tree. They were quarreling, and one took a mouthful out of the other one's tail, but they skipped out of sight before we had a chance to cheer the winner. Just about this time a native woman came from one of the boats anchored at the pier. She spoke to us in the most perfect English while introducing herself. It took a few minutes to figure out just who she was and why she was making such a fuss over us. In the meantime, we were invited on board to meet her family. The mystery was solved, for her son Billy, a fine looking chap, had traveled on the SS *Malaita* with us. He had been quite ill, and Father Lebel thought he might have to anoint him on the way. He had a heart condition and was returning from Sydney. The family was interesting. The father was a distinguished looking Englishman who had been shipwrecked

40 years ago somewhere on the islands. Thirty years ago he had married a half-caste Solomonese, and they had three children. The two daughters reside in Sydney—one a teacher and the other married. They own a whole island and give the impression of being in good circumstances. The mother is a Catholic, and the husband has strong inclinations that way. He appeared much older than his wife and is not well. She asked us to pray for his conversion, as he has cancer and may have only a short time to live. It was really an unusual combination, and this cultured gentleman seemed very much out of his element; however, the lady was a charming woman. Her hobby was growing orchids, and she gave us some lovely ones to take on board. Some were dainty little white orchid flowers, and others were spotted like tiger lilies.

While we were waiting on the wharf for our launch to come by and pick us up, we watched the fish in the crystal-clear water. You would almost think they were butterflies instead of fish. They were of all colors, all sizes and all shapes. There were yellows and blacks, some with blue and pink spots on them. Each group stayed close together for protection. Once in a while a big fish would come along and gulp down a whole school of small fish without slowing his speed or deviating from his course. Sharks are plentiful, and the island we were on today has crocodiles. They follow a little fresh water stream down to the ocean and lie in wait for a luckless victim.

It is now 10:30 P.M., and we are up late as we hoped to have a look at the island of Nila that the ship expects to reach sometime tonight. We are all rather anxious to see the place for which we were first destined. Tomorrow morning, we shall arrive in Kieta, so we have all been busy packing. Don't know how it happens, but everybody expects the other to have room in her bag for "just this little package," which often turns out to be a five-gallon cookie jar. We have had a glorious trip on the grandest little vessel that ever traveled the South Seas. After 21 days, we really feel a bit sad at leaving. About 8:00 A.M., the missionaries will land with bags, barrels, boxes and trunks and plenty of good will and enthusiasm to begin the great work for souls.

December 6, 1940

Today, the Sisters of St. Joseph arrive in Kieta, Bougainville, the headquarters for the Marists Missions in the North Solomon Islands.

*T*his was, indeed, a gala day in our life as new missionaries. Since early morning we had been traveling along Bougainville Island just a short distance from the shore. By 8:00 A.M., we were able to see the red roofs of Kieta. No one lingered over breakfast. We were all dressed in our freshly pressed white and were anxiously scanning the shore for the mission buildings. At last we saw them, and several priests and sisters were waving to us from the top of the hill. We passed all the inspections—the doctor, passports and then customs. Formalities were brief. We all hurried down the gangplank and were transported to the bishop's launch. Instead of one bishop, there were two; one from the South Solomons and our own Bishop Wade. We experienced momentarily a little lull of expectancy, of questioning anticipation as we were to meet our bishop for the first time. He gave us a hearty welcome, and in five minutes everyone was at ease. He has a contagious good humor, and made his greeting as informal as possible. We were sorry to learn that he was going to Rabaul on the SS *Malaita* that very afternoon. His last words were, "Now everyone stay right here until I return."

It was about 12:30 P.M. when we reached the shore, and the Marist sisters were there to take us to the convent. Several little girls came along to carry our small pieces of baggage. We had to walk about three quarters of a mile up the hill, but it was not too hot and the sun was hiding behind a cloud. The convent is a large frame building on the top of a hill overlooking a coconut plantation sloping to the sea. Within a few minutes after our arrival, we had a real tropical downpour. Such rain. The drops were as big as eggs and tons of water fell in a few minutes. We stood on the wide veranda watching it rain over the valley below.

The dinner bell broke our reveries. This was our first meal of mission fare. There was soup, then boiled taro and tinned salmon, for it was Friday. For dessert there were red and yellow bananas that were very good. The little ones are called ladyfingers and are sweet.

After lunch, everyone took a siesta for an hour, as the heat is intense between noon and 2 P.M. Our beds are made like army cots with canvas stretched tightly across. They are three feet wide and six feet long. Mosquito netting hangs from above and covers the entire bed. One tucks the netting in all around to keep out night prowlers. It was First Friday, and we had holy hour from 5:00 P.M. to 6:00 P.M. We said some distracted prayers for we were intrigued with the singsong prayers of the natives. The church is of moderate size with backless benches. There are three altars, as this is the main station and the missionaries gather here for retreat.

December 7, 1940

*W*e spent our first night in the Solomon Islands, and no one was captured by a headhunter nor bitten by a centipede. One large cockroach walked through the pale rays of the lantern as it stood on the floor nearby. His large, skulking form threw panic into our midst, and in a few seconds the four of us were after him with a long pole. It was quiet until a noisy alarm broke the silence. It is quite dark until a half hour before sunrise at 6:00 A.M. We observed that at Mass the natives all received Communion first, and the sisters, last. The explanation may be forthcoming.

Right after Mass we had to do our washing and hurry to get it dry before the next shower. The sisters have a nice little washhouse with a cement floor. It is made of sac-sac, but well equipped. The small washing machine is a great help. Clothes must be hung just so high from the ground, as the place is swarming with goats of all colors and sizes. The tiny ones hop around on the most precarious ledges. A native takes care of them during the day, and brings them home at night to be milked. Goat milk is used entirely at this mission. Food is something of a penance, but we had plenty of delicious bananas. Chickens wander all around the yard and forage for themselves. They like coconuts and look plump and healthy. The roosters are well trained and seldom crow until after five in the morning. In the course of the day, an army of pigs drifts in from the woods and usually winds up in the struggling little rose garden. The six little ones are only a few weeks old and round as footballs. Their mother weighs about 400 pounds, and she can plow up a half an acre in five minutes; then she disappears, trailing her squealing family behind her.

There are approximately two-dozen native women and children on the grounds. They sleep in little sac-sac houses and wander around in wide-eyed wonder among the five strange missionaries. There is a small house where they do their cooking, the mission supplying the food, principally taro, coconuts and bananas. One of the sisters teaches them the three "R's" and they assist at Mass and evening prayers. The rest of the time they just amble about smoking newspaper cigarettes with a little tobacco in them. Then, too, betel nut is in evidence. Nearly all of them take it between smokes. No one hurries or worries except the new missionaries, and so far, we haven't learned the Solomonese way of living today and letting tomorrow take care of itself. The missionaries do not interfere too much with the native customs, so the older folks teach all the old customs to the babies. Even tiny three-year-olds carry pipes if they have them, and the women carry theirs behind their ears. Tobacco is given them in payment for work and is considered a delicacy. Likewise, depriving them of it is a means of punishment when discipline is necessary.

December 8, 1940 Feast of the Immaculate Conception. *W*e remembered you all at Mass this morning, and how we wished you could share a few minutes with us in the chapel. The pastor is a little old French priest and as nervous as a hen with a flock of ducklings. After vesting for Mass, he rounded up two couples for a double wedding. It took several minutes to figure out what he was going to do as he did not use pidgin in speaking to them. A few sharp commands finally induced the bashful pairs to join hands in front of an audience. In a few minutes, the ceremony was complete to the relief of us all. At Communion the men go to the rail before the women. During Mass, a catechist says a few decades of the rosary, and then leads the singing of a hymn or two. The singing has a great deal of force, for they seem to put their whole heart into it and perhaps their lungs.

Since this is a special feast day, a High Mass was sung in the church down in the town. We left about 8:00 A.M., followed by a dozen natives in single file. It is a good long walk, but it was comparatively cool that early. The church was filled, women on one side and men on the other. There must have been 300 or 400 packed close with the small ones on the parents' knees. Everything was usual until it came to the sermon that was delivered in pidgin. It was impossible for us to keep our composure, and we hope no one saw us. We were sitting in the back. It may be simple when one gets the system. All men are called "boys," the women are "Marys," small boys are "monkeys," babies are "pickaninnies," and Our Lord is "big fella number one."

December 11, 1940

The last few days have been spent doing odds and ends like washing, ironing and writing letters. Our trunks are down by the wharf in a little place known as the mission repair shop. We went down and opened them today and found everything as neatly packed as the day we left Orange. How good it seemed to have them this far in perfect condition. We took a few things out as we have been living in a suitcase for two months, and now we need extra supplies. The two Marist brothers are getting the bishop's boat in readiness, so we hope to see our things going on board for Hanahan.

This morning we went down to the goat pen to watch the milking. It certainly is an art. One little black native woman takes the critter by the horns, a second one kicks it, while a third holds a small pan in one hand and makes a pass at milking with the other. Meanwhile the animal resents such indignities, inasmuch as its small offspring is in another pen bleating dismally. The mother goat proceeded to lie down and end the performance. The girls muttered things we didn't understand. Finally, one of them took the obstinate creature by the middle and hoisted her onto her feet again. Presto! We had a pint of milk for the morning coffee.

You would laugh to see us combing the beach for coral and shells. There are the most beautiful shells and so many varieties. Many of them are inhabited by hermit crabs, so we call the native girls to pull them out of their shells. When the ocean is very rough the large shells are washed up on shore, some of them as big as washbasins. The smaller ones are useable as holy water fonts, soap dishes and ashtrays. Mother Francis is making a collection to bring home with her. Someday, perhaps we too, can send some home if we have time on our mission to gather them. Father Poncelet, one of the Marist priests, has a hobby of collecting insects, and has sent specimens to museums in different parts of the world.

December 12, 1940

After breakfast, Sister Irene and Sister Hedda started out for their first visit to the native hospital. Brother Paul met us at the pier and took us across the bay in a small motorboat. The ride was delightful, as it was quite early and fairly cool. The ocean is very warm, and the water looks clear and inviting, but it's full of sharks. Besides, there are many kinds of poisonous fish that would paralyze a swimmer within a few minutes. In fact, there are too many hungry things in the beautiful blue Pacific to make bathing a pleasure.

We arrived at the hospital about 10:00 A.M., and already many natives were waiting their turns for treatment. The doctor and several native assistants had all the equipment sterilized and ready to begin. We watched a couple of intravenous treatments being given, then we took a hand at it, and gave six without any difficulty, locating the veins in several small arms. The medicine is a form of salvarsan, which is given in various dilutions. It is the standard treatment for yaws, [8] and other tropical ulcers. The small children who scream and kick too much are held down while it is given intramuscularly.

After the intravenous treatments were given, the lineup was made for dressings. Things were done with neatness and dispatch that appealed to our systematic souls. Each patient was carefully examined and then passed on to the next assistant for the application of ointment and a dressing. You ought to see how they use adhesive here. When the ulcers are almost healed, plain adhesive is strapped over the open sore directly on the skin, and the results are very good. This is a government hospital, and they have all the supplies they need. All infectious diseases must be reported to Kieta—for example, dysentery, meningitis, leprosy, and pneumonia.

December 13, 1940

*T*oday we made another visit to the hospital, and this time it was of particular interest as we saw our first group of patients with leprosy. They came across from their village on a nearby island and waited in line for their injections of leprol. It is given intramuscularly twice each week and very little effect is noticed until it has been continued several months. Some have very good results, and others do not respond to the treatment at all. The advanced cases do not receive much help from it, and they are such pathetic looking human forms. Some have lost fingers on both hands, and still others have open lesions on different parts of the body. The eyes and ears have ulcerating nodules on them. They lose sensation in the affected area, but when the joints are involved, all movement becomes very painful. They live in the native village, and a boy who has been instructed in doing dressings is assigned to the village to care for them. It is difficult to distinguish the disease in the early stages, as the discoloration of the skin is very slight and the patches of lighter brown are not readily noticed.

After finishing with the lepers, we gave several intravenous injections to patients suffering from yaws. We had to pass inspection for a certificate from the government officials. In this we succeeded with very little difficulty. We started for home and got there in time for Benediction. Each Friday we have Benediction from 5:00 P.M. to 6:00 P.M. The natives make a short visit, but they tire easily. After the evening meal, the native girls sat on the veranda and sang Christmas carols for us. They have very good voices and it made us homesick to hear the old favorites. We can hardly believe we are in the season of Christmas. We are surrounded with all this tropical loveliness. There are only 11 days until Christmas, and tomorrow morning we expect to start out on the last lap of the trip. Just watch us cramming things into our suitcase. There's the same old story, "Sister, do you think you have room for this very small package?"

December 14, 1940

*W*e didn't have to be called the second time, as this is the day of days, and we start for Hanahan. We assisted at four Masses, including Bishop Wade's. Right after breakfast our bags were lined up for the boys to carry down to the pier, and by 8:30 A.M., we all started down the hill to go on board. It was fairly cool so early in the morning, and we walked slowly. As we arrived at the wharf, we experienced a strange sensation on seeing the two boats in readiness. The *Ludwig* is Bishop Wade's 23-ton schooner. The other, a small motor launch, was to carry our baggage, for there was not enough room in the hold of the *Ludwig*. Before leaving, Bishop Wade, Mother Francis, and Sister Isabelle had to go to the government house to present our passports, so we did not go on board until 10:45 A.M. The Marist sisters who came down with us remained until we were under way. At last the engines started, and we were soon out in the open sea. There were three priests on board. One is the captain of the schooner and the other two are returning to their missions. Father Lebel, who came with us from Sydney, is going to Tinputz. The crew consists of six husky natives. They seem to be able to take care of all the mechanical contrivances, and Father Lebreton walks around to supervise. Father Lebel led the prayers for our safe journey. About all one has to do in this small boat, is to sit still in a deck chair. There is considerable motion, and it may not be long before someone shows signs of seasickness.

At 11:30 A.M., one of the native boys served tea on a small table among our deck chairs. It was refreshing, and we enjoyed it. At noon we arrived at Tunuru, the station where Father McHardy spent most of his mission life. We anchored some distance out and went ashore in the small motorboat. You should have seen us climbing over the side and landing right side up in that tipsy little thing. It is only a short distance to the shore. We were happy to visit the church that has been built as a memorial to Father McHardy. Two priests and several natives were there to meet us when we landed. We walked over to the church and found it one of the finest we have seen in the islands. We all knelt and said a little prayer for all of you at home. Then Mother Francis took a couple of pictures of us on the church steps and of the grounds. We paid a short visit to Father Lebel's house. Like most such structures, it is built some distance up from the ground. This allows more ventilation and is drier during the wet season. The house was quite cool, and we sat down for some lemonade and fresh pineapple. The pineapple was deliciously sweet and juicy—the best we have had in the islands. They have about half of an acre of them, and Father Weber gave us six big ones to take on board. We were back on the *Ludwig* in another half hour and on our way to the next mission, where we plan to stay for the night. The afternoon went very quietly, at least for two of us. Sister Isabelle and Sister Hedda had eaten too much pineapple, and it didn't ride well on the salt water, so the two invalids buried themselves in their deck chairs while the others enjoyed hot tea and sea biscuits.

We traveled a calm sea along the coast of Bougainville

Island. The schooner wound its way in and out among coral reefs, and the breakers dashed among the reefs with great white crests. The coral is white, and the clear blue water gives it the appearance of bright green. It is beautiful to look at, but so treacherous. One of the mission boats was wrecked on a reef a few years ago. They were able to save the cargo, but lost a splendid boat. The whole afternoon was really delightful, and we arrived at Asitavi about sundown. We dropped anchor and rode in to shore in small boats. The sun dropped from sight, and we had at once a beautiful full moon. In the distance, we could see two white forms awaiting us. They were Father Fluet from Lawrence, Massachusetts, and Brother Henry from New Zealand. They helped us ashore while the natives pulled the boat upon the beach. They took us to our quarters where we prepared for supper. We made a visit to the church on the way to Father's house for our meal of fried sweet potatoes, fish, fruit salad and those delicious little bananas called ladyfingers. The native boys had prepared it and served us first, and then served the priests after we had retired to our house. We found the building to be made entirely of bamboo and sac-sac leaves. Our cots were comfortable, and we had been doubly assured that centipedes did not live there. One had been seen five months before and had been killed, so Brother Henry told us. Before putting out our lanterns, we decided to look around, however. We found two huge spiders as big as our California tarantulas. We killed them both with a 12-foot pole, while one of the sisters covered her eyes until the dreadful deed was done. Finally, we settled into bed and slept as well as could be expected. Morning revealed one of the sisters sleeping on the table. It seems that a small python wound itself around the WICKER LOUNGE ON WHICH SHE WAS SLEEPING—so we were told. The transfer had been made immediately.

December 15, 1940

*W*e were awake at the crack of dawn and ready to go out exploring, but the rising bell had not rung, so we had to stay in bed until it did. How hard it is to stay in bed when you are in a strange land full of interesting things to be seen. First, we assisted at two Masses and listened to a very good sermon in pidgin by Father Fluet. We understood enough to appreciate his noble efforts to explain the gospel to his natives. He is such a fine person, and we shall always remember his kindness to us. He had the boys make special efforts to prepare things we would like. For breakfast that morning, we had big grapefruits from a tree that Father Lebel had planted when the mission was first started. Now it is large and is bearing the most delicious fruit. Then we had pineapple, papayas, fried eggs and bread and butter. We felt like queens having all these luxuries. During the course of the meal our hosts made anxious inquiries about our night's rest. We evaded questions, even the most pointed ones, as we did not want them to know we were the least bit nervous about insects. They all seemed to enjoy us, particularly because we could laugh and enjoy a joke on ourselves. We have noticed that same spirit among the Marist priests. They have a delightful sense of humor, and a cheerful and happy spirit. They are wonderful missionaries and have done much for the Church.

After breakfast, the two sister-nurses went to the dispensary to help Father Fluet with his patients. Several who had come from 15 miles away were waiting for dressings. First, the intravenous medications were given, then the dressings. We observed that poor Father did not even have a forceps to handle those dreadful ulcer dressings. His dispensary was something like Old Mother Hubbard's cupboard. He knew how to put on a very neat bandage and could give an intravenous with his eyes shut. Everything had to be used sparingly, as so many came for dressings, and it doesn't take long to use a big supply. Another problem is the lack of cooperation on the part of the natives. They remove the dressings and go down to the ocean to bathe the affected areas. It requires infinite patience to deal with them due to their lack of understanding of treatment. The women are uneducated, and few can even speak a word of pidgin. The work that has been accomplished on these missions is little short of miraculous. Some of the priests are so young, yet they have often to go to a new center to organize the natives and build up a church and school, as well as a house for themselves. It is pioneering work of the hardest kind, and we consider it a privilege just to pass through these stations that have been established by these saintly men. Many have already gone to their eternal home, and others have come to bring Christ to these poor souls. Do pray constantly for missionary priests and their work, for their lives are so much harder than ours, and you will never know how much they need the help of your prayers and little sacrifices.

This afternoon we had dinner about 2:00 P.M., and it was a special occasion. There was fried chicken, sweet potatoes and all kinds of delicious fruits. Father Fluet opened the cake that Sister Isabelle had brought to him from his mother in Lowell, Massachusetts. He was so happy to have direct news from his people, and you can well imagine how acceptable was a piece of his mother's homemade cake. We had music with our dinner. The priests played records on a little creaky phonograph. Later in the afternoon, we went for a walk around the grounds and up the hill to get a wide view. The vegetation is very dense, and we followed a little road about half a mile to see the plants and trees. There are so many tall trees, and they seem almost to touch the sky. The top branches spread out and vines climb up the trunks, making it almost impossible for the sun to penetrate. It was quite dry as there had been no rain for a week or ten days. The climate here at Asitavi is very pleasant with a cool breeze from the ocean. We do not travel on these small boats at night or on Sunday, so we have the opportunity to spend this time at the station. There aren't any sisters here, and how we wish we could stay to help with all the work that awaits these missionaries. Truly the harvest is great and the laborers few on these islands.

The day passed quickly, and we made preparations for our second night in the sac-sac house. The nights are almost as bright as day when the moon is full. It was up at 7:00 P.M.

We should like to be able to describe the beauty of a full moon on a tropical island, but dare not wax poetic on the subject. It is everything one can imagine. Even the natives react to its magic and have special programs of song and dance during the short space of full moon. They make flutes from bamboo and instruments from shells to put their emotions into music—they, at least, think it is music.

December 16, 1940

*T*his is Monday morning, and we are all ready for an early start. Our captain, Father Lebreton, said Mass at 6:00 A.M., and right after breakfast the boys took our bags to the schooner while we folded our blankets and put the little sac-sac house in order. Our stay had been so pleasant we were all sorry to leave. It was sad to leave the two missionaries alone. Father Fluet and Brother Henry accompanied us to the beach where our rowboat was pulled up on the beach. We were obligated to make a fast run and jump into it as the waves receded. We got in amidst much laughter and were green with envy because Father Lebreton was taken to the *Ludwig* in an outrigger canoe—a pleasure still in store for us. These canoes move swiftly through the water as they are light and could be described as streamlined. The outrigger helps them to maintain the proper balance, and is propelled by paddles. The space to sit in is very narrow, so a long journey is trying in the extreme. The natives travel long distances in them and seem to withstand heavy seas. The outriggers are hewn from large logs and vary in size.

Our engines began to purr, and we were off. The morning was beautifully clear. As we petitioned our Blessed Mother for a safe journey, we left behind one of the finest missions we have seen so far. Off in the background stands an active volcano sending up its tiny spiral of white smoke. Occasionally it erupts, but it is three or four miles from the mission, and all they notice is the rumbling in the earth. All of the statues in the church are securely fastened with a piece of stout wire. Our Lady of the Immaculate Conception stands above the main altar with a heavy wire across her chest to keep her safely on her pedestal. The church and the whole mission, for that matter, was erected by Father Lebel, the American priest who had traveled with us from Sydney. After five years, he had been transferred to another mission, and Father Fluet took this one over. The landscaping and plan of the mission is very fine. The church is made of substantial poles of hardwood, and the walls are of woven bamboo, while the roof is of corrugated iron. It is finished nicely inside and shows careful attention to details. There are three altars, and the church is large enough for about 500 people. The pews are simple benches without backs, and have narrow boards on which to kneel. One of the most impressive scenes is the Communion of the natives.

Those half-naked black men go up to receive our Lord and so devoutly. During the sermon, some of them were so absorbed that they leaned forward on their elbows to listen most attentively. There are between 50 and 60 boys living on the mission compound at Asitavi. They have regular hours for class, and part of the time is allotted to gardening. Their food consists principally of taro, sweet potatoes and fruit. Strange as it may seem, these tropical fruits must be cultivated and replanted periodically to make them produce. We always thought they just grew. The sweet potato is dug up and a piece of the vine is planted so that four or five months hence a new crop of potatoes will be ready. The priests have a great deal to do as even the raising of poultry takes considerable time. Ducks do very well in some parts of the islands and they have a large flock in Asitavi. A strange friendship grew up in the barnyard. A black rooster adopted eight little guinea hens and proudly takes them around in search of worms. Whenever he finds a choice morsel, he takes them to enjoy the feast. Father Fluet is anxious to try to raise turkeys at the mission, for fresh meat is a problem. The pigs in the mountains are wild, and the meat is not very good. Some of the stations have goats, and the meat is tasty when the animals are young.

We are puffing along the shore of Bougainville Island expecting to reach Tinputz by evening and to stay there for the night. We are about three miles off shore and can enjoy the beautiful scenery. Since most of the island is mountainous, travel by land is difficult. Elevations often go straight up from the western edge. We had a little engine trouble, but Father Lebreton rolled up his sleeves and got good results after considerable hammering. Now we are sailing right along at the top speed, and the *Rosa* is following along in tow. Once in a while we strike a rough place and are tossed from side to side. During lunch, our plates of tomato soup almost landed in the ocean. We did some fast rescuing and promptly disposed of our soup. We have a small table in the center to hold our cups, spoons and plates. Essentials only are supplied. We have tinned meat, butter and jam with hot tea. Sister Isabelle has a mild touch of seasickness, but the others are fine. There is a cool breeze on deck, and we are trying to realize that we Sisters of Saint Joseph are really in the Solomon Islands. It seems like a dream but such a happy dream to be a missionary. Who knows which privilege is the greater, that of doing the actual work or, that of staying at home and praying for those who serve.

At 3:30 P.M., the *Ludwig* slowly wound its way into the harbor of Tinputz. The late afternoon sun sent its rays through the tall trees and rested on the mission buildings at the top of the hill. We were glad to be on land once more, and the Marist sisters came to welcome us. We climbed the steep hill to the convent and soon were refreshed with tea in pretty blue and white cups. It is so good when one is tired, and we enjoyed hot tea even though we were in the tropics. There are three sisters at this station, and they have about 30 native children of all ages.

Many of the Marist sisters are French and speak very little English. The superior here has been in the islands about 32 years. They spared nothing to make us comfortable in spite of our unexpected arrival. You see, there isn't any way of communication in advance, and the arrival of a boat is announced by the sounds of its engines. The stillness is so profound that the chugging of an engine causes great excitement among the natives, who run to the mission to announce it. This mission was established several years ago, and it is here that the one lumber mill in the Solomon missions is operated.

In the evening, we were entertained by the natives who sang in the moonlight and then completed their program with native dances, to the music of bamboo drums. These are made from stalks of bamboo six to eight inches in diameter and three to four feet in length. The drum is firmly held in one hand while the ground is beaten, and the sound travels up the hollow tube weirdly betraying its pagan origin. The crouching contortions of the dance added to the intensity of the eerie scene. The little tots are put into the center of the circle to get them out of the way. Their loud wails convinced us that it is not exactly a place of honor.

December 17, 1940
Tomorrow, the Sisters of St. Joseph arrive at their new mission assignment, Hanahan, on the island of Buka.

*F*rom this high elevation overlooking the harbor, we watched the most gorgeous sunrise. Later, we started on a tour of inspection. One does things as early as possible in the morning as it is very hot by 9:00 A.M. We went to the sawmill, the pride and joy of the Marist missions. It has been operating about eight years, and just before the war in Europe, they received a special diesel engine that burns wood and produces steam power to run the big saws. Special hardwood is used for lumber, and the trees are cut and hauled on a trolley to the mill. The logs are two and three feet in diameter and approximately 20 feet long. All sizes of boards and planks as well as heavier square pieces for posts are turned out. Then it is supposed to dry in the sun, but there is such demand for lumber that it does not have a chance. Green lumber shrinks and leaves large cracks in the building. They tell us that our house at Hanahan was built from lumber made at this mill. The *Ludwig* acts as a lumber and passenger boat as well, and they are loading some lumber now while we wait to go on board. As soon as that is finished we shall start out.

We sailed at 11:00 A.M., and Father Lebel is coming with us to make a sick call at one of his missions 25 miles from Tinputz. After fulfilling these duties, he will walk back to the station. We are making good progress toward our next stop, which is Buka Passage. After about two hours, we struck a rough place and the little *Rosa* bobbed up and down like a cork. We were all worried, as all of our belongings are on it, and its safe arrival is of the greatest importance.

At 5:00 P.M., we arrived at Buka Passage. This is a narrow channel separating the island of Bougainville from our little island of Buka. It is a quarter of a mile wide, and very choppy; therefore, boats find it difficult to anchor. The government officials are stationed on the island of Sohano in the middle of the channel. Our mail will be taken off the SS *Malaita* here and brought to us by carrier. We were greeted at the wharf by Laurie Chan, a Chinese who was educated in Sydney at the Marist Brothers' College. His wife was with him. She is a graduate of the Sisters' School in Rabaul. They speak perfect English and have a very nice little store at the Passage. He buys many things from Sydney and also imports some goods from China and Japan. He gave us a refreshing drink, and then we started out to the nearest mission three miles distant. Father Caffiaux came with us and assured us it was only a little walk. We started at 5:30 P.M., and got there at 7:30 P.M., so you know how little it was. Later, we learned it was three miles—no wonder our tender feet were tired. After supper and a visit to the mission, we returned to our boat. Coming back, Father Lebreton led the way through a partially moonlit jungle. At the Chinese store again, we had a cool drink to quench the everlasting tropical thirst. It was 11:00 P.M. when we again got on the *Ludwig*, so we sat on deck in our chairs and dozed until 2:00 A.M. Then Father Lebreton said Mass with his altar arranged on a tool chest, with two lanterns giving out a pale light. *The Ludwig* swayed gently with the motion of the water. All around us were the recumbent forms of the boat's native crew. We knelt in any space we could find and assisted at Mass and Holy

Communion. The occasion was impressive as we realized that we were 10,000 miles from home. As the Mass ended, the motors were started, and in a short while the *Ludwig* and her satellite were out in deep waters. It is a three-hour trip from Buka Passage to Hanahan. The atmosphere is so clear and the moonlight so brilliant that we were able to read some of our prayers. Shortly after sunrise we saw in the distance the hills and the little frame building that was to be our future home.

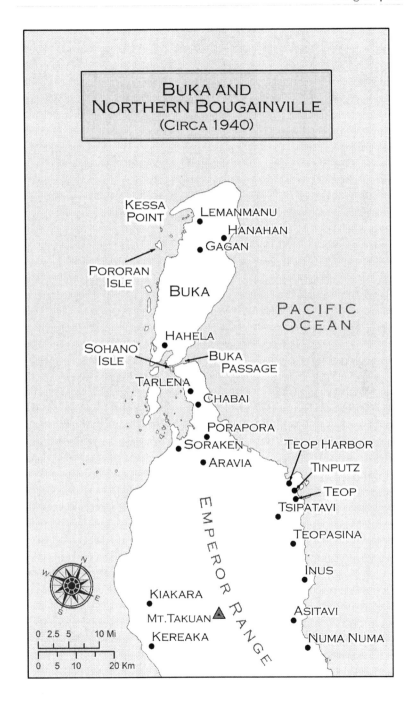

BUKA AND
NORTHERN BOUGAINVILLE
(CIRCA 1940)

KESSA
POINT
LEMANMANU
HANAHAN
GAGAN
PORORAN
ISLE
BUKA

PACIFIC
OCEAN

HAHELA
SOHANO
ISLE
BUKA
PASSAGE
TARLENA
CHABAI
PORAPORA
SORAKEN
ARAVIA
TEOP HARBOR
TINPUTZ
TEOP
TSIPATAVI
TEOPASINA
INUS

KIAKARA
MT. TAKUAN
KEREAKA
ASITAVI
NUMA NUMA

EMPEROR RANGE

N
W   E
S

0 2.5 5   10 Mi
0   5   10   20 Km

CHAPTER 4

The Arrival of the Holy Molys

December 18, 1940

*T*his morning is just three months from the day we left Orange. How happy we were to know that at last we had reached our destination. Owing to the coral reefs, we were unable to reach shore in the *Ludwig*. We stopped some distance out in deep water, and a large outrigger canoe came to get the passengers. Even the canoe could not reach the shore, and two stalwart natives carried each one of us through the surf. The whole village had gathered there to look in wide-eyed wonder at the new sisters. They did not know what to call us, as they noticed that we were dressed differently from the other sisters, so they hit upon the bright idea of calling us Holy Molys, a title that amused us much. On the shore, also awaiting us, was Father Joseph Lamarre, our pastor. He is a young American priest from Brunswick, Maine, with four years of mission experience, six months of which have been spent in Hanahan. Two Marist sisters destined for Kieta welcomed us and took us up the cliff to the mission. What a climb! The elevation is over 300 feet up a zigzag trail. In some places, one must set one's foot carefully on a jutting coral to rise slowly step-by-step. The sisters served us with a cup of coffee before taking us on our tour of inspection. There were natives everywhere staring at us. After giving us brief instructions, the Marist sisters went down to the *Ludwig* to return to Kieta. The newness and the strangeness of the situation overwhelmed us. A temporary assignment of duties was given to each one of us, and we gradually got our bearings. We rolled up our sleeves, but about all we were able to accomplish was the placing of our bags and boxes. Meanwhile, our five tons of freight had been carried up the cliff by the natives. How Mr. Tobin's icebox got up that hill we shall never be able to fathom. We noticed that the twine and packing were disappearing as soon as they were removed, but we hardly realized that they had any value. In the following Sunday's sermon, we were startled to hear Father say, "*Me shame too much long you fella, you steal plenty rope blong Sister.*"

Sister Celestine took charge of the native girls, Sister Hedda the kitchen, and Sister Irene the church and dispensary. Mother Francis was our right hand man and how things did move. Sister Isabelle helped her with the unpacking. When the sister-cook was bordering on despair, Mother Francis came to the kitchen and saved our lives by cooking a large platter of pancakes.

Our house is really comfortable and thank goodness it has two stories so we can come up the stairs and be ourselves for a few minutes to escape the noisy natives. There are four bedrooms, each containing a table, a washstand made from a kerosene box, a kanda bed, and one homemade chair. I may mention that a kanda bed is a native invention. The hammock part is made of woven kanda vine fastened to the framework. The community room seems to be very nice, though we have been so busy piling things into it that we haven't had time to admire its attractive features. It has plenty of windows and always a breeze. Downstairs are the refectory, storeroom and a small reception room. The kitchen is a separate house a short distance away, as it is too warm to have a wood stove with all its smoke and ashes in the main building. There is a wire fence around the porch to keep out the goats, chickens and other animal life, but it fails miserably in its purpose. There are goats everywhere, and a brand new one just arrived. Soon we hope to get things sorted out and running on schedule. In the meantime, we laugh at all the funny things that happen to us. We are somewhat handicapped in not knowing the language. All we can say is, "*Me no savvy,*" which makes the natives laugh heartily.

In the afternoon of the first day, a little black infant was brought to us. She weighed about four pounds and was eight days old. Sister Irene fixed her up in a packing box, and we gave her a bottle of goat's milk. She seemed starved, as her mother had been dead about four days. Now we have four babies in the nursery, all under the age of three months. We feed them goat's milk and also use Lactogen that we brought with us.

About all we could do the first day was to remember the holy presence of God and work like fury. It is still a mystery how the natives were able to climb that steep hill with those heavy boxes and trunks. Everything arrived in fine condition; not even a drop of water on any of it, and when we opened the boxes, they were just as perfect as the day they left Orange. The drug boxes are still unpacked as there is still a good supply for the present. In the dispensary, we found a quantity of drugs, and a few surgical instruments, most of them obtained through Father Carosche's Medical Missionary organization in Washington, D.C.

The mission compound consists of a large church accommodating about 700 people. It is a frame building with a corrugated iron roof and rows of plain benches. Also, there is a rectory, a convent, a small dispensary, a school, and a nursery.

Our water supply is rainwater that is caught in large metal tanks. Our dear Lord has been good to us, and has kept them full for we have needed plenty for cleaning and washing. It has been four weeks since it had rained, but the day after our arrival we had a heavy downpour that filled them all. We have a little shed for the laundry with an iron grate over some stones for boiling the clothes. Fortunately, there is plenty of wood for the fire, but as yet we are not skilled stokers and half of the time the fire goes out. In the kitchen, one feeds the fire with one hand and anxiously lifts the lids from the kettles with the other to see if there are any signs of boiling. It is exasperating and slow, but we are hopeful.

The kitchen is just a few steps from the house, and we bring the food all prepared to the refectory. The icebox has been installed, and what a blessing it is in this hot climate. Father Lamarre was the only one with any mechanical ability and the courage to attempt putting it together. He labored and perspired over the book of instructions and innumerable bolts and screws, and at the end of a week was rewarded with a glass of iced tea. Now we can keep food that would otherwise spoil overnight. The second day we were here the native boys killed a goat and brought all the meat to the poor sister-cook, who did not know what on earth to do with it. She managed to clean it and tuck it into the icebox. If those annoying creatures do not stay out of the kitchen, we shall have fresh meat every day. Do not let anyone tell you that they live on tin cans. They come into the kitchen and eat whatever they can find in the vegetable room. Father Lamarre promises to build a fence in the near future to keep them away from the house, and that thought alone rejoices our hearts.

Until Christmas, we were busy unpacking and trying to get settled. Progress is slow as we have to cook our meals and once in a while have a few minutes to rest. Still, we are encouraged and feel we have done a lot in this short time. Preparations for Christmas were hurried along as quickly as possible. The natives decorated the church with colored leaves and ferns and made a beautiful crib. The statues were good and the little scene was very realistic. We all dressed in black for midnight Mass, and after the second Mass, came home and had some breakfast. There were at least 1,000 natives present, and Father Lamarre distributed about 700 Communions.

Christmas day was a busy one, though we did find some time to recreate together when our work was finished. For dinner we had roast chicken, sweet potatoes and baked squash with fruit cake for dessert. We had tried to cook some dried lima beans, but after simmering them all day, they were still too hard to eat. We learned that soaking them overnight was the secret. The sisters have been very patient with the amateur cook, and so far, everyone's appetite is good.

We take our five grains of quinine every day and an extra five grains once a week. There are not many mosquitoes here, but enough to carry malaria. They tell us that anopheles mosquitoes come out after sundown and disappear at sunrise. We use mosquito nets on our beds. They protect us from centipedes and scorpions, too. The first night, while we were preparing for bed, we found a large scorpion, and Sister Isabelle killed him with a single blow while the rest of us got up on chairs and wrung our hands. We have never seen so many spiders in our whole lives. They are all sizes and colors and shapes. They weave webs around everything in a few hours. Throughout the tropics we have noticed that insidious conspiracy of nature to conform all things to itself. Rust corrodes, mildew destroys and thousands of insects eat through clothing, food and wooden buildings. Even the jungle creeps up to the house and threatens to envelope it unless it is kept in check. Truly, it is a constant warfare.

We have been here nearly three weeks and are beginning to formulate a system for our daily routine. Things are shaping themselves gradually, and our hearts are a bit lighter. It isn't such an effort to smile, and our weariness isn't so pronounced. Amusing things happen which we think you will enjoy. The hens came into the church and laid an egg in the excelsior "straw" of the Christ Child's crib. Then the dogs killed one of the native's pigs and almost caused a riot. Pigs are prize possessions. Tonight, one of the tiniest goats got lost, and we found him after night prayers behind the cupboard in our refectory. There he was yelling his head off, and all the time we thought he was outside in the yard.

We have a guest with us for a few days—one of the

secular nurses from Pororan. These nurses come from Australia to do missionary work. There are three at the station at Pororan, and we hear that they are doing splendid work. They take care of the tiny babies and then return them to the relatives when they are old enough to subsist on native foods. They have an experienced boy to do the cooking and another for the housework, which leaves them free to do the nursing in the dispensary as well as to visit the villages. Miss Menzies, who is visiting, came over on a bicycle, and had traveled all day to get here. She was very tired when she arrived. It was kind of her to come and offer her assistance while we were getting settled. She helps us with the dressings and injections each morning, and we are asking all sorts of questions about the routine at the clinic. She was the first to give us a course in pidgin English.

Today, we received Reverend Mother Louis' radiogram, and how happy we all were. Each one read it over about ten times, and now we are anxiously waiting for the SS *Malaita* to bring us some mail. We haven't heard a word from anyone since leaving Orange, and we are all wondering how folks are at home. Just picture us devouring the contents of the mailbag.

Do write to us often and pray for us every hour, not alone for us, but for all missionaries. How well Saint Therese, the Little Flower, understood their needs and offered her weary footsteps for them. She smiles serenely at us from many niches in the convent and in the church, and it refreshes us and makes our steps much lighter.

January 4, 1941

The only item of interest for the journal is that our mission cat, Arabella, had four kittens. We found them on the kitchen table when we went to light the fire in the morning. There she sat in their midst, proudly displaying them to our astonished eyes. We found a packing box and installed her in the woodshed, hoping that her presence will have some effect on the rat population.

Today, we finished painting the little room which is to be known from this day forth as the *parlor*. It really looks elegant, and pictures of the Holy Family, our Pope, and Bishop Wade are securely hung on nails. We have a place for Reverend Mother as soon as we can locate her picture in the trunk. We have a three-piece set of wicker furniture that Mother Francis purchased from a plantation near Asitavi. It just completes the room and is our pride and joy. We sit in there only on very special occasions. The refectory is due for a going-over next week if the paint holds out. These two rooms are very poorly lighted, and the white paint brightens them up so much. We have a little corner fixed up for a shower, and everyone gave it a Saturday try-out. It is a pail fastened to a rope in the rafters. There is a gadget that releases the water when pulling a cord.

An exciting moment came for us on Friday. Father Lamarre and his cook-boy brought us ten live lobsters in a bag, saying, "Here's something for dinner." We were panic stricken, as we had never met lobsters except in tins. Recipe books failed to give any directions for procedures with live ones. A native girl, laughing at our ignorance, prepared a large kettle of boiling water and showed us how it is done.

It may be of interest to you to know how we trade with the natives. They bring us taro, tomatoes, eggs, fish, bananas, and pineapples. They take in exchange tobacco, material for lavas, kerosene, fishhooks, and soap. Our garden does not produce a sufficient supply of fruits and vegetables.

The Monday after Christmas, school was officially opened with an attendance of 20 boys. The building is a little sac-sac house on Father Lamarre's side of the compound and nearly all of the pupils were formerly taught by him. Sister Isabelle teaches the boys from 9:00 A.M. until 11:30 A.M. Later, Sister Celestine will start a class with the girls. We have 17 teenage girls who help us in a half-hearted sort of way. We have to coax or bribe them to get the few chores done. What they really like to do is to sit and smoke.

January 6, 1941

*T*his is the feast of the Epiphany, and our thoughts are with you all in Orange. Today, Sister Hedda renewed her vows for one year, and Sister Irene picked all the flowers in the garden to celebrate the event. We spent our recreation on the porch in the moonlight, and played a couple of records on an old wheezy phonograph. To us it sounded better than anything the Metropolitan Opera could produce since we haven't heard music for a long time. Sister Isabelle has not yet unpacked her trumpet.

Some day we promise to take a few minutes off to admire the scenery and write you about it. This is a beautiful spot, and we have a marvelous view from here. The clear blue of the ocean shows through the lacy fringe of the palm trees. In all this brilliance, the most dazzling of all is the picture produced at night by flashes and chains of lightening. They illuminate the white surf in the distance and outline the coco palms against the sky. Our night skies are a constant fascination to us. From our upstairs veranda we view splendor. The stars are particularly bright and scintillating, and among them we eagerly search each night for the Southern Cross.

January 18, 1941

*W*e have just returned from taking Mother Francis down to the boat. She is starting on her long journey home. It has been a trying month for her, and she is very tired. She pushed the work along as quickly as possible, and thanks to her, we have many of the things that go to make a house a home. She scrubbed and cleaned and painted and perspired with the rest of us. Even the Sacred Heart statue in the church received a coat of paint. Mother Francis left on a little Japanese schooner for Buka Passage where she will take a boat to Rabaul. From there she expects to fly to Sydney and avoid the long and dangerous trip on the SS *Malaita.*

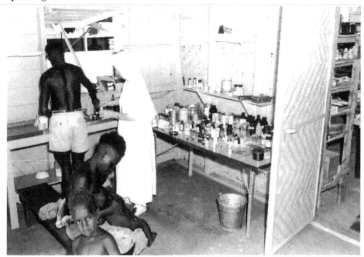

Sister Irene treating a patient with yaws

Father Lamarre proudly rides his motorbike

Sister Hedda with one of her tiny charges

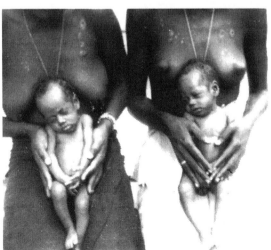

Fragile babies lovingly cared for

Sister Irene bikes to a local village

Sister Irene demonstrates how to bandage a wound

Constructing a house

An outrigger canoe paddled by experts

May 12, 1941

*O*n the feast of Corpus Christi, we had a procession. The schoolboys worked hard to decorate. The ground is nearly always wet, so fair sized shrubs were cut and stuck in the ground all along the roadway leading to the outdoor altar. This was about a quarter of a mile from the church and it was really a picture. The boys do very well when it comes to arranging leaves and shrubs. There were long ferns and colored crotons as well as branches of palms. In the procession, the schoolboys carried the canopy and the best singers walked at the head with Sister Isabelle who conducted the singing. The men followed and the women came last with one of the sisters leading. There were about 600 in the procession and it couldn't have been carried out more perfectly. It was the first time the whole congregation had taken part in a procession, and everyone seemed to enjoy the ceremony. It was a beautiful clear morning, and the sun very considerately hid behind a cloud until we were back at the church. We were all so happy that everything went along so smoothly, and the schoolboys sang exceptionally well. Everyone was very orderly both coming and going. The catechists walked at the side and "shushed" those who became too talkative.

June 8, 1941

*W*hen we wrote last we were anxiously awaiting the arrival of our cargo. On the fifth of June, a small boat was able to anchor outside of the reef and unload our things into a canoe to bring ashore. Mother Francis had made some very necessary purchases in Sydney, among them a new stove. It was great to sleep on a mattress again. We had been using the kanda beds, and it is a bit hard to fit one's shoulder and hip bone into a comfortable crevice. Aside from the dry goods, we were mighty glad to see a whole sack of flour and some real sugar again. The rough sea made it impossible to bring everything in, so a boy had to make the 50-mile round trip to the Passage to bring us a tin of tea and a small amount of flour. The shortage obligated us to try native foods, and we found it very filling, especially the taro. We tried to bake it, and steamed it as a substitute for bread and found it very good. Now we understand why the natives are not satisfied with anything but taro. We had a busy day unpacking when things arrived, and it made us think of last December. The schoolboys had a day's vacation to carry things up from the beach, while we hunted around for containers so that we could store things away in the cupboards. Everything with a tight fitting cover is priceless in our house, as dried foodstuffs have to be protected from insects.

The next important event was a visit from Bishop Wade. It was announced the evening before by a note from Father Lamarre. It read, *"Bishop Wade will arrive from Lemanmanu about 1:00 P.M. tomorrow afternoon. Pleasant dreams."* You can imagine how pleasant our dreams were with practically nothing prepared, and this was his first visit. Sister Hedda killed a duck and got it ready, while Sister Irene hustled over to the sacristy to unpack the proper vestments, and the other two busied themselves with the dozens of little duties that had to be done.

The bishop's stay was very short. He arrived by bicycle about 4:00 P.M. and left for Buka Passage the following day at 1:00 P.M. We all enjoyed his visit, as he is so cheerful and encouraging. He came to make his official visit about 10:00 A.M. After chatting with us for a few minutes, he broke the news of the division of our little group. Two were to go to Hahela and take care of the center there. Sister Isabelle was to be one of them, for he wishes that to be our headquarters. Hahela is more central and communication is easier. There is a wireless service there from the government headquarters to Kieta. Needless to say, we were all a little heartsick at the thought of separation, but after we had time to consider it, we realized how fortunate we were to be together the first few months. We are now better able to cope with problems arising in a new center. It has been decided that Sister Irene remain at Hanahan and take charge of the mission with Sister Celestine. Sister Isabelle and Sister

Hedda will go to Hahela. The house is not ready yet, but they expect to leave sometime before Christmas.

June 21, 1941

About the middle of June, the two bicycles arrived from Buka Passage. Father Lamarre rode one back and brought us mail and a special treat, some Irish potatoes. They do not grow at all on the islands, so we only have them on rare occasions. It is a real task to balance a sack of potatoes on a bicycle but all arrived safely.

A few days later, one of the nurses came from Pororan for a little visit and gave us lessons on the art of riding. If anyone thinks it is easy we advise them to try it. We fell in the ditch and got bruised and scratched and full of mud. Sister Hedda came home with a sprained ankle and had to use a crutch to limp around with for a few days. Sister Celestine had a skinned knee and couldn't kneel to say her prayers while Sister Isabelle just hurt all over. In spite of it all, we persevered and finally got our balance, and now we can hop on and go where we please. Sister Irene looked on while we struggled to master it. She can ride well and had given us instructions on pumping up the tires and oiling proper gadgets. Two of us go seven miles to Mass on the Sundays that Father Lamarre goes to another village. They make it in an hour and are home before dinner. It is the first time any sisters have attended Mass there. The first Sunday we went, the natives came out to the road to look at us and wanted to shake hands and kiss our hands as well. They are very friendly and seem so happy if you talk to them and particularly if you notice their children. They are like all proud mothers the world over. Sister Hedda and Sister Irene went the first time, and it made quite an impression on them. We left about 5:00 A.M. and rode rather slowly as the ground was wet and slippery. We reached the little sac-sac church about 7:30 A.M. It is a pathetically shabby little structure. As we entered, Father Lamarre was sitting in the confessional where he had been since early morning. There was a line of natives waiting their turn to be heard. Outside, the early morning sun was scattering its first brilliant rays upon the scene. About 250 men, women and children stood talking in little groups patiently waiting for Mass to begin. Finally, the wooden gong was sounded and everyone entered to take their places. The church soon filled to capacity, and everyone seemed to share in the solemnity of the occasion. Truly, there is not a more sublime privilege on earth than that which is conferred upon a missionary priest. Father Lamarre frequently gives Communion to 300 or 400 natives and after Mass baptizes several babies. Often on the way home, he is called to give Extreme Unction to someone who is dying in an out-of-the way village.

July 15, 1941

Recently, we have had three funerals from the church. You know they cling so tenaciously to their native customs regarding burials that it is difficult to induce them to change. Usually children are buried right in the huts, but not long ago, several people were sent to jail for a month in an attempt to make them bury the dead in a cemetery. The father of one of the schoolboys requested to have his body laid in a plot near the church, and since then two others have been buried there. The services are an attraction, and we sisters sing in Latin. Sister Isabelle has taught the schoolboys to sing *Jesu Salvator Mundi*. The funeral is held in the later afternoon between 3:00 P.M. and 4:00 P.M. as it is too hot in the early forenoon or afternoon. One funeral was held about 1:00 P.M., and everyone was so hot and uncomfortable. Father Lamarre's black cope is very heavy, and he was just dripping with perspiration. This plot is very well situated for a cemetery, and it is only a ten-minute walk from the church. Towering coconuts sway to and fro and large ferns grow all round it. After the coffin is lowered into the grave, they put in the clothing owned by the deceased, such as his blanket and lava-lavas. Sometimes a fair sized pile goes into the grave. A colored croton is planted at the head and one at the foot of the grave. Each native throws in his handful of dirt and of course all tears have been wiped away by that time. These people do not show their emotions except at the time of death. They go through a long series of moaning and crying over the body as soon as the person dies, and they are pretty well all cried out by the time the funeral takes place. A body has to be buried within a few hours as they do not have any way of embalming, and the heat causes rapid decomposition.

About the middle of July, we changed our cook-boy. After a few months, the monotony of kitchen routine irks them, and they become lazy and indifferent. This one used to sit by the stove and scratch his feet and then lean on the windowsill while the sink was full of dishes to be washed. Then, too, he was beginning to complain about the work and seemed to think the laundry-boy had it much easier. So he went back to his village, and the new one was installed. A new broom always sweeps clean, and this new boy tries very hard to do all that is expected of him. He is cross-eyed, and we cannot tell when he is looking at us. We had a good laugh at his cooking the day we went to Gogohe to Mass. We told him to make the dinner, so he boiled the kow-kow or potatoes with the skins on and then served it on a big plate. But they were good as we came home hungry and the meat is always ready—just open a tin. Notice the word "tin." The Australians do not use the word canned and it is beginning to sound strange to us. Everything is "tinned" out here!

July 21, 1941

For the last few weeks, we have all had a special interest in gardening. Some time ago, a neighbor from a nearby plantation sent us some cucumbers and we planted a few of the seeds. They all came up and were flourishing when a prolonged dry spell came upon us. Our water tanks were too low to spare even a drop for our precious cucumbers. Fortunately, we remembered a water hole on the trip across the island, and it is comparatively close to the garden. We collected all the pails and containers we could find and sent the boys to carry water. Now we are getting ten or 12 nice big cucumbers every other day. Tomatoes are purchased from the natives so we have some very nice salads. But we must tell you about that mud hole. It is about 15 feet square, and the pigs come and wallow in the mud. It is the dirtiest place you ever saw. Well, Sister Hedda took five of the little girls who stay with us here at the mission and went for the water for the garden. They were dipping it out with a leaf curled up to form a cup. It was too slow, so Sister Hedda proceeded to show the girls how it could be done faster. While standing on a log to dip it up, her foot slipped and she fell into the mud. It was almost to her knees and such a mess. It took all the water in the mud hole to clean her up so she could come back to the house.

Mother Francis will be interested in hearing that some very special work has been done on the fence that surrounds the convent. From early morning until late in the afternoon, the natives labored on that fence which was supposed to be goat proof. They used new posts and strong wire, and Father Lamarre made hourly inspections of the progress. He would confidently announce that at last the goats were conquered and would never again enter our sacred precincts. We were overjoyed at the mere thought, and we tried hard to believe his rash promises. Finally, the famous fence was completed, and we drew a sigh of relief and settled down to enjoy a peaceful life. No sooner had we finished breakfast the next morning than we saw six of them drinking out of the ducks' pen. Now there are more goats than ever. Some jump over that four-foot fence, and the smaller ones can squeeze through a two inch hole.

You will be happy to know that work is soon to be started on the new hospital at Hanahan. Some of the timber had been sent from the saw mill at Tinputz and is down at the Passage. The parishioners of Our Lady of the Sacred Heart in San Diego, under the direction of Father Hannon, sent a donation of 50 dollars that was forwarded to Bishop Wade for the hospital. We will be happy to have a good and convenient place to care for the sick. During the last two months, the two nurses have made many trips to the surrounding villages. They often see eight or ten sick people. However, one trip is not enough for the majority of them, and it is practically impossible to get them to take medicines you leave to be taken the next day. We do the best we can and leave the rest to the dear Lord. Most of them get well. We think our efforts are more than rewarded.

Recently, we have obtained a very good doctor-boy to help us. He goes with us to the villages and carries the medicine kit and interprets for us. We usually go alone on the bicycle if the village is on the top of the cliff. Quite a number of the natives live along the ocean front, and we have to walk as the cliff is impossible to go down in many places. Two villages we visited have a log with steps cut to aid one to climb upon a ledge of rock and then proceed up the cliff. It is comparatively easy to climb up but certainly not easy to go down. We often take one of the dogs with us, and even it is too frightened to make the attempt. The natives carry it up for us. One has to stop and rest every few yards, and one is all out of breath when the top is finally reached. It is still a mystery to us how those native women carry a big load and manage to descend without a mishap even when it is wet and slippery. We keep an old pair of shoes for that purpose and carry a stout walking stick to support us.

As one travels along the beach one notices a remarkable provision of Divine Providence. Little streams of fresh water trickle out from the cliff and run down into the ocean. They are never without drinking water. You know they haven't any way of conserving rainwater. We see them sitting at these little streams dipping up water with a curled leaf and filling their coconut shells. They clean the meat out of the coconuts and fill them with water and plug the hole with a folded banana leaf. How we wish we had one of those little springs in our backyard. In spite of the heavy rainfall, we are always more or less worried about water. We keep a lock on our tanks so the natives cannot use it. They think nothing of using 20 gallons to take a shower under the faucet. As this is being written, we have been without rain for three weeks, and the situation is becoming serious. Our tanks are empty, and you cannot imagine how we stretch a pint of water. We have only had sponge baths and not too many of them. On Monday, we could not do the laundry, so we are using our clean clothes rather sparingly. However, we are grateful that our dear Lord has been so good to us in other ways so we really can't complain.

Yesterday, the boy returned from the Passage with the mail and what happiness it brought to everyone on the mission. Our good sisters from the different missions sent us money that came at a very appropriate time. The mission account was pretty low, and the pastor was really worried about funds. He was hoping we could pay the cook-boy and also the laundry-boy whose salaries are about a dollar and 70 cents a month, and joy of joys, some money came to tide us over. Our sincere appreciation to those sisters who took the trouble to collect pennies for us. They go a long way out here when paying for labor and you'll never know how much these boys help us. One does the washing and all of the ironing. He does it really well, and our cornettes and veils are starched. The cook saves us endless hours of monotonous dishwashing and the cleaning of vegetables, and we are not nearly so exhausted as we were the first few months. We would all come to recreation to yawn the whole time. We were too tired to even talk.

We must not forget to tell you how very much we like the magazines you are sending us. *Sponsa Regis* is priceless and we each have a new copy for spiritual reading. *The Tidings* is like a letter from home, and we read even the ads. Sister Irene received a gift subscription to the *Catholic Digest* and Sister Celestine receives the *Readers' Digest* and the *Sacred Heart Messenger*.

This report would not be complete without a paragraph about our barnyard. We have several little goats. One goat had twins, and they are the cutest things you ever saw. They were so tiny we kept them apart in a little pen until they were several days old. When they are small they are so playful and hop around and kick up their heels. We have 38 baby chicks. The monarch of the chicken coop is a little duck—the only one to hatch from a setting of eggs. A mother hen worries about him all day. We see him climbing out of a pan of water, and she acts so nervous about it. We give him food in a coconut shell, and after he has taken all he can hold he climbs in to finish it off with a bath. He is so amusing and even Father Lamarre has to stop and play with him. However, we do not like the ducks so well, as they are the hungriest things and even eat the little chickens. Not long ago an iguana came into the chicken house and injured a couple of setting hens. Sister Celestine has charge of the poultry, and when she heard the noise, she ran to see what was the matter. She struck the iguana with a stick and then held him down while calling for help. He was extra large and seemed very vicious; and we were slow coming to the rescue, and he got away. Iguanas are large reptiles about three feet long and will put up a good fight when cornered. We often see them scurrying out of our way.

Last week we tried a new experiment, and it worked out very well. It was making soap from coconut oil. Father Lamarre got an inspiration to make some for the schoolboys, as it is rather expensive to keep them supplied with soap to wash their lavas. He put them all to work to extract the oil and then brought it over to us to convert into soap. We had a recipe which we had taken from an Australian magazine, and the results were very good. Even our dear Sister Anthony would delight in its velvety suds!

The dry weather continues, and we are having the schoolboys carry water from the little spring down on the oceanfront. It has a salty taste, but it isn't too bad when made into cold tea with a little lemon juice. Everything is so parched and dry, and fires are seen in many places in the bush. A number of large trees have been blown down with this high wind. They were quite near our house and at first we would hear a cracking sound and then a big crash. The coral prevents the trees from sending down their roots deeply into the soil. Then the heavy wind comes along and finishes the work that has been well started by the white ants.

August 16, 1941

Yesterday, the feast of the Assumption, we had a High Mass. The boys sang very well. Sister Isabelle had a severe cold in her chest, and we were afraid she would not be able to conduct the singing, but she went through it very well. We had a very special treat for dinner—an apple pie. The Chinese storekeeper at the Passage sent us five apples and we all donated our apple toward the pie instead of eating it raw. The cook had good luck with her pie and everyone enjoyed it. That same evening Sister Irene made some candy, and we celebrated the day royally.

A few nights ago we were disturbed by a noise. The chickens were cackling and flying around in the henhouse. We had just settled down for the night so Sister Celestine lit the lantern, picked up an axe and started for the chicken coop. She found a large snake all curled up and making a meal out of two of the little chickens. Loud cries for help soon followed, and we all got there in time to see the snake being hewn to bits.

Last night Sister Irene discovered a bush fire burning quite near the mission. It is so dry, and there are a lot of dry brush and leaves all over the ground. This catches fire when the natives throw aside their lighted torches at night, and of course, a fire always looks worse in the dark. We sent for some of the boys from the school to come and investigate as there was a strong wind blowing, and we were afraid some of the buildings might catch fire. Reports came back that there was no cause for the alarm so we went to bed. The pastor is away saying Mass in other villages for a few days.

On Sunday night, after four weeks of dry weather, we had a heavy rainfall. The natives were overjoyed, and you cannot imagine the excitement it caused. It meant that their taro gardens were saved. We had been praying for rain for several days; a few drops fell on the roof the night before and awakened all of us. We were just about ready to grab a towel and bar of soap and go out for a shower. However, it was a false alarm, so we all went back to sleep. The shortage of water was a real hardship, and we measured every drop as it was very difficult for the natives to carry water up that steep cliff. They would carry 16 pails every other day, and we found it contained a small amount of salt as well as other minerals. This prevented the soap from making suds. However, we had planned to use it for a little washing as we were frantic for clean clothes after going two weeks without having them laundered. When the rain started, it filled the tanks in a few minutes, and the next day the laundry was going full force. How grand it is to have a clean gown once again. It surely makes us appreciate God's goodness in sending us as much rain as He does. Needless to say, the garden is flourishing, and by garden we mean the half acre of cucumbers. We pulled them through the dry spell, and the rain stimulated their production. Now we are getting 15 to 20 big ones every day. They are new to the natives. We are teaching them to eat them and later we will give them some ripe ones for seed to plant in their own gardens. We all like them so much and have them for every meal. They grow ten inches long and about six inches in circumference. We sent a basket full to Lemanmanu and another to a plantation.

You'll be interested to know that peanuts grow well on the islands. Father Lamarre was cleaning his storeroom and found some seeds so he sent them over for us to plant. We shelled them, and Sister Hedda dug the holes while Sister Isabelle planted the peanuts and the native boy covered them over. We have five plots, and we are anxious to see if they will grow. Things come up in about 24 hours if they are going to grow. At the mission near Buka Passage, at Father Hennessey's center, they harvested about 30 bushels. In the event that ours do not germinate, we will get some seed from them, as we must have peanuts by Christmas. We have about 20 little berry bushes growing. They are a mixture that came from the ice box at St. Joseph's Hospital. We collected a few of the choicest berries from each crate and here's hoping they produce. We are told that they will not bear fruit in this climate, but you know hope springs eternal in a gardener's heart. We had the boys build a canopy to protect them from the sun. They cut four poles with a "Y" formed by the branches. These are stuck in the ground at the four corners of the plot. Then longer poles rest in the "Y" shaped crotch, and this makes the framework on which is laid palm branches to give shade.

It will be of interest to know that Father Lamarre has just finished a catechism in the native language. We are all helping with the typing as he wants each catechist and the schoolboys to have a copy. He mimeographed a few but ran out of ink for his machine and has to wait for some to come from Sydney. It is a tedious work to type the native language and we all have a crick in our neck except one sister who is paying to have hers done by saying rosaries for the typist. It is a splendid work and will aid the natives to understand the teaching of the Church so much better. So far we have not accomplished much in the study of the native tongue. We learn a few words and understand more than we did. So many of them understand pidgin, and it is so much easier for us so we do not make the effort we should.

Tomorrow morning, we are planning to make the trip to Buka Passage on our bicycles. It is 26 miles, and we expect to take it rather slowly and arrive there later in the afternoon—tired and dusty. We are all excited about the long trip, and great preparations are being made today. It is a real task to squeeze three clean gowns, a pair of extra stockings, some hankies, a veil, cornettes and a toothbrush into a package large enough to fit on the handle of a bicycle. Oh yes, and a substantial lunch in case we have "car trouble" on the way and have to stop at the house at Lonahan which is halfway to Buka Passage. We are taking a boy with us and hope to start about 5:30 A.M. as soon as we receive Communion. Wish you could see us take off. It is so funny we have to laugh at ourselves. The two who are going are Sister Isabelle and Sister Hedda, as they want to see the new center where they are scheduled to go and get some idea of what to bring from here in the way of medicines and household supplies. We will give you a description of the journey in the next report.

This brings our love and best wishes to all our sisters at home. Your letters mean so much to all of us, and please forgive us for not answering them individually. We share all of our missionary work with each one, and we beg the aid of your prayers to carry on for souls.

September 1, 1941

*O*ur last letter to you stopped at the beginning of our big adventure—the trip to Buka Passage on the bicycle. Everything was planned for the next morning and during the night a heavy rain came, so we were forced to delay our trip until the following week. At last the morning arrived and two boys accompanied us on bicycles. One carried a small suitcase with our change of clothing, and the other had a big basket full of cucumbers to take to Laurie Chan, the Chinese storekeeper. Just as we left the church to walk down to the road a heavy shower came, and we had to duck under our rain capes in a hurry. It soon passed, the sun came out and we had fine weather the rest of the day. The road was dry and we sailed along, stopping after 10 or 12 miles to take our lunch. You would have enjoyed seeing Sister Isabelle and Sister Hedda sitting on the floor of the keop's house, a roadside shelter built especially for travelling government officials. Beside us were a substantial lunch and a couple of coconuts to drink. The natives flocked around to have a look at us as I think we are the first sisters in this section to travel by bicycle. We gave the tultul (a village chief) a large green cucumber that he gratefully accepted. He then asked us for "*pickannies blong em,*" meaning he wanted some seeds for his own garden. We sent him a good supply as soon as we returned to Hanahan.

After a short rest we went on, stopping now and again for a drink of coconut milk. It was getting on towards noontime, and the sun was blistering hot. We wore those large straw hats that Mother Francis bought for us in Sydney, and they gave us a splendid protection. As we neared Hahela, there were two very steep hills. The boys took our bicycles down and then up the other side, while we walked slowly behind, stopping often under a bit of foliage to escape the sun. By the time we reached the mission, we were pretty tired and how good it felt to have a wash-wash as the natives call a shower. No one knows how good it is to have a cool drink and a bath after a trip. Shortly after we were safely indoors, a heavy rain came and lasted throughout the night.

Next morning it was clear and sunny, so we went down to Chinatown, three miles west of the mission of Hahela. Chinatown is little old New York to us out here and is made up of three Chinese stores standing side by side like those little country stores one sees in the wilds of Montana. The same large printed signs are above the door giving the owners' names and telling the world that they carry general merchandise. They have everything from bicycle tires to sewing machine needles. Everything is displayed in two glass showcases or at least as much as can be squeezed into them, and the rest hangs on a hook or rests on shelves behind the counter. The mail is brought there after it has passed inspection at the government office. You can well imagine what important places those stores really are, especially when you have been out of tea or salt for about two weeks. Incidentally, it is the local newspaper—in more ways than one—the principle one being through Laurie Chan's radio. A graduate of St. Joseph's College in Sydney, he types the world news as it comes over the wire and sends out reports to the missions so they will have some idea of what is going on. It is a service which we all appreciate, particularly at this time when we are wondering what will happen next.

After a little shopping we started out to visit the other places that we had planned to see. The government hospital for the natives is on a small island out in the channel that separates Buka Island from the larger island of Bougainville. It is only about a quarter of a mile across, but a very swift current rushes through with the change of tide. However, we went across in a small outrigger canoe and spent the afternoon visiting the medical officer and his wife and making rounds of the hospital and dispensary. They can accommodate about

400 patients and the doctor-boy from each village is supposed to send all patients with very bad sores, etc., to this hospital. The medical officer makes rounds at intervals covering all the villages on Buka Island and examining the people. They pick up the lepers and enforce the law in case of epidemics such as dysentery or any contagious outbreak. It is a big job as there are always some who squirm out of going for the necessary care. We cooperate with the hospital in reporting and urging the bad cases to go there. They have to walk 25 miles and that is the big drawback, though they could go by boat if they really wanted to. The hospital has a building for men and one for women, and it is built on the ground, native fashion, so they can have their beloved fires if they want them. Food is supplied and a blanket and pillow as well as a bowl of food. The medical officer supervises, and he has several native doctor-boys to do the routine work. One is trained to take care of the records, and he was sitting at the chart desk filing cards and admitting new patients. We had a very pleasant afternoon and had tea with two of the officials and their wives. They urged us to stay until 4:00 P.M. for the news broadcast from San Francisco, which we were only too willing to do. Were we thrilled just to hear a voice from home! It came through perfectly, and when the announcer gave the time signal, we figured the difference to be 17 hours. We have a whole day's work finished before you are out of bed.

Our next visit was to Chabai to visit Father Hennessey's school. In the event that you have not heard of this famous man, we will tell you briefly. During Bishop Wade's last visit to America, Father Hennessey volunteered to come for five years to the Solomon Islands. The school at Chabai had been started by Father McConville and was taken over by Father Hennessey. He has done a marvelous piece of work. He has a dynamic personality and is the type of man who gets whatever he goes after. Everyone likes him out here. The school he has built is splendid. It is a large one story building made substantially from lumber from the sawmill. The desks are the real schoolroom variety, and the blackboards are the full length of the room. Nearby are a study hall and dining room and a well-arranged cookhouse. Five large iron kettles are suspended on wires over a fireplace. You have seen pictures of those big black pots which one always associates with cannibals—well, that kind. Then a special oven is built to roast or smoke fish. They throw a piece of dynamite into the water, and the shock stuns all the fish within a certain radius. Then boats go out and pick them up as they float to the surface. The garden is large, and all kinds of native foods are grown, such as corn, taro, beans, sweet potatoes, peanuts, and pumpkins. Father Hennessey bought a mill to grind the corn and then taught the boys to eat cornmeal mush. He has done a lot of experimenting with fruit trees through the Department of Agriculture at Rabaul. He has two very promising looking avocado trees. We feasted our eyes upon them and took down the Department of Agriculture's address. On the opposite side of the playground across from the school are the boys' dormitories. We visited them, and everything was as neat and orderly as a new pin. Each dormitory had a large water tank beside it, and during the long dry spell they had enough water to tide them over. The grounds are beautifully landscaped and flowering shrubs of many kinds were in bloom. Clover, used as a ground cover, is effective with the gravel pathways and gives such a spacious appearance to the compound. There is also a dispensary for the schoolboys only. Chabai is strictly for the training of catechists, and there are not any native villages close by, so they are not disturbed by the constant coming and going of natives as is the average mission.

We visited the school in session, and Father Hennessey conducted a singing period that we all enjoyed. He knows his music and has trained the boys to sing in parts. He asked us what we wanted to hear, so we told him *Old Black Joe*. It was splendid, and they seemed to put so much enthusiasm into it. They also sang the *Kyrie* and *Way Down upon the Swanee River* and a number of short songs in three parts. They harmonize so perfectly. Maybe the Chabai choir will make a record for you some day. It is a never-ending miracle to us to listen to these native people sing the parts of the Mass as well as the liturgical hymns.

Chabai is on the west coast of Bougainville and is about 12 miles south from Buka Passage. We went there by boat, and as soon as we were out in the channel, the rudder came loose and we had to stop while the boys fixed it. These little shore boats are called a pinnace and are operated by benzene. Usually, the native boys are trained to handle them, but it does make one nervous to see them fumbling around the engine. After a half hour's wait, we were all set and continued our journey to Chabai, arriving at that unwelcome hour of 11:30 A.M.

The Marist brothers from St. Joseph's College in Sydney have taken over Father Hennessey's school, and they had been there only three weeks when we made our visit. Father Hennessey is returning to the United States as he has completed his five years of missionary work. Everything was so new to the Marist brothers, and we felt sorry for the poor new missionaries as we still remember those first trying weeks when one seems to be working in the dark. They were most gracious hosts, and one prepared the dinner while Father Hennessey hurried around to get us a cold drink and entertain us while dinner was cooking. Secretly we enjoyed seeing the men do a little worrying over meals for once, as we have had our share of fretting over meal preparation here in Hanahan. One of the Marists is an excellent cook as well as a high school teacher. He made some cupcakes that were better than *Van de Kamp's Bakery.* After dinner and the visit to the school, we returned to the boat to go to Tarlena. We arrived there in just a few minutes, as it is only about two miles north of Chabai. The Marist sisters are stationed there, so they came down to meet us and we had tea and a nice visit with them at the convent. They have about 15 children of all sizes, and we met one of the sisters who was here at Hanahan when we arrived. It was getting dark, so we went back to the pier to go aboard as we were anxious to get back before too late. Brother Paul, who visited Orange on his way out, came with us, and we were glad to have him to oversee the engine in case of trouble. More trouble was in store for us, and as soon as we were out beyond the breakers, the boat sputtered and stopped. Sister Isabelle started the rosary and the rest of us hung onto our wet benches and waited for the worst. Fortunately, the ocean was calm and a half moon was well up in the heavens, so it was a bit easier to inspect the engine. An extra tin of benzene was found, and soon we were chugging along towards the Passage. It was 9:00 P.M., when we two weary travelers had some supper, but we were very happy to have had the opportunity to visit the two centers in one trip.

The next morning, we started for Hanahan and had a perfect road all the way and not one drop of rain. We made the 25 miles in six hours as we rested several times and had our usual refreshment of coconut milk. Coming home we each carried a fair sized load on our wheels—a few supplies for the sisters such as toothpaste, sandshoes, beads, and clay pipes for the five children. We also collected a few plants and seeds at the different stations. Hanahan looked pretty good to us after our three days' absence, but we were glad to know a few of the details of our new center at Hahela. We expect to make the transfer before Christmas, and we have already started packing a few things. We will take a few linens and medicines, as there is very little to begin our work there.

The following week Sister Irene had to make a sick call to Lemanmanu, 14 miles from here. Sister Celestine accompanied her and they had a good trip going, but a heavy downpour overtook them on the way home. They were simply drenched and full of mud as the slippery roads caused the wheels to skid. Sister Irene treated the sick patient, and since then he has made a good recovery. It was the usual thing, pneumonia.

Two weeks ago, work was started on the native hospital. Trees were cut and the ground cleared while different villages sent their donations of native cut poles for the huts. The dispensary is to be made of special timber from the sawmill, but the sick wards are to be native houses. These people are not happy unless they can sleep around a fire, and they just will not stay in a house built on stilts as the cold air at night freezes them. We have them provide their own food, and in this way they can cook it right in the hut. Usually four or five relatives come and stay with the patient and wait on him. Those who are able will come to the dispensary for treatments. Some stay two or three weeks, and the relatives make trips back and forth to their villages for loads of food.

As the work progressed more trees had to be cut and one morning there was considerable agitation among the schoolboys. Father Lamarre had given the order to cut down a large mango tree that has menaced our garden for some time. All of the natives dearly love mangoes, and they eat them long before there are any signs of them being ripe. In order to get at our tree, the youngsters climbed over the fence and broke the wire that protects the struggling little garden. We just couldn't keep them out, and of course, we did not get one mango from that big tree. That explained the deep-rooted sorrow of the schoolboys as they got their share of mangoes, too. But we are rejoicing over it as it was so annoying to see half a dozen youngsters swinging on branches at all hours of the day. Ask Mother Francis how she used to try shooing them out.

The next tree to go down was a coconut. As it crashed to the ground each one of us thought of the delicious salad the center would make. When it was brought to the kitchen a dozen natives came to the door looking for a hand out. It is quite a large piece and resembles a heart of celery. The new leaves are all folded in the most exquisitely formed layers, and it is tempting just to look at them. We cut it in stalks and eat it like celery with a little salt.

Right in the center of the grounds is a large tree that the natives call a pomelo. It bears a fruit resembling our grapefruit, only very much larger. It is slightly sweet and can be sectioned just like an orange. The blossoms come twice a year, and the second crop came in blossom in September. For a couple of weeks, the air was permeated with the most delightful perfume. It reminded us of the orange blossoms at home.

Along with the preparations for the hospital, our garden nearby is being cleared and made ready for planting.

We have been too busy with other things to bother much with a garden, but there are a number of pineapples which need transplanting and that seems like a good place. Pineapples grow close to the ground and send out new shoots around the mother stalk. These are cut and transplanted and produce fruit the following year. The pineapple season is once a year and that comes around Christmas time with an occasional fruit during the year. The tops of the fruit will grow and this produces a much sweeter type, but it takes three years. Father Hennessey has some thornless pineapples at Chabai that he obtained through the Department of Agriculture. They send out a catalogue telling about the cultivation of tropical fruits. Father Hennessey tells us that strawberries and other berries will not produce in this latitude. The leaves grow luxuriantly, but the plants produce no fruit. They do well in the higher elevations—about 8,000 feet above sea level and are plentiful in the mining section of New Guinea. So we will have to be contented with the memories of our strawberry patch at Orange.

About two weeks ago Sister Irene and Sister Hedda made a trip to Gagan for Mass on Sunday. As they were walking up to the church, an elderly woman met them carrying the tiniest little mite you ever saw, a twin. She wanted to give the baby to the sisters as these people have the fixed idea that they can only nurse one baby at a time. So the stronger one is chosen, and the other usually dies from intentional neglect. The sisters were a bit reluctant about accepting it until Father Lamarre had sanctioned the agreement. He was hearing confessions, so they waited until after Mass when he baptized the child and instructed the relatives to carry it to Hanahan, a distance of seven miles. We didn't dare take it on a bicycle as the constant jarring might be harmful. In due time, the mite arrived and we had its bed and food ready for it. We are sure it did not weigh quite two pounds, but it seemed lively enough, and these native babies are all very small at birth. For two days we showered it with attention, but its frail little body was too weak to sustain life. A messenger was sent to notify the parents, but they replied that they wanted us to take care of the burial here. Sister Irene found a small packing box and while she was lining it with white, Sister Hedda made the cover and tacked a small cross on it. Father Lamarre came with the schoolboys who were carrying lighted candles, and little Emma was taken to the church and then to the cemetery.

We still have the two babies that came with the mission. They are growing fast and recently have been started on taro mixture that has to be eaten with a spoon. There were loud protests when the bottle was not forth coming. One of them is just about old enough to return to his relatives. The mother is dead, but the relatives seem to have a deep affection for the child.

Recently, there have been a number of sing-sings in the surrounding villages. During the full moon they gather together and make merry. Several days before, the women make a sort of nut cake from taro and gallip nuts beaten to a pulp and baked in banana leaf. Pigs are killed and roasted over a big fire, and the feast is on. They keep up a racket the best part of the night, singing and beating on those wooden drums. The sound carries for miles and is rather weird. Some of the drummers have a few fancy little taps to intersperse with the regular beat. They also have drums of different sizes with two or three drummers playing them. Little flutes are made from bamboo, and the sound is quite musical but is limited to two or three notes. Large sea shells are used most effectively as church bells. Noise, and lots of it, make up a sing-sing. Quite often they send Father Lamarre a piece of pig and a taro cake. The meat is tied up in a vine and a loop made by which to carry it. They are clever at making little devices to carry live lobsters, live chickens or other articles of food. One can find a vine anywhere to serve as string as so much of the vegetation has runners.

About two weeks ago a double wedding took place. One of the teachers and a schoolboy were the grooms. Father Lamarre married them before Mass, and it was so funny we could scarcely keep from laughing. Father made all of the arrangements and thought all was settled so went to the sacristy to put on his surplice, etc. Then he came to the altar rail and waited for the two couples. The men came but the two women were shy, so they slipped out of the side door. Then Father sent the two who were to be the witnesses to round up the brides. They caught one by the arm and shoved the other ahead of them up to the altar. After the ceremony, they returned to their respective places in church. The brides had on new wedding rings, a dime-store variety supplied by the pastor, and all the other girls craned their necks to have a look at the new rings. A week after the marriage, the celebration takes place—a big sing-sing and the roast pig to go with it. The man Maria married was one of our first patients. He was half dead with T.B. and had a huge abscess on his back just below the shoulder blade. We brought him up the cliff and fixed a little room for him in a little shack near the priest's house. We opened the abscess, and it drained for weeks. The doctor who came to see Sister Irene examined him and said his condition was serious and that it was only a matter of time. As the days went by he gained strength and weight and is now teaching the native language to the new students before they are passed into Sister Isabelle's classroom. He gives all of the credit to the sisters, and he seems very grateful.

When we hired a boy to help in the dispensary with the dressings, our former patient sent a formal note of protest to Sister Isabelle, telling her all the new boy's faults and weaknesses. It was very amusing, and we did not pay any attention to it. They have their friends and enemies and try to arrange it so their friends will get a coveted position. Sometimes it takes weeks to analyze their schemes as they go about it in a very adroit way. Father Lamarre understands them very well and is always a couple of jumps ahead of them.

September 8, 1941

*I*t does not seem that a year ago at this time we were finishing the last details in preparation for our trip. How good it is to be here and all settled in our work. Time slips by so fast for us that it is always a surprise to look at the calendar and see that it is time for another report.

We have a woman staying at the mission who has been ousted from her village. She is expecting an illegitimate child, and the man in the case had made threats upon her life, so we are giving her a home until the storm blows over. She helps us with little duties around the house, and we have taught her to take care of the two babies. We often think how differently these children are raised, and yet they seem healthy enough. The newborn babies do not wear a stitch of clothing. During the day it is warm, but at night the fires are kept going in the hut. Sister Irene and Sister Hedda made a sick call late one night and that hut was a picture we wish you could have seen. It was so close and warm inside you would wonder how they could breathe. The boards on which they sleep are about three feet wide and five or six feet long and raised about six inches from the ground. No blankets are used, but a few smoldering embers are placed between each bed, giving warmth all around as the positions are changed. Dogs sleep inside with the family. The mother usually has a couple of the smallest children sleeping beside her regardless of how sick she may be. To give light inside, a certain wood is put on the fire that ignites quickly and burns with a bright flame.

We are beginning to notice a slight change in the atmosphere as the so-called spring months begin. The intense humidity is returning which envelops everything in a mantle of dampness. One is covered with a fine perspiration just about all the time, and one's clothes feel damp when one dresses in the morning. The rain can be heard some distance away in the bush, and gradually the area widens and the deluge reaches the mission and goes out over the ocean. The changes in seasons are so subtle they pass almost unnoticed. At times a little breeze and the rustle of dry leaves suggested the fleeting sadness of fall, and at this time about all we have to tell us spring is here is the way dew hangs on a lily pod in the early morning.

All of us seem to enjoy the rain, and it is coming down

heavily while this is being written. We are so dependent upon rain for our water supply and the garden that we often say a decade of the rosary for a little shower. The cucumbers are still producing, and we let a number ripen so we could give seeds to the natives. They like them so much, and I think we have supplied everyone who wanted them. Never saw so many cucumbers as we have had from a comparatively small patch. The peanuts we planted came up but only five plants survived. The rats must have eaten the others. The five that are left are growing luxuriantly and we hope to get enough to give us a good supply for seed.

On the feast of Saint Teresa of Avila, we received word from Bishop Wade that our retreat was to begin on the evening of October 19th and end October 24th and that it was to be given by Father Conley, S.M., from the island of Nissan. Needless to say, we were all very happy—first, because it was over a year since our last retreat and second, because an American priest was to give it. We will listen closely and try to tell you a little about his conferences. Perhaps a retreat given to missionaries may contain special emphasis on certain points of religious life that will be of interest to you at home.

In the meantime, all of us are scurrying hither and thither to finish up the little duties by way of preparation for the retreat. Sister Irene is working at the church, and Sister Isabelle is teaching her last session for the week at school, while Sister Celestine is brushing cobwebs from everywhere. Sister Hedda is trying to think of new ways to cook pumpkin and taro. Our cargo has not arrived, and we are short of everything, even salt. However, we find the ocean water a good substitute and boil it down to get the crystals for table use. From six quarts of water we collect about four tablespoons of salt. Then we extract oil from coconuts and use it to make cakes and cookies. Of course, during the shortage of flour we make coconut macaroons, and you would envy us if you knew how really delicious the freshly grated coconut is. Another delicacy are the mushrooms. We have them quite often as the natives hunt them in the woods and bring them to us to sell. During the dry spell the natives gather clams along the river bottom. To cook them, we roll them in flour and fry them in deep fat. At first we did not know how to get them out of the shell much less how to cook them. One is so helpless with all these new things.

Last week, the workmen took down the old shack that had been used for the two babies and the five little girls. They salvaged the nails and the metal roofing to use on the new dispensary. We were all happy to have the eyesore removed and now we can look out to the west of our house and see the road. The children have smaller quarters in a house not far from the kitchen. It was made in a couple of days from native timber and covered with sac-sac and some metal roofing. The natives chop a certain tree and use it to make boards about six inches wide. They are splendid substitutes for real lumber and look very nice when finished. The only drawback is the white ants. The ants dearly love that particular wood and move in by the billions. In a comparatively short time, the wood is reduced to a crushable shell.

This morning, we received some medical supplies from Sydney. Nurse Richardson, the head of the Marist Medical Mission in Sydney, made a few very necessary purchases for us. The most important is N.A.B., the abbreviation for neoarsphenamine that is used in the treatment of yaws. We were all out of it and have had to turn patients away for several weeks. We have 16 waiting in the hospital now, and it is the only thing that will clear up those dreadful sores. The three houses for the natives have just been finished, and each day a new family arrives from somewhere with two or three children and a load of taro. We were quite excited when the boxes of drugs arrived. We also ordered some adhesive and some tonics for the sisters as the samples we brought from home have all been used. Now we will have to get all the saints in heaven busy to help us pay our 12-pound drug bill. The N.A.B. is about ten cents an ampule, and we received 300 ampules. This particular brand is made in England by the *May and Baker Company* and is much more effective than some we used a few months ago from the United States.

October 18, 1941

*O*n Friday afternoon, Father Conley arrived. Shortly before evening prayers at 5:00 P.M., he called to see us. After the usual formalities were over, he told us the surprising news that two of our sisters were coming from California, and that last minute preparations were being made to obtain their passports. To say it took our breath away is putting it mildly. We could hardly wait until he was gone so we could ask one another, "Who do you suppose is coming?" We are all aflutter and how anxiously we await news from Reverend Mother. Evidently, our bishop has been doing some work by cable. In the meantime, we are so glad to know others are coming to join us. We are wondering what surprises the bishop has for us. Will they stay at Hanahan and Hahela or will a new center be opened? Even out here, we try to read the mind of the Holy Ghost.

October 19, 1941

*W*e are very happy for the privilege of making our retreat under the guidance of Father Conley. For the last year, we have listened to first one and then another sing his praises until we have concluded that he is just about ready for canonization. To meet him in real life, he gives the impression of being just another facet in that regal gem which makes up the Marist Congregation.

The times for conferences were scheduled for the same hours as we have them in Orange. However, the length of the time given to each was much shorter. This was done because of the heat during the day. The usual subjects were covered with special stress laid upon the importance of union with God in accomplishing the work of saving souls. Only occasionally was our special work as missionaries brought into the conferences. The same means of winning souls for Christ applies to work here as well as at home, namely purity of intention, sacrifice and prayers. He mentioned the fact that the difference in climate, changes in living conditions as well as the quinine, make it doubly important for us to be on our guard against even the slightest relaxation in self-discipline. Perhaps the most helpful suggestion of all was the fact that we had asked to be given the privilege of coming here and should remember that trials, disappointments, sickness, and misunderstandings, etc. were fully understood and willingly accepted. The conference had a serious tone and he was the soul of brevity. He did not preach to us, just reminded us in a most persuasive way of our obligations and the reward that awaits those who fulfill them faithfully.

October 24, 1941

*O*ur retreat closed, and we all felt spiritually refreshed and ready to meet the next big event, namely, the separation of our little community. In the meantime, Bishop Wade is scheduled to make a visit to Buka Island to give Confirmation. All of the centers have been preparing classes, and each morning after Mass the catechists spend about an hour preparing the students. They say, *"They school em long Lotu"* meaning they are teaching them about the Church. It is amusing the way they use the word school. It is applied to everything one is learning. When we were learning to ride the bicycles they would pass us on the road and say *"Sister school em long wheel."*

During the last couple of weeks, there has been a shortage of food among the natives in this part of the island. The long dry spell, followed by heavy rains, destroyed the taro crop and that is to them what bread is to us. We see them munching on coconuts and pieces of sac-sac. They cut the sac-sac tree and bake it in large sections over the fire. It contains a mealy substance with rather an insipid taste but it seems to satisfy their hunger. These natives could have so many other things to give variety to their food as well as substitute for taro during a shortage but custom seems to prevent it. They follow the plan laid out by their ancestors and "what was good enough for grandpa is good enough for me." So many experiences with hunger will not change them. The government tries to induce them to grow sweet potatoes, corn, peanuts and larger banana plantations, but still they go on in the same old way. At times, it is exasperating to stand by and see them live year after year without lifting a finger to improve their living conditions. Coming from a country that has so many conveniences it is almost unbelievable that human beings can exist with so little. God provides for them in a thousand different ways and they accept it with the minimum of exertion. Half of the world thinks these South Sea Islanders are a happy carefree race. We have not found it so. They, too, are bent with sorrow and trouble and sickness the same as the rest of mankind. They work hard to get food. In sickness, they sit beside the members of the family to comfort them. They feel it just as keenly as we do, but whatever comes is accepted with patience. Even death is not feared; they face it calmly and await the appointed hour to go. Quite often they seem to know in advance the time they will die. A man died in the village recently, and before going to bed, he told his family that he was to die before morning and sure enough it happened just as he had foretold.

They are a strange but interesting race. An amusing incident occurred last night that we think you might enjoy. Father Lamarre's house-boy was sent on an errand, and upon arriving at his journey's end, he did not receive the customary allotment of food from the storekeeper. He returned very tired and seething with indignation. Later, he recounted the painful details of his trip to us. We sympathized with him and this was his reply, *"Em he alright now, Father he talk he kill him finish long letter."* which in pidgin English usually describes the situation perfectly after you get it untangled, which meant that Father would settle the matter by letter.

The biggest event of the year took place about 3:00 P.M. last Friday. That was the butchering of our large Hereford bull. The natives are especially fond of meat and they had been looking forward to his killing with the greatest interest. The animal was large and had two of the most vicious looking horns you ever saw. In fact, everyone was afraid of it as it seems these animals go on the rampage when one least expects it. We were even afraid to go down the road on our bicycles while it was eating peacefully by the roadside. Now we have just the cow and a six-month old calf that we plan to kill later on. These animals run around loose and eat all the young leaves from the natives' banana plantations. Other pastures are always greener and this makes the natives very angry. We really can't blame them, so we decided that some of the animals should be killed. It is a big nuisance to keep track of them in the bush, and the cow is never here on time to be milked. One of the natives milks the cow and also the goats, so that is a big help to us. We get about two and a half quarts of milk a day, so we have enough for our own use as well as the two babies. Well, to come back to our story about the bull. Bokkie, the half-caste carpenter, who is helping with the building, took care of the whole thing and three of the sisters went to a safe place to watch the bloody affair. He took careful aim with the rifle, and that huge animal just dropped in its tracks. In a few minutes it was strung up and partially skinned. There were dozens of natives everywhere and they were all very excited. It did not take long before kerosene tins full of fat were coming to the kitchen. Then came a huge liver that filled a dishpan. This was followed by enormous hunks of meat carried by the natives on a pole. They lined up in front of the kitchen, and we picked out the cuts of meat we wanted for our own use, and Father Lamarre gave the rest away to the hungry-eyed mob standing around. He gave a piece to representatives from each village, and they in turn divided it. How we wish we would have taken some pictures of them sitting on the grass and cutting up the pieces of meat. Even the head and feet were carried away.

The next day the fun began with two enormous hindquarters of beef to be quickly prepared for preserving. Sister Hedda and a native cut up the two quarters while Sister Irene supervised the fire under the outside grate where we had the kerosene tins of solution boiling. The pieces of meat from which all the fat had been removed were dropped in the hot salt solution and allowed to boil for a half hour. That is called corning beef out here, and as it is our first experience, we are just hoping it will keep well. The salt is pretty strong and the meat is weighted down in the brine, and we have a guardian angel sitting on each tin. What a day that was. We obtained about four kerosene tins full of grease. We had all the fillet mignon we could use for days as well as some real honest to goodness hamburger with onions and a little garlic. We packed the steak in the ice chambers of the *Frigidaire*, and it was well preserved.

Two days later, we heard the report of a rifle, and low and behold, a wild pig had been shot in Father Lamarre's yard. The schoolboys hung it on two poles and carried it over for our inspection. The natives were excited all over again, and in two minutes a fire was built and they were holding the pig over it to burn off the hair. Not more than 40 seconds later it was opened, cleaned and sectioned. How those natives can work when it comes to preparing a meal. Their knives are as sharp as razors, and of course it was just getting dark and they had to hustle. We lit the lanterns and went out to watch them. Of course we did not want any of the meat, as those wild pigs have a strong taste and then, too, we had just about all the fresh meat we could handle. Father Lamarre came and had it divided equally, so that pieces were sent to several of the nearby chiefs. Pig is a rare delicacy and they relish them, tame or wild. Our dogs caught and killed a small native pig, and the owner was furious and came and demanded payment of ten shillings or $2.50. We compromised by giving him the dog.

A couple of nights ago as we were preparing to retire, a shrill call for help came from Sister Celestine's room. "Hurry! Quick! A centipede!" As often as we hear that word, it makes our blood run cold. We keep a long forceps hanging on a nail in a prominent place so we all made a rush to get it for sister. Sometimes a strong light is directed on them and they will remain perfectly still, thus giving one an opportunity to kill them. This one, however, was very restless, and as it moved away Sister Celestine made an attempt to set the lantern on it to hold it down. She had barely touched it when the thing changed its course and started right towards Sister Hedda's feet. A piercing scream followed, and everyone was so unnerved that it got away. Everyone looked for it except the sister who was standing on a chair trembling with fright. It couldn't be found anywhere, so we all retired and tucked in our nets very securely and dreamed of killing centipedes by the dozens. The next day Sister Celestine, who always has an uncanny way of seeing them first, saw this one sleeping on the wall just outside of the room where it had been the night before. The only thing handy was an axe, which she used to strike it. We measured it and found it to be ten inches. During August and September, we did not see very many, but as the summer season approaches, we can expect to find them anywhere. Scorpions too, and long black bugs that bite just like a centipede.

November 19, 1941

*L*ife in Hanahan is just one big suspense after another. Today we learned that the shipment from Orange had arrived at Soraken. We also had a letter from the Chief Steward, Mr. Casey, on the SS *Mariposa,* saying that he had seen Mother Francis at Wilmington shortly before the boat sailed, and that she was arranging for the shipment to us. To think it is really here in the islands so soon! Now we are all on pins and needles wondering if you heeded our repeated warnings to send invoices with every single box of medicine. Sister Irene wrote down the full details as given by Father Lamarre so there would not be drawbacks at this end. Otherwise all of the things will be opened for inspection and duty. Two messengers have been sent off to Buka Passage for the invoices and we will know tomorrow.

December 1, 1941

*T*his morning another big event took place. Bishop Wade arrived by bicycle, accompanied by one of the Marist brothers from Chabai. We knew he was on his way up the coast, and that Confirmation was the main reason for his trip. We have everything in readiness.

     The schoolboys went to the bush to gather flowers and

ferns. We find those colored leaves called crotons very pretty for altar decorations. They then placed young coconut palms in tin cans covered with green paper. The church really looked lovely. After all of our preparations, the bishop decided to postpone Confirmation until Christmas. However, we had our best linens ready for his Mass. Our bishop is very short so we had to hunt for an alb of the right length. All of our vestments are made of such heavy material and lined and interlined, and the surplices are of heavy linen and crocheted lace. Just imagine how the priests perspire if the Mass is late in the morning, for instance around 8:00 A.M. or 9 A.M. The perspiration from the black cassock stains everything and we nearly always have to hang things up to dry after Mass. How we wish we had those thin materials like those we have at St. Luke Hospital. No matter how gorgeous the vestments are, the priests all request "the lightest ones you can find." Even at 6:00 A.M., it is very hot at this time of the year and more so just before a rain.

After the bishop's Mass the next morning, he and Brother Donatus came to visit the school for about an hour. The first period was singing and the boys did exceptionally well. Sister Isabelle has done well with the choir here, and their repertoire has been put in book form ready for printing. They sing the Mass and many of the liturgical hymns in both Latin and pidgin English. After the visit to the school, the bishop came to visit us at the convent. The chief topic of conversation was the two sisters who are expected from Orange. He is most anxious to open the center at Hahela though he wants three in each place according to Reverend Mother's wishes. The conclusion of the interview was that we would go to Hahela and then besiege St. Joseph with petitions to see that the other two arrived safely. A very inspiring conference was then given in the church. Then we all hurried around to get things ready for dinner. Father Lamarre's house is some distance from the convent; the food is sent over on trays in hot covered dishes and the two boys serve. After dinner, the bishop left by bicycle for Lemanmanu where he is installing the new priest. Three guesses who it is? We were all so surprised we could scarcely believe our ears. He has induced Father Hennessey to stay another year in the islands and to take charge of Lemanmanu. He is now our next door neighbor 14 miles away.

At the close of this report, we must tell you a little joke on Sister Irene. She was sitting quietly in her room reading when a chicken flew down from the top of her clothes closet and began cackling for all it was worth. After shooing it out of the door, she decided to get upon a chair and see what the hen had been doing up there. On the top of her brown suitcase were three fresh eggs. Did you ever think Sister Irene would keep chickens in her room?

This is the last report of the year. We try to send one every three months, making four reports a year. We would like to have you tell us if they reach you safely and we will give them numbers one to four. This is number four for this year.

We all join in sending you our prayers and good wishes for a holy and happy Christmas. We will be with you in spirit at midnight Mass and we know you will whisper a little prayer for your sister missionaries. Do pray for us always. Every tiny little offering aids us to win souls whose happiness you will share in eternity.

News Flash: December 7, 1941, (December 8th on Buka)—Japan bombs Pearl Harbor. The United States declares war on Japan. On December 16, 1941—Guam and Wake Island fall to the Japanese.

CHAPTER 5

We Will Remain at Our Station

December 17, 1941

A few days after the December report was mailed to you, we learned that America and Japan were at war. The suddenness of the attack on Pearl Harbor was a great shock to us. We had seen the harbor when we made the tour of Honolulu last year, and it is hard to visualize the destruction of American ships that were peacefully anchored there. We were fortunate in receiving the news only two days after, and it was not altogether a surprise, as the situation has been tense so long. We are glad our sisters are not traveling in these dangerous waters. We know, too, that you are feeling some concern about us way out here. This is bordering on the danger zone, and the Australian government sent us a "Public Notice," an extract of which reads as follows:

> **The Commonwealth Government has decided that women and children, other than female missionaries and nurses who may elect to remain, are to be evacuated**

compulsorily. Stop. Cost of fares will be borne by Commonwealth Government. Stop. This will be handed to you by Mr. Green, to whom you are required to state in writing, whether you elect to remain or to be evacuated.

The position, in brief, is that if we choose to be evacuated, we must be prepared at any moment from now on to proceed to the point of embarkation. Transport will be arranged to take us to that point, but it is essential that we be prepared to board the boat the moment it arrives at the set location.

Further details regarding regulations for those remaining include blackouts at night on those windows facing the sea, using local-grown foodstuffs as much as possible to conserve tinned provisions, and providing temporary shelter in the bush in case of quick departure.

It sounds very alarming, and we must admit it frightened us a bit when the notice was given to us. However, the clause excepting missionaries helped us to make a decision quickly.

Our pastor had gone to Buka Passage, so we had to solve our own problem. We chose to remain. We sent the following letter to the District Officer:

December 17ᵗʰ, 1941
We received your letter this morning through Mr. Green. Inasmuch as it is not compulsory at the present time for missionaries to be evacuated, we wish to state that we will remain at our station until we receive further word from you.
Sister Isabelle, Superior

In a couple of days, we settled down to our daily duties and forgot all about raiders and sampans. The other women on the islands, including the four nurses from Pororan, left a couple of days later for Australia. So, we are the only white women here, and we feel a bit lonely knowing the nurses have gone. Their station was closed, and their supplies were divided between Lemanmanu and Gagan. Father Hennessey and Father Caffiaux were going over the day after Christmas to take care of things and to close the station. We will have to take care of as much of the medical work as we are able. Two of the sisters are going to Lemanmanu to give shots to the natives after Mass on Sunday.

In the meantime, the shipment sent from Orange is at Buka Passage awaiting transportation to Hanahan. The little Japanese schooner that operated up and down the Solomon Island Coast has been confiscated and the owner put in a concentration camp for the duration of the war. We hope to find someone to bring the supplies up for us, as we are all so anxious to get them up here safely. How fortunate we are to have that cargo at this time, as it may be several months before a boat will come from Sydney. You may well imagine how excited we'll be when it comes time for us to open those boxes.

As the Christmas season approached, we made preparations with so much joy and enthusiasm. Everybody worked. We had to leave the church decorations until the day before, as Father Lamarre spent the greater part of the preceding days in the church hearing confessions. Imagine listening to 1,180 confessions. He finished at 10:00 P.M. on Christmas Eve after spending the day in another village hearing another 300 or 400. We took advantage of his absence to decorate the church. All of the natives took part in it, and how they worked. Some sat outside stringing flowers and colored leaves on long vines while those inside, by means of long poles, fashioned them into garlands. One does not have to hesitate about driving a nail anywhere when it is a question about decorating. Tall palm leaves were placed around the walls. The altar was beautiful; the schoolboys cut down half a poinciana tree and the blossoms are a bright red, which made an ideal Christmas decoration. Then we covered two five-gallon kerosene tins with red crepe paper and arranged coconut palms on the floor on each side of the altar. The two side altars were banked with flowers and ferns, in fact, so banked, that one of the altar boys almost tripped over one with the lighted lamp when he went to light the way for Father Lamarre to give Communion. We all managed to get 40 winks of sleep before 11:00 P.M. We arose to have a cup of coffee before Mass. Just as we were ready to bite into a sandwich, somebody remembered it was a fast and abstinence day, and no one had asked for a dispensation. We choked down the first mouthful and sheepishly made the sign of the cross and hustled over to the church.

December 25, 1941
The Japanese take over Hong Kong.

*F*our lanterns supplied the light in the church, and the large reading lamp that Mother Francis got for us in Sydney was used on the altar. The church was packed to the brim; in fact, we estimated the number to be well over 1,000. For a half-hour before midnight, there was considerable shuffling and the murmur of voices as each new group came in to hunt for a suitable place to sit. Tired babies cried almost continuously, and the occasional yipping of a dog would tell us that someone's big foot had stepped on his boney carcass. At last it was time for Mass. The boys' choir burst forth with *Silent Night* while Father was vesting. They sang exceptionally well, and it gave our hearts a little tug as we thought of you at home singing it at the Motherhouse with the organ accompaniment, the tall poinsettias, and the brilliant lights. As the Mass proceeded, the choir sang the different parts, trying hard to follow the words by the faint rays of the lantern. Then came a favorite hymn in pidgin, *Adeste Fideles,* and it just about raised the roof. Everybody sang as loudly as possible, and when they sing, the main idea is to outdo the other fellow in volume. Nearly all of the villagers know it well, as it was transposed into pidgin in the good old days of long ago. Finally, it was Communion time, and it took 45 minutes for Father to give 780 Communions. He has a large ciborium with a capacity of 600 hosts if they are packed carefully in rolls; then he has a smaller one holding 250 hosts.

Some of the people have the same good manners as the folks at home. That is, they climb right over the other fellow to get there first. We enjoy these natives so much, as we see the same manifestations of human nature, and it does make one gasp to see how very much they are like us, and we like them. It was about 2:15 A.M. when the second Mass was finished on Christmas morning. We came back home to warm up the coffee and finish our sandwich. In the meantime, Santa Claus had been here and left some dainty little packages for each one. We opened them with much laughter as we recalled how each sister had been desperately digging down in the depth of her trunk in a last-minute effort to find a suitable something for a gift. It was 3:30 A.M. when we decided to retire, and Sister Isabelle had warned us not to waken the others when we got up. About 6:00 A.M., we quietly put one foot out of bed, dressed noiselessly, and left our rooms to tiptoe downstairs; who should we meet but Sister Isabelle, all dressed and stealthily leaving her room. We all met and went over to the church. As we were saying our prayers, Father Lamarre rode by in the pouring rain to go seven and a half miles to say the third Mass. He came back about 11:00 A.M., and went straight to bed, too tired to even eat Christmas dinner. It rained a greater part of the day, but in between showers, we went to visit the patients over at the "sick house," and brought them each a piece of cake, some holy cards and a piece of newspaper to roll into cigarettes. The latter struck the most responsive chord. Smoking is the joy of their lives.

School was closed for the Christmas holidays, and with four of us at home, it was an opportune time to visit the other villages to give shots. Sister Irene and Sister Celestine made the trip to Lemanmanu and had a very busy day there. Father Hennessey, who had charge of this station for a year, had rounded up all the sick ones and lined them up for shots. The small children receive N.A.B. intramuscularly, and the grownups, in the vein. We have a small kerosene stove with a pan of water boiling continuously to sterilize the syringe and needles. One sister writes down the name and village of the patient, while the other gives the shots, so it goes rather fast. Sister Irene gave 102 shots while there. When they returned from Lemanmanu, we began our Triduum in preparation for Sister Hedda to make her final vows. We had three conferences each of the three days, given by Father Lamarre. Everyone emerged with renewed enthusiasm and courage, and on the morning of January sixth, Sister Hedda made her perpetual vows.

A few days later, the welcome news reached us that a boat had arrived bringing mail and cargo from Sydney. We were overjoyed at the thought of hearing from home, especially with Christmas mail. A big stack came for each one, and as usual, all work stopped until we had glanced through it and listened to the letters from the Motherhouse. You cannot imagine how interesting every little event is to us. We thoroughly enjoy knowing about the changes to different missions, and we greatly appreciate having the mission list. [9] We studied it very carefully and feel so relieved to know just where each sister is placed. You'd almost think it was a part of our responsibility. But you know this little island is so small, and now we rarely see an outsider to bring us material for general conversation. News is brief and at long intervals, for the only radio is down at Buka Passage. So, you see we talk about the same old things, and each one tells the same joke about 20 times, and we know the thing by heart, but always manage to be very interested and laugh at the right time. Our world is so small, and for that reason, one's peculiarities stand out like a sore thumb. Just the way sister so-and-so pours her soup is irritating, while someone else is annoyed at a similarly trifling action. There are so many little things in missionary work that make it profitable for those who spiritualize it. For instance, the boys who work for us unintentionally give us many of these kinds of pinpricks. In the kitchen, the cook-boys can take time out to scratch their heads while they are frying pancakes, or as one did not long ago—and don't be shocked, dear sister, leaned out of the window and blew his nose without benefit of hanky, and then resumed his dish-washing. A few days later, the same cook-boy was nonchalantly mixing the bread in the wash-basin. We took one gulp and turned on our heels and said, "All for you, dear Jesus."

This mission has something the rest of the islanders may justly envy— Father Lamarre's *motorbike,* as the natives call it. It belonged originally to Father Lepping, and it was purchased in San Francisco about four years ago when that group of missionaries came out. Last year, Father Lepping was transferred from Lemanmanu to Faisi or Nila and he gave the machine to his friend, Father Lamarre. However, the tires were all worn out as rubber deteriorates in this climate and then, too, it has had several hundred miles of wear and tear on the coral. Nevertheless, Father Lamarre was overjoyed with the gift, and as soon as he could, he sent an S.O.S. to Mother Francis for a set of San Francisco tires. All accessories on U.S. made goods, particularly bicycles, have to be sent from America, as they are not handled in Australia. It was a long wait for the reply to his letter, but at last it came saying the tires were on the way. The promise of an electric train at Christmas could not have brought more joy. When the shipment arrived, the first thing to be bailed out of customs was the set of tires. Home they came, bundled on the front of a rickety old bicycle. The tired boy handed them over to Father Lamarre, and he sat down on the porch and worked until the wee small hours assembling them correctly. The next day we were not prepared for the whir of a motor, and it just about scared us to death. Two minutes later, we saw Father sailing off down the road and a swarm of natives looking after him with mouths wide open. It has been working ever since, and he makes the trip to Buka Passage in an hour and eighteen minutes. He can make the round trip on a gallon of benzene. When he went down to see about a boat to bring the supplies up, none was available, so he brought a few things on the motorbike—a five-pound tin of peaches, pears, and some *S & W* coffee. Were we glad! You cannot imagine how grand it is to have some things from home. And real honey made by honest to goodness American bees! Well, how can we tell you how much it is appreciated?

Although the war news was encouraging, the bishop sent word to us to have a house built in the bush in case we have to make a hurried escape. We packed a few tins of food in a tin trunk and have our suitcases ready to leave quickly. One man came up from the beach and told us about a hidden cave that he thought would be suitable, but we didn't like the idea of a place with only one entrance. The natives are upset about the whole thing, and are puzzled about the "fly ships" that make rounds over the islands. We have returned all the orphan children to their relatives, including the two babies. We were sorry to lose them. Paulo was the elder of the two babies—a year and five months. He is a cunning little fellow. A few days later, we were down in the village and dropped in to see him. He was so happy and reached out for us to take him. After playing with him for a few minutes, we turned to go, and it just about broke his little heart—not to mention ours.

They are happy living like the other children on the sandy beach near the water. That lovely white sand and inviting water! The coral reef protects the children in swimming, as it is quite shallow when the tide is low and there isn't any danger from sharks. Some of the boys around 10 and 12 make surfboards with a few poles and ride the waves in to the shore during a high tide. They also attract sea birds by throwing rocks to imitate jumping fish, and when the birds are all excited, they turn on them and kill them. The favorite pastime of all is lying on the sand, flat on their backs with a leaf to protect them from the glare of the water and a pipe full of tobacco. They look so comfortable; it makes us a bit envious, especially as we pass them when we are hot and covered with perspiration, trudging along to make a sick call. The children play all day along the water's edge. Some hunt for flat stones or pieces of shell to throw skimming along the surface of the water. Others catch tiny colored fish and wall them off with sandy partitions in the water. A cruel amusement that they particularly like is to catch a large beetle, put a piece of wood through its thorax, and then suspend it on a long slender fiber. A sharp flip with the thumb and middle finger sets it in flight, and the poor thing buzzes for hours without getting anywhere. They do the same with large butterflies, using a delicate piece of fiber to enable the insect to lift its own weight. Another outdoor sport is to catch baby possums, which are about the size of a large field mouse. They are the most helpless little things you ever saw. They are hairless, have large bulging eyes, and cling desperately to anything for support. The youngsters put them on their heads and carry them around in much the same way an American boy would do to a pet white rat.

One thing that really takes the prize in the "art of killing time" is making smoke bubbles. These natives are skilled in the science of plain and fancy spitting. They spend hours practicing it. Some can spit through the teeth as far as from here to there. Others can make fancy moves to the accompaniment of harmonious gurglings and the long wiping of the mouth on the back of the forearm and hand. With all this experience comes the ability to make incredible smoke bubbles. First, the mouth is filled with saliva and a big puff from a "seegar" is drawn into the mouth. Then, the tongue and lips are manipulated in such a way that the saliva covers the smoke, and the filled bubble is carefully deposited on the palm of the hand for the admiration of all. When one wearies of this, there is always the old standby—hunting and killing lice on the other fellow's head. I'll bet the folks at home think that only the monkeys at the zoo do that. 'Taint so. Here, everybody does. Last, but not least, in the way of evading monotony, pain or hard work, is the chewing of betel nut. It grows everywhere, and it is equivalent to three mortal sins to steal one betel nut from another fellow's property. They mix it with a bit of lime made by burning coral several hours in a very hot kiln. It produces varying degrees of intoxication. Children begin to use it as soon as they are able to chew. The reaction from a betel nut can be similar to the effect of alcohol. Some laugh and talk incessantly, and others can't walk a straight line. The effect wears off with a good sleep.

On January 3, 1942—Manila falls to the Japanese.
On January 12, 1942—Japan invades the East Indies.

January 22, 1942

*W*hat an eventful day! Yesterday, Father Lamarre went to Buka Passage to see about our things in storage there and to learn what is happening in the war zone. He stayed at Hahela with Father Montauban, and about midnight a message was sent to the mission telling them that a large number of Japanese bombers were destroying Rabaul. They dressed and hurried to the church to consume the Blessed Sacrament and made ready to leave the mission at daybreak. Father had the motorbike and came right on to Hanahan to meet Father Caffiaux. The four of us were at church making our meditation when the motorbike came at full speed down the road. We all sensed trouble of some kind. Father came right over to tell us the latest happenings and that we were all to receive Communion and that the Blessed Sacrament was to be consumed. You can well imagine how nervous we were. The natives were quietly informed, and Father sat down near the altar rail to hear confessions, as so many natives do not receive Communion unless they have just gone to confession. When confessions were finished, we all went to Communion. We each consumed seven or eight hosts, and then Father consumed the ten that remained in the ciborium. It was such a solemn moment, and we all received our Lord as if it were to be the very last time. After making our thanksgiving, we came to the house to try to get things ready for breakfast. Father had told us to pack our suitcases and make ready to leave at a moment's notice.

A small house had been started out in the bush, but it was not completed, so he made other arrangements for shelter at the home of a catechist three miles from here. We put a few tins of food and blankets in a tin trunk, and each of us packed a small suitcase with a couple of changes of clothing.

About 9:00 A.M, the boys gave an alarm, and we ran

for dear life to the thickest part of the bush. Four boys came with us, and we stayed hidden until the plane passed over. Yesterday, a Japanese bomber flew right over our very heads, and we all came out on the porch to look at it, thinking that it was an Australian patrol ship. The plane was so close that machine-gun fire could have easily reached us, but they apparently were not interested. This morning, Father Lamarre told us that the Australians had fired at this same plane as it went over Buka Passage and the airdrome. Evidently, the Japanese were taking pictures of different sections of the island. About 11:00 A. M., a messenger returned from Lemanmanu asking Father Lamarre to come as soon as possible. Father Lamarre had sent Father Hennessey the news as soon as he got home this morning, so that he could be prepared for whatever might happen. Father Hennessey thought it best not to leave his station, so he asked Father Lamarre to make the trip quickly on the motorbike. In the meantime, the dispensary had been temporarily closed as well as the boys' school. We have everything in readiness to take to the bush, and quite likely we will have some of the boys stay on guard during the night. The doctor-boy is the chief alarmist and wears a police whistle attached to a cord around his neck. The natives are all very much concerned about our welfare, and some have even expressed the wish that they could give us their black skin so we could pass unseen. We do not know what the future holds for us, but we know that you are all praying for us at home, and even in the face of danger, we are happy to be missionaries.

January 23, 1942

*T*oday was ushered in by a heavy rain that cleared around 6:00 A. M. Father said Mass and we received Communion. A few of the natives came to Mass, including six very sleepy-eyed night watchmen. Later, they told us how well they had guarded the mission, but we have doubts about the time spent in watching, knowing so well their natural inclination for sleep. About 9:00 A.M., we heard what sounded like heavy gunfire south of here and later the whir of a plane. We all ran hurriedly to the bush, one sister just missing by an inch a headlong plunge into a mud hole. One of the boys nailed a couple of boards to the poles that support the barbed wire and you should have seen us run for it and climb the fence. It's a dreadful feeling, but we got under cover of the jungle bush just as a Japanese plane sailed over the buildings. It had a large circle in white and a red number in the center. More explosive sounds were heard, so we suspect the buildings at the Passage have been destroyed and with it, our 11 tins of honey. It's a good thing Father Lamarre brought one tin home so at least we could taste it. No boats were available to bring our things to Hanahan.

January 24, 1942

So far all is well. We began the day with Mass and Communion and were thus fortified to face whatever the day brought forth. It is hard to settle down to do any definite work as everyone is a bit on edge and always imagining they heard the sound of an airplane. About 9:00 A.M., Father Lamarre came over, and we all had a round table discussion about the situation in general. We poured over the map, hunting up all those little islands that are referred to in the news report. All at once Father heard a motor and told us to run. We did! He disappeared in a cloud of dust to one part of the bush, and the four of us climbed over the fence and ran to our regular hideout. The plane didn't even come near us, but it's such a free country up above the clouds, that we never know when the pilot may change his course. We came back all trembling and dripping with perspiration and tried to collect our thoughts and carry on at least part of our duties. After dinner, a news report came to us saying that "the operator" was unable to contact Kieta or Rabaul and that in all probability, the territory was in the hands of the Japanese. Later, we received word through a native that the government station at Sohano had been completely destroyed, which may account for the loud explosions we heard yesterday. We do not know if the Chinese stores still stand. We hope so, as our prized cargo from Orange is still there. Naturally, as danger drew near, the government officials left for Bougainville Island, taking whatever supplies they could carry over with them.

After 5:00 P.M., Father Lamarre received a letter from Bishop Wade encouraging us and assuring us that we are as safe here as anywhere at the present moment. He mentioned that the Apostolic Delegate expects the Japanese to respect the missionaries. The bishop asked us to make the Stations of the Cross daily for the safety of the missionaries, especially the sisters, and for God's blessing on decisions that he must now make. His letter made us very happy. Father Lamarre was greatly relieved, as he has been quite concerned about our safety. We feel that our choice to remain was best, and we are quite ready and willing to accept whatever God has in store for us. We are most grateful that we have daily Mass and Communion.

Yesterday and today, everything has been very quiet. We expected Father Hennessey to come over, but a message arrived late stating that he was unable to get away. Shortly after Father Lamarre started Mass this morning, someone gave the alarm that a plane was heard. Everyone scattered like flies. Father went over to the nearest window to see where it was headed and then proceeded with the Mass. The plane was some distance out at sea going southward. We thought it was in the direction of Kieta. Since then, all has been quiet and we feel like mice that have missed the cat by half an inch. We are peeking out of our holes, full of curiosity. We would like to have a bird's eye view of Buka Passage and surroundings. Father Montauban sent a note telling us he was planning to go down to Hahela this morning to view the remains. Probably a boy will come back in the late afternoon to bring a letter from him. To say we are anxious is putting it mildly. There has been a drizzling rain since noon today, and it does not promise a let up very soon. It is washday, and all of the clothes are hanging on the line in a very droopy condition.

January 27, 1942

*G*ood news. The boy arrived with a letter from Father Montauban. He is at the Passage and seemingly finds everything quiet and peaceful. Even Laurie Chan was found smiling in the doorway of his store ready to carry on business as usual. Bishop Wade is at Tarlena today and expects to come to Hahela late this afternoon. Japanese officials are expected momentarily at Buka Passage. Father Lamarre is leaving shortly to meet and confer with the bishop at Hahela. He is extremely anxious to be off. He said that he intends to take out his Roman collar and put a new tape in his crucifix. He'll add a white tropical helmet. That outfit might easily cause the new administration to mistake him for a Buka Island coffee planter. He wants to meet the Japanese as he is—an unknown soldier in the international army of Christ.

In the meantime, we are anxiously awaiting the news that Father Lamarre will bring home from the bishop tomorrow. We can imagine all sorts of changes. We wonder if the new officials will be staying at the Passage, and just what we are expected to do to fulfill our role as neutrals.

January 28, 1942

*W*e have all been patiently waiting for a message from the Passage. How time drags! Finally, at 5:00 P.M., while we were at evening prayers, the boy came back with a letter from Father Lamarre. It was brief but answered a lot of our questions. The bishop, accompanied by Brother Joseph, came to Hahela for a few hours and the three priests met him there—Fathers Montaublinean, Caffiaux and Lamarre. In the late afternoon, a plan was made to use the small pinnace of Laurie Chan to bring our supplies from the storehouse by night to Hanahan. Brother Joseph was to be chief engineer, and the natives at Hanahan were to take things off the little boat in outrigger canoes and bring them ashore. There was great excitement, and all the work-boys hurried down right after supper so they would be there on time. The moon was about three quarters full but the sky was overcast, shedding a diffused light over all. The sea was as calm as a mirror, and we thought every obstacle had been thoughtfully swept away by St. Joseph. We said rosaries and aspirations and waited expectantly for the purr of the motor, but all in vain. Finally, at 10:00 P.M., we came back to the house and said our night prayers. Even in sleep we kept a subconscious vigil and prayed for the safety of the guardians of the little boat and its cargo.

While we were saying morning prayers the boys came to tell us that they had waited on the beach all night, but the boat did not come. Father Lamarre is expected home this morning. Naturally we are somewhat concerned as we picture all sorts of surprise attacks from the enemy. At 10:00 A.M., Sister Isabelle sent two boys on bicycles to Buka Passage to offer their assistance. In the meantime, Father Hennessey came in from Lemanmanu to see Father Lamarre, and as he had not returned yet, he waited for him. He is very calm and cool and collected about the whole thing. Three enemy planes flew quite low over his house while he was outside doing his morning work at the dispensary.

About 3:00 P.M., Father Montauban came by bicycle from Buka Passage. His nerves are pretty well upset from the strain of the last two weeks, so Bishop Wade sent him up here for a few days' rest and medical care. He looks very old and very tired. Just think, he is one of the oldest missionaries and has been on Buka Island over 30 years. Surely his place in heaven must be one of the highest.

At 4:00 P.M., Father Lamarre came tearing down the road on his motorbike loaded with all he could carry from the boxes you sent to us, and news galore. He came over right away to tell us how things were and about the damage done by bombs. There were 17 bombs dropped around Buka Passage. Only a few found their objective, and on the whole very little damage was done to buildings. Some fair sized craters half-full of water may be seen around Chinatown and what used to be the airdrome. The soldiers stationed there disposed of everything before crossing to Bougainville Island to escape. We had heard the most absurd and exaggerated reports. It was worse than radio announcers after an earthquake in California. Actually, the Japanese just dropped a few bombs and flew away leaving everyone in a panic. The Japanese make frequent flights over the islands to observe, and the very sound of a motor paralyzes everyone. There is always the danger of machine-gun fire from the planes since they used it on the soldiers along with the bombing. However, they have not come to occupy the island as yet, so at present there is not anyone in charge. The district officer left for the interior for safety and has not returned to his post yet. Possibly in a day or two he will come back to restore peace and order. As soon as the natives knew the officers were in hiding, they began looting the Chinese storeroom where our things were, and took boxes of supplies belonging to Father Hennessey. Up to the present time our things have not been touched, and Bishop Wade helped Father Lamarre to transfer the boxes to Mr. and Mrs. Luxmore's about six weeks ago as they have gone to Sydney. Mother Francis will remember the house because she stayed there one night and had to pay regular hotel prices for the accommodation. The natives were not slow in exercising their new freedom. As Father came through a village yesterday he found a number of them armed with spears and axes to settle a quarrel with an adjoining village. Several were cut with knives but no one was killed. Some are still savages at heart, and though most are Catholic, their faith doesn't always go very deep.

On January 29, 1942, the Japanese bomb Buka Passage. The Australian soldiers stationed on the island of Sohano dispose of everything and prepare to leave.

On January 30, 1942, New Britain and New Ireland, including Rabaul, fall to the Japanese. The Australian district officer at Sohano flees for safety.

January 30, 1942

*M*ore worries. The quarrel between the two villages is really serious and Father Lamarre left around 10:00

A.M. to go to Buka Passage. A catechist came to see him last night and told him that the villagers had injured a number of people. Some were badly cut with knives. And just think, this is Gogohe, the village he goes to so regularly. He even said the third Mass there for them on Christmas Day. Now they are decorated with ferns and flowers and are ready for war. All of the men and young boys are lined up ready to attack the village next to them. They threatened to kill Father Lamarre if he comes to try and talk to them. The doctor-boy went with Father part of the way and stopped to dress the wounded. It wouldn't be safe for any of us to venture near them while they are so upset. However, we are quite sure Father Lamarre did stop to see them and has gone on to get help from the government officials. If the violence of the natives is not checked in time, it may spread throughout the island. The bishop is still at Buka Passage, and we are hoping the district officer has returned to his post.

What a strange and unexpected turn of events. The people here can be very superstitious, and some time ago a fanatic started a story going around that a steamer loaded with cargo was supposed to come for the natives. The yarn gathered momentum, and the officials had to take a drastic measure to check it. It breaks out periodically in different parts of the territory and causes a great deal of trouble. It has now grown into an actual battle during this very brief sojourn of the officials. Some of the natives can fabricate all sorts of strange tales, and before long, a number of the others accept and follow their suggestions. Black magic accompanies some of their rituals, and everything mysterious can have a strange fascination for them.

How fortunate for us that St. Joseph did not see fit to permit the little pinnace to bring part of our cargo up from Buka Passage two nights ago when we expected it. They may have thought their long expected cargo was being confiscated by us. They cannot understand where things come from or that we purchase them with money. The natives can be extremely jealous of white people and that seems to feed their sense of inferiority keenly. Of course, they are only a quarter of a step from paganism and their religion, as Father Hennessey sometimes says—can be a veneer. If they were not held in check through fear, they could revert to type in a surprisingly short time.

CHAPTER 6

We Are Cut off from the Rest of the World

January 31, 1942

It is reported that there are 10,000 Japanese at Rabaul, 200 miles away.

You can well imagine how anxious we were for Father Lamarre to return from Buka Passage and what a blessing it is to have the motorbike. He arrived home about 10:00 A.M. with another load from the Orange shipment plus a small bag of flour and good news. He rounded up some native police-boys, each equipped with a rifle and half a dozen cartridges and brought them to restore peace at Gogohe. The natives are deathly afraid of a gun and the effect was almost miraculous. It will require a couple of days before they cool off, but at least there won't be a general massacre. Father Lamarre is the self-appointed police master for this section until the officials come back to shoulder their responsibilities. The bishop is keeping law and order around Chinatown. He walks around saying his breviary and every time a native appears on the scene he asks him what he wants. If his answer is a bit uncertain, he is told to get out in plain English. The officer for Buka Passage had a hurry up call to go to Kieta to take over the reins of government. It seems that fear of the Japanese flying overhead threw everyone into a state of confusion and they ran for their hideouts in the bush. The natives took advantage of the situation and broke into the stores and stole right and left from anyone and everyone. The story that has reached us revealed that Marist Brother Henry took the matter in hand and made himself a deputy police commissioner. He ordered all the natives into submission. He filled the jailhouse house to the brim, put it under guard and then sent a desperate appeal to the bishop to come home at once as the jail was full and more were coming in. The bishop had a good laugh and got in touch with the district officer here who proceeded at once to Kieta. Brother Henry is an Australian, and he was stationed at Asitavi when we came up the coast to Hanahan. He is a regular clown and kept us laughing from the time we arrived until our boat pulled out. We just cannot imagine him "saving the city." He will surely have something to laugh about for the rest of his life. It's a good thing the missionaries did elect to remain.

Along with all this, we learned that we have 10,000 Japanese soldiers, sailors and candlestick makers living practically next door to us at Rabaul. It's a good thing the ocean is deep and that 200 miles of salt water lays between us. It surely is occupied territory and gives everyone an uneasy feeling. We have not seen our regular aerial visitors for a couple of days. Guess they are busy about other things. We are cut off from the rest of the world and very likely will be until assistance comes from somewhere. We can live for a long time on native products, and all we ask is that they leave us in peace.

February 1, 1942
    Singapore falls to Japan.

*W*e had two Masses this morning and best of all the Blessed Sacrament is back in the church. What an empty shell a church can be without His presence. Today, we had our retreat Sunday, and the rest of the day has been very quiet. Father Montauban is still with us, and Sister Irene is treating him for a skin infection and a large boil on his left arm. He is not feeling at all well and seems very old and tired. Father Lamarre has gone to visit Gogohe to see if they are demobilizing or what. We all feel a bit easier for a few hours. This tension and worry plus a certain amount of fear make one very nervous. One sister almost fell off her chair when the sanctus bell was rung during Mass.

February 12, 1942

*W*e have had a very peaceful two weeks. The natives at Gogohe came to terms and settled with their neighbors. There was a native court held and Gogohe, the aggressor, paid Tehete some pigs, a few lava-lavas and shell money along with a couple of dollars in cash. Bishop Wade made a trip through Buka Island to talk to them at each village. He spent a day in Hanahan and then went on to Lemanmanu and around to Pororan and then back to Buka Passage. Father Montauban stayed with us two weeks. He developed a large abscess on his left arm just below the elbow. Sister Irene lanced it and drained out several ounces of pus that gave him much relief. Then she gave him a course of N.A.B. neoarsephenamine, and at the end of two weeks, he was feeling like a new man. He has gone back to Hahela. Brother Joseph came up for a couple of days last week to get some relief for a toothache. He has three large cavities in the back molars and he had suffered so much from them. We packed them with carbolic pledgets, and we hope the nerve is dead. The doctor has gone from Kieta, so there isn't any medical officer this side of Australia. It is a real problem to have teeth cared for in these islands, and missionaries suffer so much from toothache. Everyone carries a little bottle of oil of cloves in his travelling kit but in severe cases it does not give relief.

You'll be happy to know that we are gradually getting part of the cargo from Buka Passage. At present it is out of the question to use a boat as planes open fire with machine-guns on any small boat. Father Lamarre has been bringing as much as he could pack on his motorbike and we are all so overjoyed with all the things you have sent. The soap is a lifesaver at this particular time. We were down to our last bar of laundry soap, so you can well imagine what those cases of samples meant to us. Then, too, we cannot get material to make into lavas to buy things from the natives so we can use a bit of soap to exchange for native grown foods. They won't give us one single thing unless we pay for it.

We were glad to have some tinned fruits and other things from home. There is absolutely no comparison in the taste of those packed at home and those from Australia. They just don't know how to put the meat in cans. Some of it is worse than dog food but we try to dress it up with spices and onions to make it go down. The Similac and Carnation milk will be used right down to the last drop. We tried making cocoa with the Similac and it's really good. Thanks a million for sending it. At present, we haven't any babies, so we can use it ourselves. During certain seasons the goats go dry, and we barely have enough milk for tea. The cow is dry now also, so you see everything you sent is more than welcome. The honey arrived safely and that is worth its weight in gold. We crave sweet things so much and you don't know what a treat it is to have some for breakfast with pancakes. Really, we are so glad you thought of all the things and we are surely having Christmas every time Father brings a load home. The boxes are too big for one man to even move, so he opens them and fills a gunnysack full to the brim and ties it on the back of the motorbike. He went down yesterday after Mass and came back about 5:00 P.M., loaded to the hilt. He ran into a rain storm, skidded on the slippery road and received minor injuries—bruises and abrasions on the left knee. But it surely is a lucky break for this mission that he has that motorbike. Ordinarily, it's a strenuous trip to pump a bicycle over that 25 mile stretch of road. Then it is hard to bring very much on the handlebars, as it throws the wheels off balance. About 25 pounds is about all one can carry. Father brings at least 150 lbs. each time on the motorbike and makes the round trip the same day. You can imagine what a priceless treasure that machine really is to all of us. Mother Francis didn't realize what a benefit she was bestowing on the mission when she purchased those tires in San Francisco, and sent them out to Father Lamarre. It's better than using a boat, and it doesn't take a fraction of gas and oil to operate.

Thus, time passes and we wonder how long we will be cut off from the rest of the world. We get bits of news once in a while. Someone on the mainland has a small radio, and he relays the news. Everything is so uncertain, and we do not know whether the Japanese are coming to occupy these islands or not. We carry on our duties and prayers and know that God in his good time will make everything right. We are so happy to have daily Mass and the Blessed Sacrament in the tabernacle.

February 20, 1942

*E*verything has been quiet and peaceful on our island. We haven't seen a plane for nearly two weeks. Reports reached us about the fall of Singapore, and we wonder what the reaction will be upon those occupying New Britain. We hear that raiders visited the plantations along the coast of New Ireland and took all the food they could find. They'd get slim pickings around Buka Island, so we hope they won't waste the benzene to come this far.

February 24, 1942

*T*his is a red-letter day as we had our first O.B. case; at least, we were invited. We learned that a patient in the village, the wife of one of our schoolboys, had been in labor for two days, so we jumped at the opportunity of edging our way into the family circle. Sister Irene went down about 10:30 A.M., and found the patient in a darkened room surrounded by 10 or 12 women. She was lying on a dirty old plank with a stack of leaves beside her to serve as sterile sponges. The hut was full of smoke partly from a smoldering fire and the rest from the pipes of the 12 attendants. Sister was asked to sit down and not to interfere in any way. This she did until the patient suddenly decided to move to the house next door. This is done when the baby is slow in coming; they think the transfer will speed up the process. After Sister Irene learned the reason for moving, she followed the procession and took her place in the corner as before. They insisted on carrying out their native customs; unfortunately, the baby died. However, they allowed Sister Irene to baptize it first. Sister came home all tired out from her five-hour vigil and a bit discouraged in her fruitless attempt to help. They cling tenaciously to their tribal customs, and we realize that it may take a long time before we can win their confidence. One shrinks at the filth of the native huts and the method of delivery, yet until they trust us, we stand helpless to aid them. Actually, there have been a number of births in Hanahan during the past year, and all of the mothers and babies have survived. The mortality rate is not high in spite of all of the germs. Generally, on the island there is a high death rate among children up to five years of age, caused by dysentery or malaria, followed by pneumonia. It may take years before the people can be taught the most elementary principles of hygiene; a full-fledged public health department working 48 hours a day could not easily induce them to change their ways of living. It will be so slow that we will barely scratch the surface in our lifetimes.

One thing that does a lot of good for them is N.A.B. and the general treatment of ulcers. To lance a big abscess and release quantities of pus is nothing short of a miracle to them. For the present, that will be our main work, and we are so grateful for all the medical supplies you have sent to us. We were delighted with the rolls of bandages and washed gauze and the ointments and all the 1001 things you so thoughtfully packed into those boxes. It is like digging for gold, as we never know what we might pull out of the packing. Everything is useful and especially so at this particular time.

We don't know how long we may be cut off from Australia. It gives us a strange feeling to think that every possible form of communication with the world has been closed. The two white men on Buka Island are trying to make their way on a small schooner to the New Hebrides and then across to the mainland. It's a risky trip, and it might be just as painful to face a shark as a Japanese. Some of the Australian soldiers are still here, and their presence does a lot to keep order among the natives.

March 7, 1942

*A*t last we have some feeling of safety, as the island has been put under martial law and the Australian soldiers, who were in hiding during the bombing at Buka Passage, are very much on the job. There was trouble in one of the villages, and the natives were on the verge of killing one another over that same "cargo idea" [10] that caused the trouble in Gogohe a few weeks ago. The soldiers caught two of the ringleaders and gave them each 20 strokes with a heavy kanda whip. The humiliation was almost as bad as the pain, and about all they could do was to crawl off to the bush and lie on their stomachs for a while. It made the rest of them sit up and take notice. They thought the government officials had gone back to Australia and that it was a good time to do as they pleased. It's a lucky break for the missionaries that the soldiers are here. Right now, some of the natives are digging up old pagan customs and ceremonies as well as polishing up the old spears. Then that "cargo craze" is spreading throughout the island. With martial law the Australian soldiers will shoot to kill whenever necessary, and it may come to that if the whipping post isn't effective.

We are continuing the medical work and there is plenty of it to do. The government hospital at Buka Passage was demolished by a bomb, and the medical officer is hitch-hiking to Australia. This means that all the medical work is done by we two nurses at Hanahan. We take turns in going to distant villages to give shots. We had to go to an interior village about three miles in the jungle and across a river, as it was impossible for those with bad ulcers to come to us at Gagan. The catechist rounded up a dirty old saucepan to boil the syringes for shots, and we brought a couple of bottles of sterile water with us to dissolve the neoarsphenamine. Twenty-five patients lined up in a shady place outside of one of the huts, and what a picture that scene presented. There we were in the most isolated place you could imagine, surrounded by dense jungle growth, and the whole village standing around to watch us at work. Nearby, a huge eagle tiptoed on the windowsill of one of the huts and eyed us suspiciously. He was a huge bird with enormous talons and a wing spread of at least four feet. His feathers were a golden brown, and we wondered if he could be a golden eagle like those in America. Evidently, the natives had caught him and made him a family mascot, for he stayed there the whole afternoon unchained and blinking at us with his wide-open catlike eyes.

After the injections were finished, we hurriedly packed our kit and started for Gagan, as we wanted to get out to the main road before dark. We had left our bicycles at a village on the road, as we could not use them in this hilly section. Some of the little youngsters followed us, and one took hold of my hand so she could keep pace with us. It felt good to get back on our bicycles after our trip, and in a few minutes we were on our way to Gagan, arriving just in time to change our wet shoes and get to evening prayers. We managed to squeeze in our prayers and meditation before the supper bell rang.

We had our meal at Father Caffiaux's house and then returned to our quarters as soon as we were finished. The chief of the village had sent a nice chicken for dinner and the cook-boy boiled it and made gravy and delicious soup. They grow a lot of sweet potatoes there, so we even had them mashed for breakfast with fried eggs. That night we were so tired we just hopped in bed as soon as we could and tucked the mosquito screens well around our beds. It is a sac-sac house that the secular nurses used when they came over from

Pororan to give shots, so we use it when we go there. As soon as we were beginning to doze, the rats started to play. They would chase one another across the floor and up the legs of our beds and seemed to enjoy themselves to the fullest. We didn't care what they did as long as the roof stayed in place to keep out the rain. It showered at intervals all night, and in our dreams we could see pools of water standing on the road between us and Hanahan.

Next morning it was clear but wet, so we started for home with two boys carrying our suitcase and medical kit. It took us about three hours to ride the 15 miles as we stopped often to rest and drink a coconut. It surely is a great blessing to us to have these bicycles. Our tires are getting a bit worn, but we hope they will last until we can order some from Sydney or Tokyo. When we got home, Sister Isabelle took us to see all the supplies they had received from Orange. Father Lamarre had arranged for two large native canoes to bring some of the packages up from Buka Passage. How thrilled we were to see all the useful medicines and the bottles of essence for making root beer once the war is over. You simply cannot picture our joy and especially as you sent just exactly what we need most. Everything was more than welcome, and you thought of all the things that are most useful, even shoe polish. We were on our last tin of black and all prepared to go with scuffed and scarred shoes for at least a year, when joy of joys, a whole dozen cans of black polish arrived. The black trays were grand and went into service at once. We brought one small metal tray with us when we came last year; it is used for carrying Father's meals over to his house. It is in continuous service and so many times we have wished we had a couple of large trays. These came to supply our need. Everything in tins or bottles was in first class condition, but the cereals and yeast in cardboard boxes were alive with worms. They were so long in storage at the Passage that the insects found their way in. Everything edible should be sealed in tins, as there are millions of insects ready to pounce on it and get into the tin if there is even a little dent in the cover so that it is not absolutely airtight.

March 10, 1942

 Japanese ships are spotted off the west coast of Buka. The sisters go to their hide-out for the day and take the hospital patients with them.

*T*his is being written while the four of us sit on a stack of banana leaves out in the bush. We left home early this morning. Reports reached us that a number of Japanese ships were anchored on the west coast. Father Hennessey sent word to Father Lamarre to make a quick getaway as they might be raiding along the coast. [11] We brought a few sandwiches and some books for spiritual reading, and we are going to stay here until dark. We locked the house and left a reliable boy to look after the place. Two boys came with us and cut down the vines and bush under an enormous tree and then spread banana leaves for us to sit on. Later, they will make a shaded lean to and a bench so we can sit in a more comfortable position. The bush is full of wild banana trees that do not produce fruit. They cut down the whole tree and lay three of them horizontally with two at each end to rise from the ground. Bugs, spiders, beetles, ants, and butterflies swarm around us. One huge flying beetle seemed to think Sister Celestine was a flower as it kept sailing around her in spite of all the passes she made at it.

 It is 11:00 A.M., and now we are all sitting on our banana tree bench. Sister Irene is reading a book on the life of St. Theresa, Sister Isabelle is reading the September edition of *The Catholic Register,* Sister Celestine is darning a stocking, while Sr. Hedda is just sitting. It is a clear, sunshiny day and we are about a half a mile from the mission but the jungle is dense, and we came by a hidden pathway, so it would be difficult to find us. Ten or eleven patients came with us from the sick-house, and they are resting under a tree not far from us. One native woman is sitting nearby weaving a basket from leaves. It is a restful scene with only the buzzing of insects and the occasional screech of a parrot. Two airplanes passed high overhead, and we ducked under our leafy shelter. The boys have gone to get a few coconuts to drink. One is up a tree now tossing them down as fast as he can loosen them.

It is 3:00 P.M., and we are beginning to think of home. We have finished all of our prayers and meditation. It has been a long day, and in the early afternoon we heard what sounded like bombs exploding. We hope Father Lamarre will send a boy with a message to let us know how things are and if any new developments have taken place. He consumed the Blessed Sacrament and sent the sacred vessels to the home of a catechist before leaving the mission this morning. He was afraid some Japanese troops might travel across the island and the main road goes right by the mission. The responsibility for our safety rests heavily upon his shoulders, and he made us hurry away to the bush right after breakfast.

March 11, 1942

Seven Japanese warships anchor at Kessa Point off Buka and interrogate Father James Hennessey.

*E*arly this morning, three Australian soldiers came to the mission on their way to Buka Passage. We hurried and made them some breakfast which they enjoyed immensely. They were all tired out as they had walked all the way from Lemanmanu, which is 14 miles northwest from here. Yesterday, seven Japanese warships anchored at Kessa Point, and a group of marines with an officer and interpreter came to see Father Hennessey. When he saw them coming ashore he put on his cassock and went down the cliff to meet them. They came from the ship in an awkwardly manned rowboat, narrowly escaping a dunk near the reef. They were dressed in badly tailored uniforms and ill-fitting shoes but seemingly had a firm grip on their rifles. Father Hennessey introduced himself, and the interpreter asked his nationality. He then requested to be taken to the mission. Father thoughtfully took them up the steepest road and had them all puffing by the time they reached the top. At the house, a long siege of questioning followed with special emphasis on wireless, movements of troops, boats, etc. There was little to be told, as this is such a small island. They were a bit puzzled over him and apparently did not understand much about missionary work or why he was there. Finally, they inspected the house, opening all the boxes, trunks, etc., and as luck would have it, found two cameras that they confiscated. All this was done with profuse apologies that war made such actions necessary. Father offered to serve them a cup of tea that was curtly refused. Several times during the interviews one of the soldiers came close to Father and stuck the rifle in his ribs while pulling on the string of his crucifix. Before leaving, they went to visit the church and the officer made a profound bow toward the altar while the others looked around and commented on the structure. Father was asked to accompany them back down the cliff to the beach and warned not to leave his station nor communicate with other missions. This he faithfully kept until 4:00 P.M. when he arrived all out of breath at Hanahan. We were mighty glad to see our "Japanese ambassador" and eagerly listened to his detailed account of his experience. The ships have gone away from Kessa Point, but we expect troops of Japanese soldiers to come to occupy this island.

March 17, 1942

Eight Japanese warships visit Kessa Point again and take Father Hennessey as a prisoner. The sisters begin to hide their diary behind the St. Joseph statute in the church.

*T*his is a sad day for all of us. A boy arrived at noon today telling us that eight Japanese ships came to Kessa Point on Sunday, and Father Hennessey was taken aboard as a prisoner. He had gone to Pororan to say Mass for the natives there when the ships came. Mr. Good, the owner of the plantation at Kessa, was also taken. They left this morning at 8:00 A.M., after buying a lot of food supplies from the natives such as bananas, taros and paw paws. We are all holding our breath and wondering what will happen next. Father Lamarre is going to Lemanmanu in the morning to pack and lock up

Father Hennessey's things and to make arrangements for a reliable boy to take care of the mission. We are all sick about it as he was here to see us just a few days ago, and we all joked about his visit from the Japanese marines.

In the meantime, we are hiding our quinine and a few tins of foodstuffs in the event that they come here. Sister Isabelle thinks it best to hide this diary because the information therein may arouse suspicion. We are hiding it behind St. Joseph's statue in the church, as we know he will guard it and see that you get it safely. We'll add a note often and try to keep it up to date, so you will have some record of our experiences if anything happens to us. We all realize the seriousness of the situation and are prepared as much as we can be for whatever God has in store for us. It all seems very unreal and is more like an account one reads in the newspaper. Our hope and constant prayer is that they will not take us prisoner and subject us to ill treatment. We know you are praying for us at home as the radio reports have informed you of the occupation of the territory. God wishes us to help him save souls in this particular way, so we only want to fulfill his designs for us.

March 18, 1942

The body of Mr. Percy Good, a plantation owner near Father Hennessey's mission, is found in a shallow grave. He has been shot and his throat has been cut.

Father Lamarre came over right after breakfast to let us know he had talked with a police-boy from Kessa Point. After the Japanese ships had left the harbor, the natives went to Mr. Good's house to look around. They found blood in two of the rooms, which aroused their suspicions. After investigating around the grounds, they found a freshly dug grave and in it the body of Mr. Good, the owner of the plantation at Kessa Point. They examined the body and found he had been killed with a knife—his throat was cut, and they buried him in a grave about a foot deep. Such treachery! Only a few days previously, they had taken him for questioning by other officials, so he concluded that he was safe. It makes us just sick, as we think the same fate might have befallen Father Hennessey. He was taken onboard Sunday morning after he had finished saying Mass for the natives at Pororan, which is about 16 miles from Lemanmanu, his own station. He usually stops at Kessa Point at Mr. Good's house, and takes a boat across to the island of Pororan. His bicycle was at Mr. Good's house, and after the ships had gone, a native brought it across to Hanahan.

Father Lamarre has just left for Lemanmanu. It is a sad trip. This morning we all offered Mass for Father Hennessey, either for the repose of his soul or his safety. Father Lamarre feels so badly. About noon, a heavy rain came up from the east and settled for a steady downpour. Father Lamarre came back from Lemanmanu about 5:00 P.M., drenched to the skin and covered with mud. We were glad to see him safely back at the mission. He had very little news to add to what we already knew; however, we learned that Father Hennessey was taken to Pororan on Monday, March 16th and was permitted to say Mass. The natives gave us the report, which has been verified by those in Pororan. That alone gave us a ray of hope regarding his safety. Possibly he had to prove to them that he was a priest instead of whatever they suspected.

March 19, 1942
Japanese planes repeatedly circle Buka.

This is the feast of our Holy Patron, St. Joseph, and what a lot of petitions greeted him from Hanahan alone. Our one thought is for the safety of Father Hennessey. We simply cannot think of anything else—to be taken so suddenly from our midst and not to know what has happened to him. Perhaps he is celebrating this great feast in heaven while his poor fellow missionaries are mourning their loss.

About 2:00 P.M., a plane circled around our island, and we think it may mean the ships are back at Kessa Point for more mischief. We don't know whether to run to the bush or just stay and meet them when they come. It certainly is a problem that can only be handled by God alone. In the meantime, we are spending the day quietly. We had chicken for dinner and a tin of real honest to goodness California peaches. So, you see our zero hours have a few bright spots. We have practically all of the things up from Buka Passage and how grateful we are for everything. It came just when we needed it most, and it will tide us over several months if we are permitted to remain at our station.

At 4:00 P.M., we were all sitting in the refectory having a cup of tea when who should come walking up the pathway but Brother Joseph. At first we were a little frightened, thinking he was coming from the Passage to bring us more worries about the Japanese. Instead, he had accompanied the officers to Kessa Point to investigate the reports of Mr. Good's death. They exhumed the body and found he had been shot through the head. Decomposition had taken place, and they were not able to tell whether he had knife wounds on his body. The natives said they did not hear a shot, and they were hiding in the bush only a short distance away. Everyone feels so upset over Mr. Good's death and Father Hennessey's disappearance. The conclusion is that Mr. Good was taken for a spy as he had a radio receiving set on his premises. His plantation is at a strategic place on Kessa Point overlooking a wide expanse of water, and in spite of many warnings from the Australian officers, he continued sending messages. Brother Joseph then walked across to Lemanmanu to see if any further information had been obtained about Father Hennessey. It was a nine-mile walk and he was all tired out but was determined to reach Hanahan before dark. He borrowed an old wreck of a bicycle and made the 15 miles to our place. Naturally, he was a bit upset as well as very hungry and tired. He and Father Lamarre discussed the situation with us, and it was decided that we ought to go to a less exposed center until they could get in touch with the bishop. That evening we all set to work to pack up the barest necessities and made ready to leave the following morning. It was not a surprise to us as we had been packing and unpacking for weeks. So the evening of St. Joseph's feast day was spent sorting out and packing what we thought to be most useful. We finished shortly before midnight, and each of us had two bags. The other things were packed in our rooms and locked for safekeeping.

CHAPTER 7

It Grieves Us to Leave Everything Behind

March 20, 1942

Father Lamarre instructs the sisters to bike to Gagan, an inland mission, for safety. On March 21st, the Australian government instructs the sisters to bike to Buka Passage and to leave Buka in order to find safety on the larger island of Bougainville.

This morning we put finishing touches on our packing while the boys overhauled our bicycles and helped us to tie our small traveling cases on the handlebars. Father Lamarre and Brother Joseph left for Buka Passage to send a message to Bishop Wade. We were ready by 10:00 A.M., and turned the keys of the house over to a reliable boy and started out for Gagan. How fortunate we were all able to ride a bicycle. Sister Irene rode the old wreck that Brother Joseph used to come from Lemanmanu. We had to stop every two miles so she could pump up the tires, and it was a funny sight to see her climb upon it to start out. Three of us had women's bicycles, two of our own and one that formerly belonged to the nurses at Pororan. It was a sad going away. Many of the natives came up to the mission to see us off. Some of them were crying. Along the road, many would stop us to shake hands and tell us goodbye.

It is 15 miles to Gagan, but we rode slowly and got there about 3:00 P.M. Poor Father Caffiaux didn't know what to make of it when he saw all four of us peddling down the road. We were caught in the rain and our clothes and shoes were wet; we were tired, but a cup of tea refreshed us. As we were finishing our tea, who should come in but Father Dionne from Carnewa and Brother Donatus from Chabai. You can just picture the consternation of Father Caffiaux as he made a mental picture of preparing for six unexpected guests. Fortunately, there is a little sac-sac house that the nurses used when they came over from Pororan to give shots. We were installed there and how glad we were to have a wash and get into some dry clothing. We had supper at Father Caffiaux's house with the two priests and Brother Donatus. The chief topic of conversation was Father Hennessey. The opinions were divided as to whether he had been shot as a spy or not. We returned to our house and said night prayers early as we were all in from our long trip. We did not have our mosquito nets so were a bit nervous with all the rats. First, one sister would switch on a flashlight and begin rummaging through her sheet to shake out an imaginary rat or centipede. Then, when all was quiet, Sister Celestine all but jumped out of a window because a stray dog came in and was sniffing her toes. The front part of the house where two of us slept did not have doors or windows; in fact, most of the sac-sac houses are built that way, as it is much cooler.

After breakfast the next morning, the two nurses thought they would make themselves useful by giving shots and dressing sores. The carriers had not arrived with our boxes and suitcases from Hanahan, so we did not have any needles or syringes to do the work. In the meantime, we rested a bit and did our spiritual reading.

At 11:00 A.M., a messenger arrived from Buka

Passage with a letter which read as follows:

Dear Sister Isabelle:
Orders from the government that you have to move
out of Buka immediately. So jump on your bicycles
and come to Hahela. A launch will take you to
Tinputz or Asitavi. I'll wait for you here.
Signed: J. Lamarre, S.M.

Well, a Japanese bomb couldn't have startled us more. We hurried to put our toothbrushes, etc., back into our bags, and we were ready in ten minutes. Father Caffiaux had lunch prepared for us, and after forcing a couple of bites down our nervous throats, we took off for Buka Passage. The road was dreadful. It had rained heavily, and pools of water stood everywhere. For miles, the road was up one hill and down the other, and most of the time we walked because our brakes were not too good. Sister Irene had trouble with her old wreck, and we had to adjust the wheel two or three times. It took us the longest time to cover seven miles, and we were just about exhausted when we got to the main highway to Buka Passage. We sat down while the natives got us some coconuts to drink. No one can even imagine how good coconut milk is when one is hot and tired. It was getting late, and we were afraid darkness would overtake us, so we hurried along. The last eight miles were over a good road, and we made up for lost time. There are two very steep hills, and it's real work to push a bicycle up a hill while weighed down with a heavy suitcase. We finally reached the top and actually were so out of breath that we stretched out flat on the grass for five or six minutes. If the sisters at home could have seen we refugees, they would have a good laugh. We got to the road leading to Hahela and sailed down the decline towards the mission. Father Lamarre came about a quarter of a mile down the road to meet us. We were muddy and tired and wet, since we came through the heat of the day and perspired with every step. Father Montauban met us at the door and had a cold drink ready for us. We sat in that nice big airy room and rested while supper was being prepared. Everyone tried to be cheerful and light-hearted, but we can assure you it required an honest effort to be that way. We ate very little of the nicely prepared supper and even that stuck in our throats. About 7:00 P.M., the boys took our bags, and we set out with Father Lamarre leading the way for a two-mile walk down to Kakil, which is near Chinatown. The boat was to meet us at the pier at 8:00 P.M. Brother Joseph stays at this house, as it is the property that the bishop purchased from Mrs. Luxmore shortly before the war. All of the medical supplies from Orange were temporarily stored there, and a few still remain that have not been taken to Hanahan. It grieved us so to leave everything behind—all those expensive things that are worth their weight in gold to us. At Kakil, we picked up a few supplies and one can of cocoa malt and took it on the boat with us.

Promptly at 8 P.M., the government pinnace the *Nugget* came up to the pier. We went aboard with an elderly woman from a western Buka plantation. Father Lamarre held the flashlight and handed us our bags and parcels while Brother Joseph directed the boys to steady the boat. Farewells were brief, and in a few seconds, our little boat was sailing out into the night. It was pitch dark with only a few stars peering from behind the clouds. He who calms the sea had heard all the prayers for our safe journey as noted in Matthew 18:24-27. When we got out of the Passage between Buka and Bougainville we had a mirror-like sea. How good, our dear Lord has been to us, smoothing all the rough places and showering us with kindness on every side.

The *Nugget* is a rather small motor launch and was operated by three native boys. We felt so helpless out in the big ocean in such a tiny boat. A couple of times some big swells rocked us from side to side and prompted some speedy acts of contrition. The boat crew made us jittery because they were lighting matches and smoking cigarettes right inside of the engine room not too far from the tank of benzene. However, no lives were lost, and we found a comfortable position and watched the phosphorus as the boat cut through the waves. We traveled about a mile from the shore just outside of the reef. Sister Isabelle and Sister Irene took turns at feeding the fishes, and Sister Celestine curled upon a bench and went to sleep. The other passenger, Mrs. Huston, lay down on the bottom of the launch with her pet dog beside her and slept all the way. The hours passed slowly, and at one point we noticed our launch headed straight out to sea. All of the boys had fallen asleep, so we roused them, and they hustled to turn the boat around in the right direction. The boat is guided by a rudder with one's foot.

March 22, 1942

The sisters arrive at Tinputz, a Marist mission station on Bougainville.

At 2:30 A.M., we came into the harbor of Tinputz. In the southern sky a star of exceptional brilliance seemed to welcome us to our new home. We drifted slowly in the direction of the pier, but it was so dark we could scarcely see it until we were right close. Stillness reigned supreme. It was soon broken when all the mission roosters began to crow, for it was 3:30 A.M. As soon as the launch was securely anchored, we climbed out and collected our bags, ready to climb up the steep hill to the mission. Not a light was to be seen at either the priests' or the sisters' houses. We made as much noise on the pier as we could, thinking it would awaken them and half prepare them for our arrival. This is Father Lebel's station, and you remember he was the American priest who traveled with us on the SS *Malaita* from Sydney. As soon as we reached the top, we called out his name, as we knew they might mistake our boat for Japanese and be dreadfully frightened. Our calls did not seem to awaken anyone in spite of all the force Sister Isabelle put into them. Finally, a sleepy voice from the distance answered us. It was Brother Gregory, the one who has charge of the sawmill here. He dressed quickly and escorted us to the sisters' house. The superior answered promptly and in a couple of seconds was dressed to meet us. The poor thing was very frightened, and imagine what a shock it was to meet us refugees. We were dreadfully tired as we had made that strenuous trip on the bicycles from Gagan to Buka Passage and went right on the boat after a brief rest. It was so near time for rising that we just asked to sit in a deck chair and doze until daylight. We all went sound asleep and were awakened in time to wash a bit before the 6:00 A.M. Mass.

There are two priests at this mission, one an aged man, and Father Lebel, the superior. However, Father Lebel had walked to a distant plantation to deliver a message and did not return until 7:00 A.M. He came right over to welcome us and then went to the church to hear confessions before saying Mass. It was Sunday morning at 10:00 A.M. when he finally finished confessions and began Mass. He must have a tremendous amount of energy and determination to be able to stay up all night and then all of the morning without even a drink of water. There was a long gospel, a still longer explanation and then a sermon. He finished about 11:00 A.M., and one of the sister nurses went over to take care of his patients and give the necessary shots.

After dinner, Father Lebel sent for the two communities of sisters to confer with him at his house. When we arrived, he had the chairs all arranged on the cool veranda and glasses ready on a tray to serve wine. It was a most unusual thing for us, because we have seldom even tasted wine, but this was a gift from one of the Europeans who was leaving for Australia and could not take it along. Sister Isabelle gave him an account of Father Hennessey's last visit to Hanahan. When that was finished, we were told that we were to remain here with the Marist sisters until further orders were received from the bishop. The rest of the day was spent very sleepily. It was about all we could do to keep our eyes open. Finally, at 8:45 P.M., our beds were ready, and we said our night prayers in a semi-conscious way and climbed into bed. A pile of rocks would have felt like a bed of roses to our weary bones. Instead, we had a nice canvas bed and a mosquito net. This is a small house with barely enough room for the three sisters, but they tucked four beds here and there, and we are deeply grateful for their hospitality.

March 23, 1942

*W*hen we went over for morning prayers we saw the sacristan fixing the bishop's chair, and then we knew he had arrived during the night. After assisting at all three Masses, we had breakfast and then made preparations for the bishop's visit. Unfortunately, we did not have cornettes and veils in the suitcase we brought with us; we took just the barest necessities, thinking our bags would follow shortly. It was one grand hurry to wash one extra cornette and change and wash the soiled one for the next change. We stayed in our room while one sister pressed our veils and by 11:00 A.M., we were ready to meet him. The interview was short but very reassuring. He was so calm and did not seem the least bit worried. He told us he had planned to have us go to Asitavi, a station halfway between Tinputz and Kieta. We are to leave during the night after the boat returns from Buka Passage. The bishop is going to Tarlena this evening, and the boat will collect our bags at Hahela and return shortly.

In the meantime, Bishop Wade intends to stay on Buka, and if possible meet the Japanese if they return to Kessa Point. He wants to come to some agreement with them regarding missionaries so that we may remain at our stations without fear of being molested. The Australian district officer has issued an order for all white people to go well into the interior of Bougainville for safety. All of the plantation managers have left Buka Passage for the larger island of Bougainville and at present are at various places along the east coast. Tinputz is sort of a halfway house as they travel southward and Father Lebel is a very busy man extending hospitality to all. One night last week, he had 11 men for the night at his house. They put up beds all around the porch. It keeps the Marist sisters busy serving lunches as well as cooking meals. He has a radio that he bought from one of the Europeans who was leaving for Australia, and everyone depends upon him for news. Each day he types a report and sends it on its rounds. In the evening, all of us went over to listen to the 7:00 P.M. news. It seemed so wonderful to us to hear London, New York, Cairo, South America, and Los Angeles.

At 5:00 P.M., the bishop left on the *Gabriel* for Buka Passage. He is a busy man with this large vicariate and we are all praying much for him. We were so glad he was able to get a message to Australia to notify Bedford, Washington and Orange that we were all well. Father Bergeron will relay it, and we know it will be a happy moment when the message reaches you at Orange.

March 24, 1942

*T*his morning after Mass, the four of us helped cut up a bullamacow. They butchered a beef last night and hung it up for the night. The greater part was given away to the white residents on nearby plantations. Sister Elie, the superior here, corned part of it, and also used a lot of small pieces to convert into bovril for a sandwich spread. She puts it through the meat-grinder and lets it simmer in the oven for hours and then adds agar-agar and seasonings; you cannot imagine how delicious it is. They have a number of cattle and butcher them quite often. They have many white Leghorn chickens and plenty of eggs. They also have a large flock of ducks, so they will not starve unless the Japanese come and raid all along the coast. The Japanese take anything and everything they can find in the way of food. Someone was telling us they were so hungry for fresh fruit and vegetables that they even ate green bananas and green paw paws. The natives were badly gypped in their dealings with them, and in a way it serves them right as they hustled out to meet them in canoes the minute the Japanese came into the harbor. While officers went ashore, the sailors went out to collect food. They bought pigs that the natives value at five dollars for the insignificant payment of one carton of Japanese cigarettes and some salt water biscuits. The natives are like the rest of us, always hoping to get a bargain.

March 25, 1942

*I*t is the feast of the Annunciation and here we are so far from our mission. How grateful we are to be able to assist at Holy Mass and receive our Lord in spite of all the turmoil of war. Shortly after breakfast, we heard the roar of a plane, and we all made a dash for the bush to hide. This time there were two planes and we wonder if more ships are around the point at Buka. During the day, planes were heard three times, and we hid in the bush a short distance from the house.

At noon today, a messenger came by bicycle bringing a letter to Sister Isabelle that reads:

Dear Sister,
Hope you had a good trip! The wind subsided shortly after your boat sailed, and the sea was most calm in the morning. How many rosaries did you say? Your bags arrived at Gagan half an hour after your departure. They are still there. I'll have them brought down to Buka Passage if Father Lebel can send the pinnace. Make a list of what you need in food and send it by Nima. He'll return immediately and then I'll get busy. In the meantime, I'll work on the motorbike. Hanahan is so quiet. I returned only Monday morning, and everybody came to shake hands. They thought I was clearing out. I settled things with Father Caffiaux, thanked him for his help and the rest. All investigations point out that Father Hennessey had a better fate than his neighbor.
Sincerely. J. Lamarre, S.M.

About 4:00 P.M, several of the white residents from nearby plantations came to see Father Lebel and to interview those of us from Hanahan regarding the death of Mr. Good and the disappearance of Father Hennessey. We all went over to Father Lebel's house, listened to the news report and then gave them the story. They all seem to be of the opinion that it was caused by a radio transmission set which was the property of Mr. Good. The Australian soldiers had confiscated it and stopped at Father Hennessey's mission. It was an unwise move that involved Father Hennessey, and naturally he was under suspicion from then on. Mr. Good was court martialed and shot as a spy, but the fate of Father Hennessey remains unknown.

March 26, 1942

All of the visitors stayed overnight. The men slept at Father Lebel's house, and the only lay woman in the group slept here at the convent. After Mass and breakfast, we assembled once more at Father Lebel's and had a round table discussion about current events. The important point in the whole affair is the order from the district officer to go into the interior for safety. For the plantation owners, it means leaving their homes and living in a shack and waiting in suspense for something that may never happen. Most of them prefer staying right at home but running to the bush if Japanese ships come into sight. Of course, the missionaries all wish to stay right at their posts. The sisters will leave if danger threatens, but it will only be for a day until the ships depart. The Marist sisters have a house in the bush not far from here, and their bags have been sent to this place as well as a small supply of food.

At 4:00 P.M., the guests departed, and it was a big relief to be by ourselves once more. There were 10 visitors for dinner at Father Lebel's today. We had dinner with them as we are on the "entertainment committee" with Father Lebel. Most of them were Protestants; in fact, one was a Methodist minister from Teop. Wonder how he liked sitting down with four Catholic sisters? He was very nice, and the conversation was entertaining. Everyone seemed to feel at ease and to enjoy the event. We four Hanahan Sisters were tired and bored with it all and anxiously waited for an opportunity to get away. Tinputz Harbor is spacious and very calm. It extends inland about a mile and the passage is wide and deep enough for an ocean vessel.

March 27, 1942

*W*e are beginning to feel a bit of anxiety for the *Gabriel*. It has not arrived yet. The boat we came down on, the *Nugget,* is out of order, and we heard the *Gabriel* was going to tow it halfway down the coast to anchor for repairs. The night we came there was a knocking sound in the engine, and we were somewhat apprehensive.

March 28, 1942

*T*his morning when we got up, we looked down toward the pier and there stood the *Gabriel*. How glad we were to know it was safe. The bishop came back and is going down to Kieta. We are leaving for Asitavi in the wee small hours of Monday morning. We learned today that the bombers that frightened us so many times a couple of days ago, machine-gunned Kieta. We don't know what was damaged as yet. The bishop's boat, the *Gabriel*, was anchored at Tarlena pier, and the Japanese flew very low and examined it carefully but did not drop any shells. Today, Father Lebel went to one of his substations in the bush about three hours walk from the mission. Tomorrow is Palm Sunday, and he wanted to say Mass for the natives. Many of them are afraid to come down this far. He is a very zealous missionary and does not spare himself in the least. Besides his priestly duties, he takes care of all the medical work. After Mass on Sunday mornings, he gives shots and even makes sick calls to distant villages. This afternoon, Bishop Wade heard confessions part of the afternoon along with Father Allotte. We arranged it so we could go to the latter, in spite of the fact that he protested at hearing confessions in English.

March 29, 1942

*T*his is Palm Sunday, and we have just heard Mass and finished our other duties. The two sisters gave shots for about half an hour. There were many natives at church, but only a few for medicine, quite a difference from Hanahan with the swarm around the medicine house after Mass. We are all anxiously waiting for tonight when we expect to sail for Asitavi. We have been here a week, and it makes so much extra work for these poor sisters. The superior does most of the cooking and is assisted by five or six of the small girls whom they have as boarders. She is a very good cook and has given us a lot of useful information about preparing foods that are native grown. These three sisters are French, though the superior is from Maine and from the same town as Father Lamarre and Father Lebel. She knew Father Lamarre when he was a youngster, and she came to the islands about 20 years ago. Many of her early years were spent in Hanahan, and she still has a warm place in her heart for that station. The other two sisters here are from France and speak very little English so French is used most of the time so they can follow the conversation. Sister Irene and Sister Hedda talk pidgin to them.

This afternoon the bishop came over to see us and to tell us about his visit to Hahela. We were very happy to know the priests were to remain at their stations. Father Servant has gone to Hanahan to be with Father Lamarre; and Father Montauban has gone to Gagan to be with Father Caffiaux. In the event the Japanese come to anchor off Hanahan, Father Lamarre is to go to one of the substations and remain there until they leave. He is an American and that alone may be against him. The bishop quoted a passage from scripture which was quite apropos to the situation, "The Good Shepherd stays with his sheep and does not desert them, even when the wolf comes."

At the completion of his visit, he told us we were to leave early in the morning. He asked us if we would like to have him say Mass before leaving. Of course, we were very happy to be so privileged. The sacristan made ready for the early Mass, and we all went to bed early so we could arise at 12:30 A.M.

March 30, 1942

Japan occupies Buka Island. Father Lamarre stays at his post in Hanahan.

*W*e had Mass and received Holy Communion at 1:30 A.M. It was a clear moonlit night, and the *Gabriel* was ready and waiting for us at the pier. Sister Elie made a cup of hot chocolate for us, and by 2:00 A.M. we were all on board ready to sail. The boat's crew was all at their posts ready to start the minute the signal was given. The *Gabriel* is a fair sized boat with a roomy cabin and two bunks. There is space on the back for at least six deck chairs so you know we were comfortable. The engine was functioning properly, and the sea was calm. The bishop started the three Hail Mary's for a safe journey, and we were off to Asitavi. When we were well out beyond the reef, the skyline in the east became very black, and for a few minutes the bishop was a bit worried. All of us began praying to St. Joseph for all we were worth, and within an hour the clouds dispersed and we felt safe enough to curl up and have a little rest in our deck chairs. The bishop went down to the cabin to rest. We traveled rather close to the shore just outside of the reef and, at 4:30 A.M. the first faint rays of dawn appeared. Soon the bishop was out on deck to ask for more prayers. The early morning hours are the most feared as that is when planes make their rounds, and if we were seen, there might be danger from machine-guns. It was an anxious hour, and we kept St. Joseph very busy until the church of Asitavi was in sight. In a few minutes, we were ashore greeting Father Fluet.

It was a grand and glorious feeling to be safe and on dry land and at the end of our journey. There was a bit of hurried moving by Father Fluet and Brother Paul. They transferred their things to the sac-sac house and gave us their house. It is larger, and it would be easier for us to supervise the cooking and housework from there. The bishop was left to shift for himself while all the packing and unpacking was being done. They were all most solicitous for our welfare, and beds were put up and mosquito nets unpacked. After dinner, we took a rest, as we were so tired we could scarcely think. We all had extremely sick headaches from sitting in the sun, and aspirin only made it worse. By 4:00 P.M., we were able to say our prayers and take out some clean clothes. Fortunately, the cook-boy took care of preparing the food, so we were free. After all these weeks of moving, we are able to land in a strange house and feel right at home the minute we open our suitcases. We all retired early and had a most profound and refreshing rest.

March 31, 1942

This morning the bishop said Mass at the main altar of this beautiful church while Father Fluet said his at the same time at the St. Joseph's side altar. During Mass, two heavy planes sailed high above us, but the building is so well hidden among the trees that little thought was given to them.

After Mass, we came back to the house still enjoying that feeling of relief to know we were safely in Asitavi. We took a few things out of our bags and put our rooms in order while the cook prepared breakfast. It was a beautiful morning, and as we have already told you this is one of the most beautiful stations we have ever seen. After living in Hanahan, it is like coming to paradise. The entire grounds are covered with clover. Neatly trimmed hedges border all the pathways. Two rose bushes in full bloom grow right near the entrance to the house. At the side, a real grapefruit tree stands loaded with fruit. Throughout the property, paw paws grow by the dozens, and the bananas hang in huge bunches everywhere. They have about 2,000 banana trees. Pineapples grow by the hundreds in a garden not far from the house. You can imagine the four of us feasting our eyes upon such a scene. In Hanahan, we have to buy all of our bananas, paw paws and pineapples. It's a rare treat to have pineapple there.

The breakfast bell called us back to earth, and we sat down to enjoy a real honest to goodness Arizona grapefruit. No sooner were our spoons raised to our lips than the cook rushed in and with bulging eyes told us two Japanese warships were coming into the bay. We were terrified. We ran to our rooms and threw things in our bags as fast as we could. In a few minutes, the bishop came over and told us to eat our breakfast and then make ready to leave as soon as he sent the word. In the meantime, curiosity got the best of us, so we found a protected lookout and saw our first Japanese warship. It was a huge thing and was slowly moving toward the harbor at Numa Numa. One look was enough to speed up our breakfast, and in a few minutes all our bags were ready at the door for carriers to pick up. We took everything, including a bundle of *Los Angeles Times* newspapers that Father Lamarre had thoughtfully put on the *Gabriel* for us. We had a hurried visit to the chapel and were off with a dozen boys carrying our luggage. Our last view was of Bishop Wade standing in front of the house calmly looking out at the battleship as it glided slowly around the reef to anchor. He was anxious to interview some of the officials and come to some understanding about the missionaries. Father Fluet stayed with the bishop.

We started the rosary and walked quickly up a hidden road to our mountain retreat. At the beginning, the ascent was gradual, but after an hour's walk we had some real climbing to do. We reached the house shortly before noon, and how good it was to sit down and have a drink of coconut milk. About halfway up, Brother Paul caught up with us. He understands the language of these natives. It is entirely different in each section, so our Buka language would not be of any use.

The house we found awaiting us was built about two months ago; it is made of bamboo and covered with sac-sac, and the government officials used it as a hideout. The house is small, about the size of the refectory at Saint Joseph Hospital in Orange. We have four chairs and three canvas beds. We used some bandages to put up a line so we could hang up our clothes, then made up our beds and took a little rest. We had brought our blankets with us. Later, we hunted around for a little food, and found some tins stored away out in a little shed. There are several bags of rice, but they are full of worms. Moths lay eggs, and soon little white worms hatch and make cocoons and the whole bag is one moving mass. At Hanahan, we spread the rice out on a sheet and put it out in the hot sun to kill the worms, and it works like a charm. In the storeroom, we found a small amount of kerosene and a tea kettle. Hunting a little more, we found a tin of salmon and soon supper was ready. Two suitcases, with the *Los Angeles Times* spread over them, served as a table. We had a loaf of bread and a few spoons with us, so we managed to take our meal in picnic style. There wasn't any water, but during the afternoon a heavy shower came, and we held our cups under a drip, catching enough to quench our thirst. It wasn't too clean, as the roof of sac-sac is a favorite haunt of spiders, ants and bugs of all kinds. Toward evening, one of the natives went down to the river, and filled a kerosene tin for our use. We were so glad to have the little kerosene stove, as it boils water very quickly. We found a package of cocoa and removed the top of the contents because it was wormy and used the clean part to make our beverage. It was a delicious meal, as we were hungry after our five-mile mountain climb. During all these hours we were praying for our bishop that everything would go well in his dealing with the Japanese. We could see four ships anchored a few miles from the coast.

April 1, 1942

*W*e had a peaceful night, and after prayers and breakfast, we were ready for whatever the day brought forth. The villagers were most curious about the whole thing. Some of them came to our house to look at us. They had not seen sisters before and watched every move we made. In this section, it is quite primitive; many have not been baptized, and they are afraid of white people. We saw a number carrying bows and arrows that looked powerful enough to send anything into the great beyond. About 9:00 A.M., we were called to see a man with a large ulcer. We dressed the sore and then gave him a "shoot." Two small children were then brought to us, just covered with yaws, which we treated. When we had finished, we decided to take a little rest, as we were weary from the day before. We had just settled down for a nap when Father Fluet and a dozen carriers arrived to bring us back home. The ships had gone, and the plantation at Numa Numa was stripped of everything that would fit into a battleship. The Australian soldiers stationed there made a hasty retreat to the bush, but were unable to take their food with them. Bishop Wade did not see any of the Japanese officials, as they did not come to Asitavi.

It did not take us long to pack and start down the incline for the mission. The heavy rain made the road slippery, but we dug our heels in and hurried along. We were so glad we weren't in India or Africa where the jungles are full of snakes and dangerous animals. Those poor missionaries must have a bad time of it. We had a splendid view over the mountain crests rising throughout a stratum of cloud. Steep vine-covered precipices were on both sides, and we heard the rush of water in the river below. White cockatoos flew overhead, and brilliantly colored parrots scolded incessantly in the cocoa palms. The vegetation is very dense, and enormous trees partly shelter the pathways from the hot sun. We wore our large straw hats and found them invaluable. A native walked ahead and at the crossroads placed a piece of wood indicating the direction. We arrived there after carefully studying the sign, deciding it meant the other way. We soon discovered our mistake and turned back to find our guide at the crossroads laughing at us. When we reached the house, we found the table set with the mission's best tablecloth. A large bouquet of flowers supported a still larger picture of Saint Joseph. On the porch a small table with four chairs, a pitcher of fruit juice and glasses awaited us. Beside them was a note from the bishop that read:

Dear Sisters,
Saint Joseph welcomes you back for these days of special prayer and recollection. He has a cup of tea ready for you, and Miko, the cook, says that he has a

*kai-kai ready to finish. "Em I sorry too much blong
you fella." You must be very tired, so fall to, then
rest and I shall call later.
Sincerely, T. Wade, SM*

How happy we were to receive such thoughtful
kindness from the bishop. We have given Father Fluet and
Bishop Wade so much work and worry during our short stay.
Perhaps we can make it up in some way. If not, Saint Joseph
will have to dig into his purse and do it for us. After dinner,
we went over to help Brother Paul decorate the altar for Holy
Thursday. Two of us made rounds to pick every flower in
sight, while the other two arranged them in vases. It was
finished by 6:00 P.M., and it was beautiful.

April 2, 1942 Holy Thursday

*I*t is hard to realize that this is Holy Week and that all of the
beautiful ceremonies of the Church are being renewed
throughout the world. Circumstances prevent their being
carried out here in full. This morning our bishop gave the
priests, brothers and sisters an inspiring message before Mass.
He reminded us of the serious times through which we are
passing, and of the greater need of living close to God. At
8:00 A.M., the bishop began Mass with Father Fluet assisting.
The schoolboys sang the Mass under the direction of Brother
Paul. There are only 20 schoolboys remaining at the station,
and many are only 10 or 12 years of age. After Mass, the
Blessed Sacrament was carried in procession. Throughout the
day, the sisters have been going in turn for half an hour of
adoration. The bishop has been there the greater part of the
day. Tonight from 8:00 to 9:00 P.M., we shall have Holy
Hour. During the latter part of the afternoon, it has been
raining steadily. In our free moments, we have ventured to
take a few things out of our suitcases. Upon opening a
package of medicines and dressings, we found a note dated
March 24th. It read:

Dear Sister Isabelle,
Many thanks for your letter. Glad to know you arrived safely having a good sea. The Holy Ghost inspired me to go to Hahela and Kakil today. There I found your letter and the bishop's, so immediately I made for Gagan on the motorbike to have your cases brought down at once. You will have seen Nima by the time this letter reaches you. Tell him of anything you need, and I will have it sent down. Everything and everybody is well at Hanahan. I'm going right back there now, and will see the bishop tomorrow. Give my best wishes to Father Fluet. Treat him well. Remember, he is a silent man. Thanks for prayers.
Yours sincerely,
J. Lamarre, S.M.

Even though it was several days late, we were happy to have some explanation for the delays with our baggage. Transportation is such a problem when moving with several suitcases and a heavy medicine kit. Our usual pay, tobacco, is used up, and that is the one thing the carriers like best of all. A woman will carry a 50 pound bag of anything almost any distance for a stick of tobacco.

CHAPTER 8

Our Hearts Were Heavy

April 5, 1942 Easter Sunday

Things have been happening so fast we scarcely had time to jot them down. With all of the excitement, we have been able to carry out the Holy Week Services. Bishop Wade has been with us since our arrival here. On Good Friday morning, while we were kneeling in the chapel, we heard rapid footsteps coming up the center aisle. It was Brother Henry, who had arrived at daybreak to find the bishop, for it has been reported by radio that he had been taken. Four Japanese warships visited Kieta. A large number of soldiers landed, and all the brothers and priests were taken at the point of bayonets to headquarters to be interviewed. The interpreter was a Japanese who had lived on Buka Island a number of years and had spent his time gathering trochus shells. Profitable pastime! He knew the priests and brothers well, and you may imagine their relief at seeing a friendly face among the serious group. He spoke excellent English and had quite a conversation with them. To be brief, nothing was taken from

Kieta mission except a few trinkets. The priests and brothers were permitted to return unharmed with instructions to remain strictly at home. If it were necessary to go by boat, they were to use a Japanese flag, but no promises were made that they would travel in safety. The soldiers left them with an uncertain feeling about their security. After they were gone, the natives came to the mission to tell them that Bishop Wade was in Asitavi. Brother Henry left at nightfall to verify their report.

This afternoon, the bishop gave us a conference in the church and broke the sad news to us of our impending separation. Sister Isabelle and Sister Irene are to go with the bishop by boat this evening to a station between here and Kieta. Having our safety at heart, he thinks it best to divide us into two groups, so we won't all be taken at once. Sister Celestine and Sister Hedda are to remain in Asitavi.

At 6:00 P.M., as the last rays of the setting sun illumined the sky, we said farewell to two of our sisters. A rowboat took them from the shore to the small launch *Teresa*, and the bishop followed in a few minutes. Our hearts were heavy, but we managed to keep the tears back. They waved to us from the boat, and as darkness was coming quickly, they made all speed to get beyond the reef while it was light. Two sad hearts hurried to the chapel to say a prayer for their safety. They are expecting to arrive about 4:00 A.M., and it is an hour's walk from the beach to the mission. The bishop will stay there for a short time while they are getting settled. From there he will walk over mountains, rivers and swamps to visit and encourage his missionaries. No one knows where he is, or where he will appear next, but Saint Joseph, to whom the missionaries are entrusted, will guard the beloved bishop.

April 28, 1942

The days have gone by so fast we almost forgot about the journal. It is in hiding behind Saint Joseph's altar in the event of a surprise visit from the Japanese. Sister Celestine and Sister Hedda did not waste any time mourning over the loss of half of the community. There was too much work to be done. Sister Celestine took over the boys' school, the poultry raising, the laundry and the mending, while Sister Hedda took charge of the medical work, the kitchen and the sacristy. The days have been full to the brim, but we are happy to be useful in some small way to repay this mission for giving us refugees a home. Sister Celestine teaches an hour in the morning and an hour in the afternoon. In between times, the boys work in the garden under the direction of Brother Paul. Sister Celestine uses her spare moments taking care of the small chickens, ducks and guinea hens.

Father Fluet has quite a poultry farm and a fine place for supplying them necessary food. There are chickens and ducks setting all the time, and new families of chickens are put into little pens and fed several times a day until they are old enough to scratch for themselves. The little ducklings are more delicate and require careful handling for about three weeks. We have plenty of corn and papayas to feed them so they grow fast. The newest family of guinea hens just curled up and died, and we couldn't account for it in any way. They build nests out in the woods in the tall grass and it is too much for the little ones. Father Fluet found a family of ten and put them in a pen, and they all lived. Now they are old enough to fly up on the perch in the chicken house and sit beside their parents. It's strange, but the older guinea hens protect and feed the little ones, and they all travel around in a flock. Woe to anyone who dares to pick a small one up. It surely is fascinating, and we stand and watch those fluffy little things while they pick up cracked corn. There is a great deal of work attached to it, and we cannot see how two men were able to accomplish as much as they have.

Father Fluet is an American, and he has been in the islands about five years. In fact, he came with Father Lamarre as they were ordained at the same time. He is interested in everything around the farm, though it is doubtful if he ever saw a live chicken before he came here. When he isn't kneeling at the altar railing praying, he is out chopping down a tree or building a fence or putting a gadget in the chicken house. He has very little to say and is most considerate of others. This is the first time sisters have been stationed at this mission, but we found everything in the sacristy as neatly folded and packed away as any sister could possibly have done it. It really surprised us to see the delicate lace surplices hanging just so, and three little camphor wood boxes with finger towels, purificators and amices all in order. He has beautiful vestments and altar linens given to him by loving relatives and friends before he left for the foreign missions.

About two weeks ago, we heard through Father Lebel that all the priests on Buka Island were safe and well. After the Japanese officials occupied the government station at the Passage, they sent for all the priests to come and register. The interpreter was a Catholic, and he was very courteous to all of them. He even offered to supply them with food if they were in need. Father Lamarre wrote the message and sent it to Tinputz telling the good news. No one can cross the Passage—not even a native—and all messages are sent through the officials. Father Fluet had sent Brother Paul to Tinputz to get news about the other missions, and the evening before he arrived, Father Lebel heard the announcement over the radio that Bishop Wade had been taken to Rabaul. He was stunned, and that evening at 7:00 P.M., started out by boat to come to Asitavi to see if it were true. He arrived at midnight and talked with Father Fluet for an hour and then hustled back to Tinputz. He has a small motor launch. How happy he was to know that the bishop was safe and somewhere on Bougainville Island.

May 17, 1942

*W*e had news from Sister Isabelle and Sister Irene. It is difficult to get messages delivered without any of the mission boats running, and their station seems to be in an out-of-the-way place. The bishop spent a week there helping them to get things in order.

In the meantime, we have been busy here. We made a five-mile trip up to a village in the mountains to see a man who was dying of pneumonia. Sister Hedda baptized her first native since coming to the islands. He died after a few days. It was an eventful trip with all of the usual transportation problems. Halfway back we met Father Fluet with a package of sandwiches, and accompanied by two boys—his rescue squad. When we reached the river, which is a rushing mountain stream, we wanted to wade it instead of being carried over. This was our first attempt to cross one of these rivers. Father mistrusted our strength against the current. The water was quite shallow, only reaching to our knees, but we had no idea of the force. We two sisters locked arms, and with a stalwart native on either side, started across. Sister Hedda lost her footing and fell to her knees. It had looked so easy when the boys carried the bicycles over. We crawled up the opposite bank like a couple of half-drowned rats. Father had given us his precious watch to carry, and we dropped it into the water almost at once. The water was clear, so we got it and dried so quickly he didn't see what had happened. We were thoroughly chagrined with ourselves as we silently pursued our way. We later learned that we had crossed through the haunts of crocodiles.

About three miles from here, there is a small Chinese colony where we called to see one of the men who was sick. We came to their assistance on Holy Saturday when a new baby arrived. Since then, a number of them have been sick and in need of medical attention. This time we lanced a large abscess on one man's back and relieved him of about six ounces of pus. Then we gave him an intravenous of N.A.B. before going home. He had a bad case of shingles previously and had been ill a couple of weeks. These poor people live in constant fear of a visit from the Japanese. They live in little bamboo houses with all their suitcases, bedding and boxes piled in a corner, but with it all, they are the cleanest people you ever saw. The wash lines are always full of clean clothes. Their gratitude for the little we do is really touching, and I believe they would give us the last thing they own if we would accept it.

A few days later, we had some more minor surgery to

perform. A native was coming across from Numa, and the water was very turbulent where a swift river enters the sea. His canoe capsized, and a piece of floating wood cut a big gash in his abdomen. He came up the walk holding this large flap of bleeding tissue in place. In our hurried departure, we had neglected to include surgical needles. We hunted around and found a rusty one that we scoured with ashes and sterilized. Fortunately, we had a few tablets of Novocain that Dr. Nall, of Santa Ana, had given us. When the local anesthetic had taken affect, we proceeded with stitching it together with some heavy sewing thread. Miko, the cook-boy, assisted and supplied all the "Oh's" and "Ah's" each time the needle was forced through the skin. Shortly our patient developed pneumonia, but we brought him through. He went home yesterday, cured. As he was leaving, big tears came into his eyes as he said, "Good bye, sister." He was an unbaptized boy from Green Island and is employed at the Numa Plantation. Later, he brought several of his friends to the mission, and they asked to be baptized. My needle and thread had netted nine souls.

We have been most fortunate in getting news from the outside world in spite of our isolation. Four plantation managers are in hiding up in the mountains, and they have a radio. They are staying at the same house that the four of us used as a hideout on the day the Japanese visited Numa Numa. They have fixed up the place with a porch and other additions, calling it the *Hotel Australia*. They send boys down to the plantation for meat each week that makes the rounds of the European residents. The large plantation at Numa has about 700 cattle and many pigs. Each week they kill a cow and give part to the Chinese, a generous amount to the mission and a supply for the mountaineers. About two weeks ago, we became heir to an icebox from the plantation. They asked Father Fluet to take care of it, as it is a nice new *Electrolux*; the owner left for Australia a couple months ago. It works like a charm. We just light the little lamp, and in six hours it is freezing. We are delighted with the simplicity of its operation. It consumes a moderate amount of kerosene, so we use it only when we have fresh meat. Its name indicates that it is made by an American firm with a branch at Melbourne.

During the last few weeks, we have been trying to use as much of the native-grown foods as possible. Fortunately, Father Fluet planted about an acre of peanuts, and now they are ready for use. We have sacks full of them. They grow exceptionally well on this island. All of our butter had long since been used, so we got busy with a few experiments. Several failures at making peanut butter did not discourage us, and finally we turned out a good product. By drying the shelled peanuts in a slow oven, we removed the red skins easily, and the nuts were put through a meat-grinder four times to get the meal as fine as possible. The next problem was to make it spreadable. The bright idea of using coconut oil came to us, and presto—a perfect product. Sugar shortage was the mother of another invention. Numerous attempts at extracting the juice from the sugar cane resulted in our using the back of an ax to pulverize the stalk. The fibrous pulp was then squeezed in a muslin cloth. After boiling the juice for several hours, we had a thick, sweet syrup—about one-sixth of the original quantity.

The bishop is dreaming dreams of a great future for Asitavi, as the soil here is splendid, and a river about a mile from here could be used for a power plant. This center could produce many things to ship around to the less fortunate stations. There are 2,000 banana trees and 300 pineapple plants producing. Father Fluet is full to the brim with ideas; he promises to import a colony of bees on the next visit of the SS *Malaita*. He has accomplished a great deal. His garden is producing sweet potatoes, tapioca, taro, corn, and peanuts. The tapioca or "manioc" is a bushy shrub with thick roots. These roots can be skinned and boiled and used as a potato, or the starch may be extracted from them to make the tapioca that we know.

A few Sundays ago, we had a little excitement. Reports came through the natives that two Japanese warships were coming down the coast. The Chinese were panic stricken. They all piled into canoes with their bags, suitcases, trunks, and children, and came to the mission. Our house is roomy, so there was plenty of space for the children to play. We gave them all the peanuts they could eat, and the place was a sight—peanut shells everywhere. We let them do as they pleased as long as they were happy. All were under eight years of age and full of mischief. The grown-ups sat uneasily around the doorway looking uneasily out to sea for an approaching ship. The native carriers sat on the grass in front of the house guarding the baggage of the refugees.

Brother Paul made a pretense of scanning the horizon with an old broken pair of field-glasses, while Father Fluet mingled with the agitated group, encouraging them and trying to be very nonchalant about it all. We busied ourselves in the kitchen preparing dinner for the guests. We cooked kettles of sweet potatoes, a big roast of beef and a five-gallon kerosene tin full of corn. We had fresh corn from the garden, which was a big treat for them. After dinner we spread grass mats on the porch for the children, or for anyone who wanted to rest. We took a brief rest period to get in our prayers and meditation.

By 5:00 P.M., they concluded that the reports were false and prepared to go home. Picture our relief as they climbed into the canoes and started off. The generalissimo of this company was the wife of a plump, placid tailor. This small, enterprising woman constantly herded her family and her neighbors to the point of exasperation on the part of some. She managed the placing of the baggage in the canoes and was last seen giving directions to the fleet while she balanced a basket of eggs on the outrigger.

That same day Miko, our cook-boy, left for the northern part of the island to take care of some of his relatives. He was gone two weeks, leaving us in charge of a smoky old wood stove and all the dishes. This boy has been here about two years and is really very good. He is a native of New Guinea, and bright, but has somewhat erratic behavior. More than once we felt like wringing his neck, but the stack of dishes, pots and pans always restrained us. After two weeks of penal servitude in the kitchen, we had just about given up hope of seeing Miko again, when lo and behold, who should appear in the doorway but Miko, with a smile from ear to ear. We wiped our perspiring brows, and tried not to look too overjoyed, but oh, what a welcome sight he was.

A few days ago, we had news from Sister Isabelle and Sister Irene. Father Fluet made the long trip on foot, visiting some of his villages on the way. The two sisters are fine and sent word to us that Bishop Wade is bringing them back to Asitavi this week. We are anxiously awaiting their arrival.

May 26, 1942

*T*he possibility of our return to Hanahan is being seriously considered. Father Lamarre sent a note to the bishop telling him that the Japanese officials at Buka Passage have encouraged the return of the missionaries. The bishop asks us to join him in special prayers to make a wise decision.

May 28, 1942

*R*eports from Father McConville and consultation with several priests resulted in the bishop's decision to have the sisters remain on Bougainville. With this change of plans, Sister Isabelle and Sister Irene are not likely to come back to Asitavi.

June 1, 1942

*W*e must tell you about an experience we had this morning. When we get up at 5:00 A.M., it is pitch dark as we are on daylight saving time. While we were kneeling in the church for morning prayers, Sister Celestine made a move to put her meditation book on the shelf of the *prie dieu*, but for some reason it wouldn't fit in its accustomed place. She groped around and put her hand on a big snake that was curled up beside our missals. She screamed and said, "A snake!" Sister Hedda got up on the bench and Sister Celestine stepped out in the aisle. Brother Paul got a broom from the sacristy and came down to kill it. Solomonese snakes climb anywhere and are frequently seen lying on a beam under the eaves. They move slowly and are fat, ugly things.

We were returning by canoe from a sick call at a village further up the coast. Since there was a good breeze the boys decided to hoist the sail and save paddling. We were nervous, for even these outriggers are easily over-balanced. In spite of that, we curled up to make the most of it, for it was a new experience. Scarcely had we settled down when a plane suddenly buzzed over our heads. The natives could see our uneasiness and lowered the sail to cover us. We huddled together and waited for the machine guns to finish us off. Nothing happened, and later we learned it was an American plane. If we had known that, most likely we would have stood up to wave at them. Hope they hurry up and send these Japanese northward.

In this section, there is an abundance of fish. The reefs surround a point near the mission where there is good fishing. Once a week a boy goes out to watch for a school of fish, and when he finds one, tosses a cap of dynamite into their midst. The fish are stunned for a short while and float on the surface where the boys hurry to gather them up. This is a special treat for the schoolboys since they are exceptionally fond of fish and even cook the heads and fins. Occasionally, we rescue a couple of heads for the cats. We have ten cats. Don't be too horrified, for they are a part of the mission's assets. They are traded for taro or native labor. A cat or a dog is worth something in this country. Some of the villages are alive with rats; in fact, they are everywhere in the bush, so a cat is a highly respected animal. Our cats live in a little storeroom near the kitchen wall so they can go in or out. At present, we have six playful little kittens, and when we mix anything at the worktable, the kittens play with our shoelaces. In the evening during recreation, they climb up on our chairs and walk around the community table, sometimes sleeping in the sewing basket.

Two days ago, Father Lebel made a short visit. We surely were glad to see him. This time he had to travel on foot, as his launch was taken by the Japanese. He had a very interesting account to give us about his visit on board a Japanese warship. Leave it to Father Lebel to get out of a tight corner. Any man who can talk the *Burns, Philips Steamship Company* into checking six tons of the Sisters of Saint Joseph's freight on their tickets can get away with anything. He has an engaging personality. The Japanese landed and ordered him to go on board the warship for questioning. He put on his cassock and mission crucifix and walked ahead of fixed bayonets. The interview probably allowed him to exercise his powers of persuasion for he was permitted to return to the mission. As the motor launch pulled out, a Japanese lieutenant gave him his best salute and a big smile. That was a close call for an American. The second visit from the Japanese was a bit different, and they took his radio and his launch.

June 27, 1942

*I*t is a long time since we have added a note to the diary. The month of June is almost finished. We have celebrated all the big feast days, including a Corpus Christi procession. We even had a flower boy scatter petals before the Blessed Sacrament. This event was unusual for the natives, but they joined whole-heartedly. We sisters and Brother Paul made up the choir, and the schoolboys tried their best to follow. We had two beautiful altars that we fixed up with some broken candelabra. We put them in tea tins and filled them with rocks and water and lovely ferns. The effect was beautiful past our anticipation. The Mass for the feast of the Sacred Heart was celebrated by Bishop Wade. He arrived the day before, and when his boat appeared on the horizon, we were all a-flutter. We had hoped the rest of our community was coming to join us. They stayed in Kieta instead. They are both well and happy and have visited Tunuru. The Japanese are still at Sohano, the government station; reports reached us that a new group is in charge, and they are not too friendly.

During the bishop's stay in Asitavi we had two visits and a conference. Needless to say, we enjoyed them. He is a very holy bishop, and every word he speaks is food for one's soul. During this very trying time, he is just as cheerful and encouraging as formerly. Many of his regular duties have been interrupted, so he is spending more time going out among the natives. In spite of adverse conditions, it appears that this will be a profitable year for souls. Many natives are seeking baptism on their deathbeds. Sickness and deaths have increased since medical work has been discontinued. Many who would have otherwise have been saved by N.A.B. are dying from large ulcers.

After the bishop's visit, the brothers assembled in Kieta and made their retreat. Brother Paul left Asitavi with Brother Gregory from Tinputz and they were gone over two weeks. Upon their return, Brother Paul brought two large pumpkins and an assortment of spices with him. These items were placed on the kitchen table with the request, "A pumpkin pie, please." The pie was made, and everyone enjoyed it, even an Australian who had dinner with them.

About this time, Father Fluet made a trip into the bush and was gone two weeks. We packed food for him and the cook-boy went along. They climbed mountains, waded rivers and Father Fluet wore out his last good pair of shoes. He baptized a large number of natives and brought a number of boys back to enter the school. Accompanying the schoolboys were six or seven natives carrying little pigs. We couldn't figure it out until a note came from Father Fluet saying the pigs had been stolen from a neighboring plantation, and the culprits were making restitution. How is that for mission work? The squealing little porkers were put into a canoe and taken to the rightful owners at Numa Numa.

Father Weber came from Tunuru to replace our pastor. He is a native of Cologne and has been in the islands about seven years. We are told he has done wonders at his station at Tunuru. He is extremely active and can do anything from building a house to repairing a watch. He takes a hand at cooking, making jams, producing vinegar from his pineapples, and raising chickens, ducks and cattle. He has a voice that sings a High Mass like a whole choir of angels. He sailed for his station in his little launch, which is only as big as half a barrel. It is named *Me Too*, because there is always a crowd on the beach when he starts out on a trip, and they always want to go somewhere, so *Me Too* was chosen as a fitting name for the boat.

July 3, 1942

*W*e had all settled down to routine when word came from the bishop that the priests were to make their retreat at Kieta. Father Lebel and Father Fluet made their plans and set out in the *Rosa*, a small and very slow launch. They took chickens, eggs and fruit as their contribution of food for the retreat. We also packed them a lunch. The day before, we had received a small tin of chocolates from the Chinese. We put it in the lunch. Father Fluet told us that he almost toppled into the ocean rather than let go of the chocolates. He had a sandwich in one hand and a chocolate in the other, when a swell came along and tipped the boat over to one side. Father Lebel accused Father Fluet of eating all but four of those chocolates, and said he had to wait until he had fallen asleep to take the tin out of his hand. They pulled into Tunuru Bay at 2:30 A.M. It was pitch dark, and they did not see four Japanese warships anchored at a stone's throw from them. Father Fluet went ashore while his companion curled up to get some sleep. He did not sleep long, for the bishop sent for him, and told both priests to hurry and say their Masses and start for home. They had a brief visit with the bishop and left to make their way by trail to Monetai. It was a strenuous hike across rivers without a bit of sleep. Sister Isabelle and Sister Irene are back at Monetai. They got out of Kieta just in the nick of time. Sister Isabelle wrote to us and her letter gives you a good account of the priests' unexpected visit. It follows:

Dear Sisters Celestine and Hedda,

Sister Irene and I were happy to receive news from you through Father Weber. He has been very good to us and, of course, the bishop is like a real father, always solicitous of our comfort and spiritual welfare. Pray very hard for him, as he is now in Kieta. Father Fluet will give you the latest news about him. Things do not look so bright at present, and I do not know when we will see one another again. Doesn't it seem a long time since we separated? Let us hope and pray that everything will turn out for the best. Remember all our dear ones at home, for they must surely worry about us.

I am glad you are both keeping well, even though the work seems a little harder. When there are only two on the mission, there are more things to look after. We manage to keep busy, but, thank God, we are both well. I was not so well for a while, and in Kieta I broke out with sores on my arms and I also had malaria. I think now, after taking a "shoot" and other medicines, I'll be better.

Yesterday Sister Irene was on a sick call when, who should appear on the scene, but Father Lebel and Father Fluet. It was 3:00 P.M. in the afternoon; they had walked from Tunuru and were exhausted. I was alone, so hurried to give them some make-believe ice water. I had hardly anything in the house, not even eggs, at the time. They said, "Don't worry. Eggs are on the way, and you'll have all you want." I got busy and fried three apiece. They certainly were tired and hungry, so they did justice to the scanty meal. Then we had an omelet for supper. Today, we are serving them a good chicken dinner. Everything that comes from Asitavi is welcome around here, because as you know, there is hardly any fruit. The trees are too young to bear, but we get along and God is good to us. We can't be too grateful these days.

While I'm hurrying to get this note off, Sister Irene is starting to get dinner. We have two little schoolboys to help us, so they take care of many little things and keep the fires going.

Sister Celestine, I am sending you a few aspirin tablets that we found in Kieta—hope they will help you. And Sister Hedda, we found a few spices that we divided up, so you might find them useful. We are always happy to get news from you whenever possible, but from now on it might not be so easy, as the Japanese are occupying Kieta. We were told that they have bloodhounds with them.

Please keep well and happy and offer your work and prayers for our dear bishop and for the missions. Love and prayers from both Sister Irene and Sister Isabelle.

July 7, 1942

*T*he two priests arrived safely in Asitavi traveling on foot and by canoe. They reached the mission about 3:00 A.M., and Father Lebel went right to the chapel to say Mass. They were both heavy hearted, for a runner had reached them at Monetai to tell them that the bishop was being taken to Kieta by the Japanese. It seems that on July fourth our sisters received a letter from the bishop, an extract from which follows:

"The Fourth without speeches, firecrackers and ice cream! Anyway, these days speech is human and silence is divine. You know only too well that there is nothing of the latter about the editor, so kindly bear with him if the Fourth call out old memories, and allow him the privilege to burst forth:

America, my country, I come to thy call.
I plight thee my troth, and I give thee my all
In peace or in war, I am wed to thy weal.
I'll carry the flag through fire and steel.
Unsullied it floats o'er our peace-loving race
On sea, nor on land, shall it suffer disgrace.
In reverence I kneel at Liberty's shrine
America, my country, command, I am thine.

Doesn't this recall memories? So, the best of everything tomorrow and a special intention that America may come out of this war nearer and dearer to God, whatever the cost."

The Japanese sent a message to the bishop saying he would be considered an enemy of the Japanese empire if he did not report at Kieta at a certain time. Thinking to conciliate them for the safety of his missionaries, he replied promptly that he would report. They did not wait for him. We do not know what the future holds for any of us, but we know Divine Providence is watching over all. Our prayers are going heavenward every hour for our beloved bishop.

Now the diary must go back under Saint Joseph's altar in hiding, as we never know what minute visitors may arrive to search the premises.

On August 7, 1942, American Marines land on Guadalcanal in the South Solomon Islands. On August 15, 1942, three Australian Marist brothers are taken prisoner by the Japanese from Bougainville. They are never heard from again.

August 18, 1942

*W*ell, the world looks brighter. Our bishop is free once more, and we are all rejoicing. On the second of August the Japanese decided to leave Kieta. They were short of food supplies and looked very "down-at-the-heels." For some time, groups had been going out to the native villages to collect food without much success. However, there might have been other reasons for leaving, as trouble was brewing in the South Solomons at Tulagai. On August sixth, we were alarmed to see squadrons of planes flying high overhead. They were so high we did not know to which country they belonged. It was a beautiful sight to see so many planes flying in formation. The next day they weren't quite so beautiful, for we learned that they were Japanese planes going to Tulagai. Since then a real land, air and sea battle has been fought. We see planes passing every day and are always hoping that they may be American or Australian. We'll be so happy to have some feeling of security from foreign invaders. The wish was so strong that we fancied that one group of 29 planes was "Flying Fortresses," and everyone on the compound waved delightedly. Father's handkerchief was not big enough, so he waved his coat.

The work of the mission goes on peacefully. More of

the natives are coming to Mass on Sunday, and also for medicine and "shoots." Last Sunday, August 16th, the day after the feast of the Assumption, Father Fluet went to say Mass in the villages down the coast. In one place there are a number of lepers who left the leper colony near Kieta when the war broke out. Most of them returned to their own villages. This particular group seems to be alone, and one leper who is not as advanced as the others, hobbles around to take care of his companions. Father Fluet would like to have them nearer the mission some place on the sandy beach, where he could supply them with food and medicine. We are hoping it can be arranged, as that is a real charity to these poor outcasts.

On August 26, 1942—Four Marist priests, Fathers Servant, Montauban, Caffiaux and Lamarre, and Marist brother Joseph are interrogated at Sohano. On August 27, 1942, three of the Marist priests, all French, are returned to their mission stations. Father Lamarre and Brother Joseph, who are Americans, are kept imprisoned at Sohano and later sent to the larger prison camp on Rabaul.

September 6, 1942

*T*oday, we learned through the natives that Bishop Wade is on his way to Asitavi. Some natives brought him from Monetai by canoe on August 21st we were at Numa Numa when the good news reached us. As soon as the Japanese evacuated Kieta, he left for the bush, traveling on foot to Monetai. He reached there suffering from an aching molar. He knew there was a set of dental instruments at the station and intended to extract the tooth himself. Sister Irene, though inexperienced in any phase of dentistry, offered to do it for him, for she knew that molars don't come out on mere invitation. Sister Isabelle acted as dental assistant, putting a deck chair on the veranda and providing a clean spoon for a tongue blade. Curious natives were gathering around, and the gentle bishop courteously offered his chair to anyone who wanted it. Father Mueller stood by to offer assistance. The "dentist" had sterilized the instruments and proceeded to inject the local anesthetic. It may be explained that there was an old French medical book at the station that the two sisters read the previous evening, with Sister Isabelle translating. The dentist recollected herself, applied the forceps and gently loosened the tooth. With a dexterous twist, she succeeded in bringing out a three-root molar on the first attempt. Although the patient perspired, he didn't even wince. The natives gazed in tense silence, then clapped and laughed as the tooth was triumphantly held aloft in the forceps. The happy patient arose and shook hands all around. During the week, 10 or 12 natives came for extractions while Sister Isabelle became more and more proficient.

The bishop stayed in Asitavi a week administering Confirmation to a large number of people. He was more like himself and seemed greatly relieved to be a free man again. To the credit of the Japanese official in Kieta, be it said that he was a gentleman. He spoke English fairly well, and though he was not a Catholic, he did all he could in the way of little courtesies.

The problem of securing wine and flour for sacramental purposes is becoming acute. Sand shoes for the staff would be most acceptable. Quinine, too, is an important item for us. We have a good supply in Hanahan, and the bishop is going to try to get more from the priests on Buka. He is leaving for Tinputz to see what can be done.

Meanwhile, planes are flying overhead daily, with both countries represented. Occasionally, a scout plane will fly low over the mission, making all of us scamper for safety. Last Sunday, while we were giving "shoots," a plane, probably noticing the gathering of natives, skimmed as low as it could safely fly and miss the trees. Japanese motors have an irregular sound, and we are learning to recognize them.

Word reached the mission that the three Australian Marist Brothers from Chabai at Father Hennessey's catechist school were taken prisoners by the Japanese. We are all stunned. It is thought they were taken as part of a prisoner exchange. They are such fine men and splendid teachers. We have redoubled our prayers for those who remain, particularly for the Americans, because the Japanese may be vindictive since the Battle of Tulagai.

September 8, 1942 Nativity of the Blessed Mother

Sorrow visited all of the missionaries today. We learned that Father Lamarre has been taken by the Japanese. The shock is almost paralyzing. The message came from the bishop at Tinputz. The four priests from Buka Island were all called to meet the Japanese officials at Buka Passage. Father Lamarre was the only American and that was against him. What a tragedy for a priest to be deprived of saying Mass and praying his breviary. He is a zealous and holy Marist who will glorify God every step of his Way of the Cross.

September 9, 1942

This afternoon Father Lebel arrived on foot from Tinputz. The Japanese are fortifying Buka and the northern part of Bougainville. The bishop thought it best for him to leave, as he, too, may be taken. He will be staying in Asitavi for a while and will give us our annual retreat. Next week, Fathers Dionne and Herbert will join their confreres here to make their retreat.

September 12, 1942 Feast of the Holy Name of Mary

How fortunate we are to have two Masses each morning. Today is the Marists' most important feast. We had our first Mass at 5:30 A.M. and a High Mass at 7:30 A.M. The three altars were decorated in blue and white, and we were very extravagant in lighting the tall candles. Our Blessed Mother received many petitions this morning from her sorrowing missionaries. Father Lebel gave a very fine sermon in pidgin asking the natives' prayers for the protection of the missions, particularly Buka.

September 19, 1942

*O*ur retreat is over, and we are ready to begin again with new courage. Father Lebel gave us a splendid series of conferences touching on all the essentials of the spiritual life. We need reminders periodically, especially under these trying conditions.

Shortly after sundown, Fathers Dionne and Hebert arrived. They were weary to the point of exhaustion, having traveled over very difficult country through torrential rains wearing ragged tennis shoes. The first thing offered to a weary traveler here is a good wash-wash followed by a substantial meal. The priests had a joyful reunion; the only one missing was Father Lamarre. It may be a long time before further word is received regarding him, as Buka is swarming with Japanese, and their fortifications are quite extensive.

During the week, it has rained continuously. All of us have to stay inside either at home or in the church. It is hard, as the new house is not yet finished, and the four priests and two brothers are packed in that small sac-sac house. Father Hebert has been ill part of the time, so we have tried to give him lighter food and an eggnog between meals. We have also given him two injections of N.A.B. to build him up. Father Dionne is very thin, and his clothes are just about gone. He is at a distant mission that is comparatively new, and the natives not far from him are cannibalistic. He lives alone, does his own cooking and washing, and darns his cassock beautifully with white thread. It is now months since boats have come from Australia, and supplies are exhausted. He lives on taro, and twice a week his catechist kills an opossum to supply him with meat. This is a smelly creature not unlike a skunk, and it is not a small achievement to overcome one's repugnance enough to eat it. Father Griswald, the elderly priest who gave us the lecture on the Solmonese Missions at Saint Joseph Hospital in 1940, is about eight hours walk from here. Occasionally, he is able to leave and spend a day with Father Dionne. He has a few chickens and pigs, and whenever it is possible, sends something over. Really, you haven't any idea what heroes these missionary priests are. What they go through for the glory of God surely merits the same reward as of martyrdom. Saint Therese, the Little Flower, says of missionaries that they are martyrs by will and desire. We have it easy compared with those priests who have to sleep in rat-infested native huts and subsist on taro when they are visiting their flocks in the villages. Half of the time their rain-drenched clothing has not dried during the night. We look at them in awe and marvel at the graces God bestows on those he loves. They are young and from our own country where every convenience and even the luxuries of life are accepted as a matter of course, yet they have given these up for this most trying mission life. What a glorious crown awaits them in heaven.

September 26, 1942

Retreat is over. Saturday morning the bell rang at 7:30 A.M. for Benediction. The priests were kneeling at their *prie dieus* in the sanctuary. Each one stood and gave a very brief sermon. Father Fluet, the superior, gave the most beautiful address we have ever listened to in the islands. In his shy and somewhat hesitant manner, he recalled the graces bestowed upon those present, and how, 12 years before, they had made their first vows together in the novitiate. He paid an affectionate tribute to one of their confreres who had died shortly after ordination. Of the absent missionary, Father Lamarre, he spoke very briefly as he knew that everyone present was feeling his loss keenly. Father Hebert followed with an address to our Blessed Mother. His plea to her made big catches in our throats. He appealed for all of our needs and those of the missionaries who had been taken away. Father Dionne restored our feelings to normal by telling Saint Joseph just what we missionaries expect of him. Really, Saint Joseph must have smiled as he listened. Furthermore, we are sure he will grant what is asked by one so deserving. Anyone who can live for three long years all alone among people who threaten to kill him deserves a whole lot. Finally, each priest knelt in turn before the Blessed Sacrament holding a lightened candle to silently renew his vows. It was most impressive, and we two sisters felt like tiptoeing out, lest out presence disturb the sacredness of their hour.

September 27, 1942

*F*ather Lebel started for Monetai to give a retreat to our sisters there. We sent chickens and other good supplies.

October 3, 1942

*F*ather Lebel returned with letters from our sisters. Sister Irene is running short of medicines and tells us she will soon have to dress sores with sunshine and a leaf. Some tree cotton grows here she says, *"and it is very useful, but we use larger quantities than the trees can produce. We are running short of everything in the line of food, but we are finding many substitutes that keep hunger away. At Asitavi we grow corn that we grind and make into bread. We also squeeze the juice from ripe papayas and boil it down for sugar. It makes a sweet syrup and does not cost us anything. There are hundreds of trees growing all over the property. The natives demand such a high price for sugar cane that we can't buy it. Taro is substantial and takes the place of bread. We fry it, boil it and scramble it, but still it is taro. The heavy rains threaten our gardens, and it will be a hardship if the taro beds are damaged. Water stands in pools in all the level places, and Father has had the schoolboys dig trenches to drain it off into the ocean."*

CHAPTER 9

The Sky Above is Swarming with Planes

October 4, 1942 Feast of Saint Francis of Assisi.

The sky above is swarming with planes. About noon today, six Flying Fortresses were attacked by Japanese zeroes and fought over our mission. We all ran out into the open to watch. The zeroes darted in and out, taking machine-gun damage from the dignified Fortresses. Apparently one of the zeroes was injured, for it limped off westward. The Fortresses serenely went on their way. We hardly know what to expect next. Your prayers and sacrifices for us mean so much; we can almost feel your united desire to aid us during this trying time.

October 7, 1942 Feast of The Holy Rosary.

Today four lepers came to the mission to ask Father Fluet for shelter, as they were short of food and hadn't anyone to turn to for assistance. He arranged for some land on the mission property about two miles from here. It is close to the seashore, and Father had them clear a space to build a house and a small chapel.

October 8, 1942

*F*ather Fluet had all the schoolboys carry taro stalks and tapioca cuttings to plant in the cleared space. The four lepers were working hard to prepare the ground for the garden. It takes about six months before the taro is ready, so they planted corn, which will mature quickly. For a few days, they will live together under a little leaf structure supported by four poles. The schoolboys are going to build their house. We visited them and brought them a few medical supplies. They have a few open lesions but manage to get around quite well. Before the war, they were at Pok Pok Island near Kieta. Since then they have returned to their villages, but it seems that they are not readily accepted by their families due to fear of the disease. Later, the house and the church were completed. Father Fluet has been warned that more lepers are going to come to join this little colony. Until their gardens begin producing, Father is supplying them with food.

October 23, 1942

*F*ather Lebel returned to Tinputz, and the bishop came back to Asitavi. We were happy to see him. What a blessing that he has been spared to console and encourage all of us. The night before his arrival, Father O'Sullivan came from the Buin section with news for him. It seems the Japanese visited Turiburi and took Father Poncelet, Father Shank, Brother Bruno and seven Marist Sisters as prisoners. The shock was just about all the bishop could stand. He wasn't himself for days. There were Masses offered with special intentions for their safety. A few days later, word came that all the priests on Buka were taken, and that Father Lamarre was last seen on a boat. We were just sick, as we were sure they would take his life owing to the circumstances and his nationality. An American plane had dropped a bomb killing a high-ranking Japanese official instantly with the result that the missionaries were suspected of transmitting messages. Our hearts were heavy with such a turn of events. News came over the radio that a bishop and seven priests had been massacred; two

Marist priests and two Marist sisters had met a similar fate in the South Solomons. This made us realize the attitude of Japan toward the Church and the missionaries. Neither the Church nor its missionaries would be respected. In the Buin section, the churches and convents were ransacked, and all vestments, linens and sacred vessels were stolen or destroyed. What they could not use they gave to the natives. All of the missions were pillaged. The metal roofing and the water tanks have been taken away for war material. We do not know anything about Buka except that it is full of Japanese. We believe everything is gone, including all of those useful things you sent us as well as all of our clothing. However, we have lived very comfortably out of our suitcases and haven't actually needed anything. We feel very grateful for the kindness and hospitality of Father Fluet. He is so solicitous for our spiritual as well as our temporal welfare.

As soon as the bishop had an opportunity to discuss the Buin situation with the priests, arrangements were made to rescue the Marist sisters who were at Sovele. Father Fluet volunteered to make the long and dangerous trip, and the bishop gave him full authority to act in his name. On October 18th, Father Fluet and Father O'Sullivan left for the Buin district. That is the center of Japanese activity; they have airdromes, anti-aircraft guns and thousands of soldiers there. The priests entered this territory very cautiously, and with the aid of trusty natives, sent word to the priests in charge to have four Marist sisters ready for an immediate escape. *En route,* Father Fluet found Father Miltrop sick with black water fever, a complication of malaria, probably brought on by the strain and excitement. He put him to bed and treated him. Father O'Sullivan took charge of bringing the sisters away from Sovele, and Father Fluet hurried back to Asitavi by way of Monetai. At Monetai, he told Sister Isabelle and Sister Irene to leave for Asitavi at once by canoe at night. They started at dark in an outrigger canoe, traveling nine hours sitting balanced precariously back to back on a board. They arrived about 3:30 A.M. As they came up the walk, they called out to us so we would not be too frightened by a knock on the door.

It was a happy moment, as we had been separated for seven months. We sat and talked until time for Mass at 6:00 A.M. We were all together when Father Fluet came to tell us that the four Marist sisters were on their way to Asitavi. We had a few days to prepare for them. We needed extra beds, chairs, tables and washstands. Brother Paul made washstands out of packing boxes by adding legs to them. The bishop visited Numa Numa and borrowed as many dishes and chairs as they could spare. All was ready when the four weary sisters arrived at 5:00 A.M. on November 30th. There were two canoes under the direction of Father O'Sullivan. Now our mission consists of eight sisters, two priests, one bishop, and two brothers. The little old smoky kitchen stove is doing double duty. Sister Irene is taking her turn in the kitchen and serves some very appetizing meals made from combined garden products. Thanks be to God for all the fruits and vegetables we have here. We use corn meal mixed with ripe papayas and baked as a substitute for bread, as we have been without flour and sugar for some time. The bishop contributed a recipe for dessert made with grated coconut, bananas, papayas, and eggs, baked as a custard. Everyone offers suggestions to give variety to our daily menu. We all accept our little privations and make a joke of them. The priests tell us that it takes a lot of faith to believe it is soup they are eating. We are well and in good spirits but heavy-hearted over our captive missionaries.

The Marist sisters are happy to be at the end of their journey. It was a hard trip over mountains and rivers, and through rain and mud, but they finally got here. They were a week on the way, covering over 50 miles, traveling by day, sleeping in native villages, and eating whatever they could buy from the natives. Today, they are washing and getting their clothes in order. They left everything behind, except what each could carry in a suitcase.

Bishop Wade is much relieved to have these missionaries safely gathered here, but he is worrying a great deal over those who have been taken. At times his face is drawn and haggard, and he is becoming very thin. We know he is suffering intensely

November 15, 1942

*T*oday, we all assembled for the ceremony of the blessing of the new recreation center down by the beach. The bishop, always thoughtful, had this little house built so we could go there for quiet hours of spiritual reading or sewing. It is so lovely and cool, and the view over the ocean is restful. Huge breakers dash upon the coral, and the deep blue of the water is a real South Sea picture. Tea was served by the cook-boys, and as usual, the bishop had a store of good jokes. We enjoyed one on Father Fluet. Father has 20 guinea hens that he prizes highly. The bishop has been coaxing him to kill a few of his treasures instead of leaving them for the Japanese. He has appealed to him as Bishop of the North Solomon Islands. Father Fluet didn't weaken. He then appealed as Titular Bishop of Barbalissos. No result. Finally, he appealed as a delegate of the Marists. Love for his Community prevailed. Father Fluet immediately agreed to a banquet of guinea hens as soon as the flock increased to 70.

November 26, 1942

*T*his is Thanksgiving Day. We are celebrating in grand style. There were 16 for dinner including our two neighbors, Mr. Long and Mr. Babbage. We decorated the tables with flowers and had roast duck and pumpkin pie. We did not have sugar to sweeten the pie, so we used syrup boiled down from papaya juice. We also had nice fresh pineapple salad. Everyone seemed to enjoy the dinner, and before the two guests departed, the bishop and Father Fluet brought them over to meet us. One neighbor lives on a plantation about three miles from us and keeps us supplied with fresh meat. They have all been very kind to us and are always ready to do us favors. In the evening we had holy hour from 7:00 P.M. until 8:00 P.M. We usually have it on Thursdays.

November 29, 1942

*L*ast night a very special privilege was given to us, an all-night vigil before the Blessed Sacrament enthroned on the altar. The news is so distressing, and the poor bishop does not know which way to turn. It is reported that the Japanese intend to pick up all the missionaries and intern them. It appalls the bishop to think of us falling into the hands of the Japanese. He asks for special prayers to the Holy Ghost to guide him. The sisters at Tarlena were evacuated secretly and are in hiding in the bush. This may irritate the Japanese at Buka Passage and cause them to take revenge upon the four priests interned at Sohano. We learned through natives that they are alive and well, and have sent out for hosts and wine so they could say Mass. During air raids, they take shelter in a rocky cave. We took turns staying an hour at a time. It was all too short. The bishop came at 3:00 A.M., and then at 5:00 A.M., he gave us Benediction followed by his Mass. Surely our Lord will solve some of these problems.

This afternoon, Father O'Sullivan left for Tinputz to obtain definite information about the Tarlena evacuees. The canoe bringing us news of them was capsized by heavy seas, and although the boys narrowly escaped with their lives, they lost their letters.

December 5, 1942

*T*oday, Father O'Sullivan returned to tell us that the Tarlena sisters are safely hidden in a native village, Tsipatavi, high in the mountains above Tinputz. Tarlena is only 12 miles from the passage, and the mission had been overrun by Japanese soldiers for the past six months. Extreme caution was necessary even to get a message to the sisters, though the natives go in and out freely. Father Lebel, accompanied by ten carriers and provided with a tin of black paint and a lava-lava for his own disguise, made his way from Tinputz to the vicinity and awaited darkness. Through an arrangement of providence, the regular Japanese guard which patrolled the mission were on the ships a quarter of a mile off shore. Father Lebel slipped into the house where the sisters were at supper and issued a brief command, substantially this, *"Be ready to leave in one hour taking only what you can carry. I'll be back."* Father McConville and Father Morrell received the same orders. An hour later, the little caravan was on the trail. Two of the sisters were on stretchers; Sister Claire, an aged sister who had been on the islands 42 years, and Sister Reme, who has a dislocated knee. Each of these sisters were carried by four natives. A native family, including Bobby the carpenter, with his wife and five children and three faithful native girls taking turns carrying an orphaned native baby, followed. Each of the evacuees labored along in the thick darkness under the weight of baggage. Sister Henrietta staggered under the burden of "pay" tobacco, for these carriers expected payment. One of her shoes came off in a boggy stream and could not be recovered. Father Morrell's frail limbs failed him, and he fell into a ravine of running water. At dawn, they met a party of Australian soldiers— Divine Providence again. Sister Henrietta's bare foot was bleeding. The soldiers took in the exhausted refugees, giving them food and care. During the night, these soldiers had received their cargo of supplies from a plane and were on their way back to their mountain hideout. The 13 evacuees enjoyed an American breakfast, for there were American packed field rations in tins flown from Townsville, Australia. Refreshed, they journeyed on to their destination at Tsipatavi.

At 3:00 P.M., Bishop Wade came to see us and tell us his plans. Arrangements are being made to get the sisters out of the war zone, and the Australian district officer, Lieutenant Reed of the Royal Australian Navy, is negotiating with the Australian Government to get us out by plane. We are to go to one center so we may be ready at an hour's notice. We are asked to pack and be ready to leave by 7:00 P.M.

December 6, 1942

*W*hile we hurried to get our things into our suitcases, the cook-boy prepared supper. The bishop came to the church to hear confessions and to give last-minute instructions. We were all nervous and excited, and some of the sisters were shedding tears. After supper, the bishop came over for a short informal visit; we all went to the church for Benediction and the bishop's farewell. It was a sad moment. Our hearts were heavy as we went up to the altar rail. He gave each one his blessing, calling us by name, "Good bye, Sister Isabelle." We hurried down to the boat, accompanied by Father O'Sullivan and Brother Paul. It so happened that Father Fluet was away. The schoolboys gathered tearfully around as we got into the little motor launch loaned to the bishop by the Chinese colony. The sea was calm, and we were all well protected by darkness. It was 9:00 P.M. when we left, and Father O'Sullivan accompanied us. We arrived here at 2:30 A.M., crumpled and very tired. Father O'Sullivan prepared at once for Mass. Afterward, the three sisters here prepared coffee for us and we each had a slice of real bread and a little sugar. It was most refreshing and restored our wilted spirits. After that, we sat on deck chairs and dozed until the 6:00 A.M. Mass. In a few minutes we start for the bush. Destination: Tsipatavi.

December 7, 1942

*W*e were tired to begin with, so we found the trip quite strenuous. Fortunately, it was a gradual incline without steep hills. We wore all sorts of old shoes. Sister Isabelle wore some funny looking sandals that the bishop had obtained from the Chinese store in Kieta. When she wore them in Asitavi, Father Fluet said she looked like a "discalced" Carmelite. It is a good thing we had old shoes, as the road was slippery and wet from decayed leaves; however, the sun was out in full force, so we used banana leaves to shade our eyes from its brightness. We crossed through swampy sections where the muddy water was well over our ankles, and again over mountain streams that were even deeper. We must have crossed the same winding river eight or ten times. We waded through the shallow places, and the natives helped us through the deeper parts. The rivers are full of stones of all sizes that are covered with moss, making them dangerous, as our tennis shoes do not easily grip the wet surface. We crossed slowly, so the force of the water would not cause us to lose our balance. It was a sight to watch eight white figures with our skirts pinned up, moving slowly toward the opposite bank. After much puffing and renewed efforts, we reached the end of the eight-mile trip at mid-day. Sister Henrietta came down the road to meet us and began telling us of their experiences with the Japanese and their relief at a place of safety. A substantial dinner awaited us and were we hungry! Taro never tasted so good. Right after lunch we went to bed, as we were exhausted. A good sleep of two hours made us feel like new.

We four Sisters of Saint Joseph are quartered in a little bamboo house on stilts. The seven Marist sisters occupy the large house about five minutes' walk from here. We are right next door to the little sac-sac church, and the Blessed Sacrament is there. We are right in the center of a native village, one of Father Lebel's substations. The people look at us curiously and wonder what it is all about. The village is surrounded by dense forest. A little river rushes down a ravine close to our house, and here we wash our clothing while kneeling on the rocks. It works well, but you have to grip your precious piece of soap so it won't go sailing down the stream. It's lots of fun, and we wouldn't miss it for a billion dollars. We must tell you that we have adopted the bush headdress, which is a veil made of navy blue dotted print. It saves washing and ironing, and we are dressed like the Marist sisters, who were unable to bring their starched bonnets. We miss our own white things, but accept the change with all the other little sacrifices.

December 9, 1942

*W*hile this is being written, Sister Isabelle is making her spiritual reading, Sister Irene is mending socks, and Sister Celestine is typing a new ordo for Father Lebel. He has a mimeograph and is preparing copies for all of the missions.

They had a press in Tarlena where Father Morrell usually did this.

We had been told in Asitavi about the pigs at this substation. They come squealing along at 4:45 A.M., so we do not need an alarm. There are many pigs in this village—little pigs, big pigs, fat pigs, and skinny pigs. They have long noses and look like those pictures that fascinated us in our first geography books. The most amusing thing about them is the way they lie down anywhere, so the children can scratch their backs. The village pups take advantage of the nursing time to join the little pigs.

December 13, 1942

*W*e have been up in our mountain home a whole week and feel very safe and happy here. There are 11 sisters and two priests. Father Lebel lives between the two places and oversees the food supply that comes daily from Tinputz. He is such a busy man, always fixing something to make it more comfortable for us sisters. On Saturday, he made a new screen door for our house, a table for washing dishes at the Marist's house, and a new *prie dieu* for all of us at the church. He works like a whirlwind and gets results immediately. There is no waiting for things to happen; he makes them happen. A few days ago, the Australian soldiers sent us a part of their food supply—a little flour, sugar and two tins of butter. It was such a treat. We make bread from half tapioca and half white flour. It is rather dark and heavy, but it is bread and we are thankful to have it. Our principle foods are taro and meat. A plantation close to Tinputz furnishes us with meat once a week. Three of the Marist sisters stay in Tinputz and prepare things to send up to us. Father Morrell has been ill with malaria. Sister Irene has been taking care of him as he had gastric fever. He is still unable to say Mass.

December 27, 1942

*S*o much has happened since we last put a note in the diary. On December 23rd, three Japanese ships paid a visit to

Rawa, a plantation several hours from here. They raided the place and burned all the buildings. Mr. and Mrs. Campbell, the owners, barely escaped with their lives. The soldiers landed very quickly, led by a former native employee. Mr. and Mrs. Campbell made their way up here as quickly as possible. They had hidden trunks and boxes in the bush in preparation for a quick get-away. These were brought by carriers. It is sad to see others homeless. Of course, as religious, we are not attached to our homes, and what is a trifling loss to us is a real tragedy to them. The following day, December 24th, we learned that Tinputz was being raided. The three sisters fled to the bush, and then joined us here. Father Lebel had boys on watch to warn us if the Japanese started up in this direction. We were all very uneasy, including Mr. and Mrs. Campbell. Finally, at 4:00 P.M. a runner came to tell us that the ships had gone. That gave us fresh courage, so we went ahead with the Christmas decorations in the church.

It didn't seem much like Christmas Eve to us. We unpacked the Mass kit and made things ready for the midnight Mass. Father Lebel received a note from Father Allotte who had returned to Tinputz after the Japanese left, asking him to come if possible. He left here at 10:00 P.M., and when he got as far as the sawmill he saw a large Japanese ship pulling into the wharf. He made a dash for the bush and got here just as Father McConville had finished the third Mass. We were all apprehensive when he came into the church, however, he made an announcement right away, asking the natives to help us pack so that we could leave at once. There were Mr. and Mrs. Campbell, Mrs. Huson, and 14 sisters.

We left about 1:30 A.M. on Christmas morning. Father Lebel issued short and snappy commands, and in less than 30 minutes, all were on the way. He warned, "Be prepared to be cold, wet and hungry. I want you to cooperate with everything I ask you to do. Move quickly and be ready for anything." We each carried a blanket with an extra pair of shoes, two tins of meat, and whatever necessaries we could stow into the pack. Each bundle was wrapped so it could be carried on one's back or shoulder. A change of clothing was put into a small suitcase for the natives to carry. We had gotten these ready during the day. Sister Henrietta had cooked some meat and a couple of loaves of bread that she packed in a basket. Father Lebel sent two small bags of rice and a tin of hard-tack biscuits with the carriers. We set out with a boy in the lead and Sister Henrietta following with a lantern and a box of eggs. Next came our gypsy caravan with skirts pinned up and packs balanced on our shoulders.

A short distance from the house was a very steep gorge that had to be taken very slowly. We crawled down in the semi-darkness clinging to bits of hanging roots or rock. The river rushed below, but the dear Lord, who always smooths out everything for us, gave us clear moonlight to help us across. The river was low, so we crossed easily, getting only our feet wet. The opposite bank was simply dreadful to climb. It was almost straight up with so very little to cling to for support. Two of the sisters had to be carried on stretchers, and it is a miracle that they were gotten up to the top by those natives. At night, things seem so much harder. The moonlight did not penetrate the heavy foliage, so the light was fitful and uncertain. Our guardian angels and prayers helped us safely up to the level trail. From then on, we made our way quickly to another village, arriving about 3:00 A.M. The natives were frightened, but Father Lebel told the catechist why we were there. We all went into the church for a short rest. Soon we were on our way, but some distance farther on we lost our trail and had to retrace our steps. By that time, we were getting pretty tired, and so were the carriers. Sister Elie passed around some biscuits as we walked along, and these gave us a little energy.

Soon the faint rays of dawn appeared, and we can assure you it was most welcome. We took brief rest periods but kept going until it was quite light. We had reached quite an elevation and could see the ocean through the treetops. Father Lebel was in the lead to give us encouragement and reassure us that we were on the right road. Finally, we came to another abysmal gorge. It all but left us speechless as we looked down and saw the native carriers winding their way down the mountainside. We must confess that we experienced a twinge of desolation—that feeling of being homeless refugees. Father Lebel had a way of appearing in our midst just when we needed a bit of encouragement; a few words, and we started down. These bush trails are always slippery from mud and decayed leaves. We simply crawled along close to the ground like snails. Fortunately, it was daylight so we reached the bottom in safety. A trickling mountain stream was crossed and then came the upward climb. It was much easier to climb up than to go down. We were all pretty tired, so Father Lebel and Father McConville set out to look for a suitable place to make camp. We all sat down on fallen logs and rested our sleepy heads on the knapsacks that we held on our knees. After a short wait, Father Lebel sent a boy to tell us to come. We did. The Campbells continued on toward the soldier's camp high up in the mountains.

The spot chosen for our camp looked anything but promising. Father Lebel was sitting on the ground with his shoes and stockings off trying to ease the pain in his bleeding feet. He was the picture of Job sitting on the dung hill. He had deep dark circles under his eyes, had not slept for 48 hours and had a three day's growth of beard. He looked dreadful. We feared he might develop a bad case of fever. We hustled and made him a hot drink. We were fortunate enough to have a small bottle of rum, and we added a good portion to his eggnog. Then we got some banana leaves, spread them out on the ground and wrapped him up in a blanket. Soon, he was off in dreamland. In the meantime, the bush was cleared and a space about 40 by 50 feet was made ready for the camp. You'll never know how useful those wild banana trees are when one is making a shelter. The natives are clever in utilizing the different parts to build the sections of a house. While they were at work, we ate a sandwich, and then found large taro leaves and lay down to sleep. We were so weary. Picture 14 sisters curled up here and there on giant leaves. Some of the leaves are six feet long and four feet wide. We had hung our provisions on vines away from the ants.

Occasionally someone would raise her head to see how the house was progressing.

About 3:00 P.M. on Christmas Day 1942, three Australian soldiers came off the trail to bring news to Father Lebel. We served them tea that was brewed gypsy-fashion in a pot suspended over a smoky fire. Enter Sister Henrietta's eggs. Sister Fabian scrambled them in a saucepan and served them on banana leaves with boiled rice, hard tack biscuits and a little meat. They told us that the ships were gone. By 4:00 P.M., the shelter was finished. It was supported by poles and covered with banana leaves, and the roof was slanting. A low platform was made to serve as a bed. It was about 30 feet long and six feet wide, allowing each sister about two feet of space. The banana stalks were used to form the bed "springs." We folded our blankets in half, using the other half to cover. One shelter has been built for the priests and one for the natives. There were 18 of us, including Mrs. Huson, and about 25 natives. We contacted a native from a nearby village and made arrangements to buy taro and coconuts for our carriers. This food arrived about 6:00 P.M. Before retiring for the night, we all sang carols, finishing the program with the *Magnificat* on the solemn tone. At daybreak we were up. While the coffee was boiling, each group knelt to say community prayers.

After breakfast, a runner arrived bringing a message from Lieutenant Reed. Father Lebel dispatched a reply requesting Lieutenant Reed to appeal to the Americans at Tulagai for help. He stated that 17 white women were in danger of capture by the Japanese or death from fever or starvation in the mountains. We packed and started back to Tsipatavi. It was a beautiful clear morning, and this time the road was dry. We broke all records coming back, reaching there at 10:15 A.M. The first thing we did was to bathe and put on clean clothes. Words cannot express what a grand feeling a good wash-wash really is. At the camp, we were a long way from the river, and the mountain was so steep we didn't dare venture down. The native girls brought water up in containers made from bamboo. The sections are sealed and the hollow tube is filled with water.

After lunch, Father Lebel went down to see his once flourishing mission. The Japanese had spent the day in Tinputz, building a fire in the church to cook their meals that consisted of the mission's chickens. The whole place was a mess. What was not stolen was destroyed. It is estimated that about 500 Japanese came ashore and put up a radio for the day to communicate with other occupied sections. They questioned the natives by asking, "Where stop missionaries?" They seem always to have gotten the same answer, "*Me no savvy.*" Father had boys on watch. Later, he slipped into the mission and collected things he had buried for safety. All the sisters stayed in Tsipatavi, anxiously awaiting word from Lieutenant Reed.

December 30, 1942

*F*ather McConville came over to our house in pouring rain to tell us the good news. We knew the United States would not leave 17 women and children stranded and at the mercy of the Japanese. They didn't. Lieutenant Reed's instructions were for us to be at Teop at dusk on Thursday, December 31st and to take as little baggage as possible. We hustled with the packing and last minute details.

December 31, 1942

*A*t 1:00 P.M., Father Lebel came to look over our preparations and to assign carriers to carry the two Marist sisters who were unable to walk. Along with the shortage of food, there was a shortage of footwear. Sister Irene was wearing a pair of Bishop Wade's tennis shoes, and Father Lebel gave his two last pairs of tennis shoes to Sister Henrietta and Sister Hedda. He was wearing a pair of heavy leather army shoes given to him by the Australian soldiers. The caravan started, single file, at 2:00 P.M. The trip down to the beach was quite difficult, as we had to cross rivers and climb mountains. To add to the strain, a heavy rain set in, and we were pretty well soaked by the time we reached the first stop at 5:00 P.M. Lieutenant Reed was on the porch of the Keop's hut with the earphones of his teleradio on, spelling out messages. He greeted us briefly, but gave us nothing definite. We sat down, drenched and nervous, and ate a couple of sandwiches and drank some coconut milk. He told us to proceed to Mr. Urban's plantation at Hakow. It was an hour's walk, and darkness was already coming on. We hurried through the winding path of his coffee fields, noticing in them a little similarity to our orange groves and snatching the fragrance from their star-like, wavy blossoms. We reached the house at 7:00 P.M. to be greeted by our good friend, Mr. Urban, who served us supper as we sat on his veranda. We waited anxiously for our next orders. Time drags so when important events are pending; the minutes seemed like hours. At 8:30 P.M., we heard rapid footsteps on the path, and Father McConville dashed up on the porch. He told us to gather up our bags quickly and start for the beach. Sister Isabelle's bag had been dropped in a river, and she was trying desperately to dry the contents around the kitchen stove; they went back damp into the bag, and in a few minutes we were off.

As we descended the steps in the dark, Father said, "A submarine is going to pick you up." Our hearts must have stopped beating for a moment. We hadn't anticipated this means of deliverance. Lieutenant Reed and two of the soldiers started out ahead with a lantern. Two other lanterns were distributed along our line that straggled single file at some length. We followed along through tall grass, little streams and boggy mud-holes, and balanced ourselves over log-bridges, occasionally skidding on the steep path. Sister Elie's voice came out of the dark, "Wait a minute, I've lost my glasses." A high-powered command came from the rear, "Move along faster; we have to be there by 10:00 P.M." Father Lebel was anxiously urging us on. We reached Mrs. Faulkner's house about 11:00 P.M. Our hostess, gowned in black lace, received us graciously and with the calmness characteristic of an English lady. She answered our surprised look with an announcement, "I am not joining your party to go to Australia." However, Father Lebel persuaded her to change her mind. Imagine the contrast. The frightened refugees enter into her little world. Subdued lights, bowls of sweet-scented plumeria and tropical ferns and flowers, and an atmosphere of spaciousness and comfort revealed her brave effort to bolster up her own courage.

We met everybody there. The first one to greet us was Father Fluet, who had made a fast trip up from Asitavi. We were so happy to see him, as we had missed him the night we so hurriedly left. All the island residents we knew were there, including Mr. Babbage, Mr. Urban, Mr. Long, Mr. Edmunds, Mrs. Huson, Father Morel, Father Allotte, and Mr. and Mrs. Campbell. The latter had walked 20 hours from their high mountain hideout under unusually trying conditions. They were exhausted and badly scratched and bruised. We greeted them all and then went off to change our wet clothing. We were a sight. We slipped into clean, dry things and discarded our blue dotted bush veils and wet, soiled clothing, emerging hardly recognizable a half hour later.

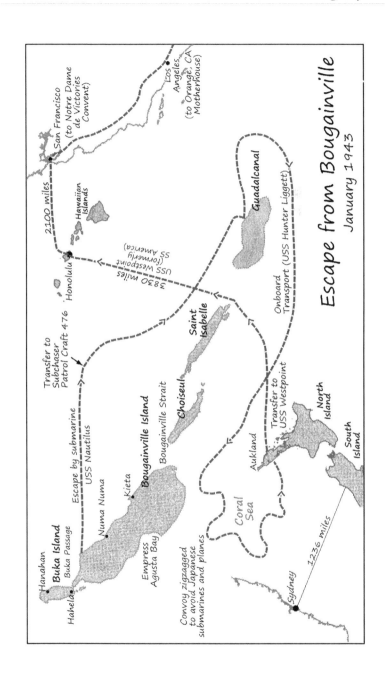

Escape from Bougainville
January 1943

CHAPTER 10

Boat He Come! Boat He Come!

January 1, 1943
Shortly before dawn, the four Sisters of St. Joseph, and 25 other evacuees including several Marist Sisters and two Marist Priests, were rescued by an American submarine.

A few minutes after midnight two of the Australian soldiers came in and wished everyone a Happy New Year. We all stood around in little groups talking to make the time pass quickly. Some of the soldiers had messages to send with us to relatives in Australia. Notes were written on bits of paper, and letters were hurriedly addressed to give us to mail. Mail had not been sent from Bougainville for over a year.

About 1:00 A.M., an excited native came running in saying, *"Boat he come! Boat he come!"* We picked up our small suitcases and started down to the shore. A motor launch was anchored about 100 yards off shore flashing signals to Lieutenant Reed. He went out in a canoe to reassure them that it was a bona fide rescue and not a Japanese plot. He was presented with a gift from the commander and crew of the submarine consisting of a generous supply of food, medical supplies—and tobacco. In a few minutes, a dozen native outrigger canoes came upon the beach and we were taken out to the launch. The subdued lights disclosed three American naval officers. No one said a word, and we waited in silence while one officer pumped up a rubber boat.

The stillness was broken by the most welcome sound in the world, the humorous drawl of an Oklahoman, Chief Boatswain's Mate F.R. Porterfield. He was jokingly commenting on the amount of air these things take. At last, it was lowered to the water. A number of us were placed in the launch with a comment from one officer about excess baggage. With that comment, Mrs. Huson tossed the larger of her two suitcases overboard. Six sisters, including Sister Isabelle, Sister Irene and Sister Celestine, together with Bobby's native daughters, clambered over the plump sides of the rubber boat that was towed behind the launch.

A native who knew the reef well, acted as navigator, winding in and out through the dangerous passage. One signal was given, and we received the reply. We started full speed ahead in that direction. We felt a bit apprehensive after traveling some distance away out in a big ocean in a small boat. Fortunately, the sea was calm. More signals were given, but we received no reply. The officers were silent, and we could feel the tension. Still we signaled. No answer. Finally, our navigator saw through the blackness and said, "*Em he stop.*" The officer did not believe him and continued his red signals. We were very close when we all saw the outline of the submarine. [12] It was huge, and the entire deck was lined with men to help take us aboard. Lieutenant R.B. Lynch, in charge of our little expedition, saluted his captain and gave his report. He asked for more gasoline to return for the nine men who were waiting in canoes at the edge of the reef.

You cannot put into words the feeling one has for those of one's own country, especially when one is miles from home and running away from the Japanese. Were we happy to see our American boys! We climbed the convex sides of the boat aided by outstretched hands from the deck. The submarine seemed about two thirds submerged. The sailors guided us along the slippery deck to the hatch, your reporter hanging on to this diary for dear life; offers to carry it were refused politely. The prayers that for the past weeks had been almost as constant as our breathing were heard. We knew that down in Asitavi our bishop was holding a night vigil before the Blessed Sacrament. The good God gave us at last a sense of security.

Once down, we were directed to the galley for coffee and sandwiches. We were half-starved, and the sight of a bowl of sugar and a cup of real honest-to-goodness American coffee was the very thing with which to celebrate the New Year. While we ate our lunch, the boys gathered around to inquire where we came from. Some of them were from New York, Boston, Idaho, Oklahoma, Fresno and even Los Angeles! If they were thrilled, we were, too. Soon the Captain, Lieutenant Commander W.H. Brockman, came to give us an official welcome. He turned his cabin over for our use, and the boys gave up their bunks. Within an hour, we were in bed, but sleep was out of the question. We were listening for the arrival of the others. They came on board just before dawn, and the ship submerged immediately. From then on, we lived the lives of sailors, submerged during the day and making full speed ahead on the surface at night.

The Australian planters gave the officers all of the information they could concerning reefs, harbors and Japanese positions. The missionaries entertained the crew with pidgin English and stories of the natives and their customs. It was touching to see the boys go to their lockers and bring out Christmas cake from home, and to see them coming to us with toothbrushes and toothpaste, in fact, anticipating our every need. The cook prepared his most American dishes; we must have been an emaciated looking crowd. Our strength returned, and we began to feel better in a couple of days.

January 3, 1943

*L*ate tonight we were instructed to be ready to leave the ship early tomorrow morning between 2:00 A.M. and 3:00 A.M. We each held a typed sheet of detailed instructions for disembarking.

January 4, 1943

*T*he patrol craft was contacted and we climbed up the hatch. We came to the surface for the first time in two days and two nights. It was drizzling rain. Heavy black clouds hung over a choppy sea. Through the darkness officers guided us over the slippery deck of the submarine. Half way down over the curved side sat our Oklahoman boatswain's mate on a rope scaffolding. Down below floated a rubber boat. "Don't drop anybody," admonished the captain. The Oklahoman drawled, "You won't drop 'em now, after going way out there to get them." One by one he lowered us into the boat. It was bobbing like a cork. We stepped into two inches of water from rain and spray and sat down quickly on the nearest seat.

We were taken, six at a time, to the waiting patrol craft. [13] Someone helped us to put one foot in the rope ladder thrown over the side. This was quite a trick, for wind and wave combined to keep us from getting a secure hold. Two strong men caught our arms as soon as we climbed up within reach and pulled us over onto the boat. This diary was wrapped up in a piece of rubberized cloth and several attempts by different sailors to help carry it were unsuccessful. This was all accomplished in silence except for staccato commands. Within a few minutes, we were all safely on the *PC476*, and our former home with all its friendly crew disappeared beneath the waves. We wiped away a tear and breathed a fervent, "God keep you."

We were all taken down to the ship's dining room where we sat around the tables. No one said a word. We just sat and looked at each dripping piece of baggage as it was deposited on the floor. About that time, a pair of dry shoes seemed the most desirable thing one could have. About 4:00

A.M., they served us a cup of hot coffee, and the officer told us we could go on deck at dawn. The coffee revived us, and we began to take an interest in our surroundings. The first thing to attract our attention was a cartoon posted close to the bulletin board, the handiwork of some of the crew. It listed the ship's activities for the past six months. It read, "One patosene tin, three planks, two barracuda, one school of minnows and two empty barrels" with appropriate illustrations. The tonsorial artistry of this crew also was amazing. Sister Irene whispered, "Is this an American ship?" There were numerous opportunities for fun.

At dawn we were out on deck; the warm breeze dried our wet clothing. The crew told us we were on our way to Guadalcanal, so we were all eyes to see that world-famous battlefield. As soon as it was light, we noticed planes circling above us. All of the men were at the ship's guns, and a man with ear-phones sat way up on top of the rigging. As we came closer to the island, two torpedo boats crossed in front of us at top speed. Then a large number of destroyers patrolled all the area in front of Guadalcanal, passing our patrol craft at the side or in front. We took a firm grip on the railing and held our breath as a plane zoomed down almost touching our ship. Ships and planes and crafts and shore boats—we were breathless.

Our boat was very fast, and we came into the harbor quickly. In the distance, a large-transport was unloading. Higgins boats were rushing to and from the ship. One came over to our patrol craft to collect we 29 refugees. Soon we were on board a 16,000 ton transport. It was 8:30 A.M. and still January fourth. An officer assigned us to our staterooms, and our first thought was of a bath and clothes. Someone produced two rolls of bandage for a clothesline. Soon our washing was floating in the breeze made by two electric fans. The ship was swarming with activity. It required considerable planning to make one's way to the drinking fountain without tripping over soldiers and sailors.

We stayed in port all day while the loading and unloading continued. Shortly before lunch, there was a brisk rap at our door, and Reverend Father McGinnis, S.J., introduced himself. He had just arrived at Guadalcanal with the troops and had not yet disembarked. He was very happy to see us and almost at once offered us financial assistance. We refused, but he insisted on Sister Isabelle's accepting $10.00. There are six Catholic chaplains with the American forces here.

January 5, 1943

*W*e kept in motion all night, returning to our base to finish loading in the morning. About 5:00 A.M., a Japanese submarine was detected, and we were warned to be at attention with our life preservers. A depth charge was dropped. We heard the dull explosion.

At 1:30 P.M., we left Guadalcanal with a convoy of ten ships. We sat up on the officer's deck and watched the planes circling above us all around the ships. In the distance, on Guadalcanal, north of Henderson Field, we could hear bombs bursting every few minutes in the section occupied by the Japanese. About 5,000 Japanese still remain at one end of the island, but they are becoming weaker through lack of food. The Japanese tried to land metal drums of food on the shore the night before we arrived, but our forces sunk all the drums and chased away the boats. We examined some of the compressed food rations that the patrol craft had picked up. It included 6 compressed cakes of rice, 2 cubes of dried fish, and 3 cakes of sugar. The whole package was about 6 inches square.

January 6, 1943   Feast of the Epiphany

*W*e are sailing along with the United States fleet somewhere in the Pacific. We do not know where we are going as no one gives out destinations. We are enjoying it very much. There are five of us in one stateroom—four sisters of Saint Joseph and one Marist sister. We have our meals in the guest-officers dining room, and particularly enjoyed mashed potatoes and real bread and butter. The first day we had a special treat—ice cream. After two years, we found it mighty nice. We all carry our life preservers with us wherever we go. At dinner we had an air raid alarm, and let me tell you, it was an awful feeling. All of the portholes were quickly closed, and all hands went to their posts. When the alarm is sounded at night, it all but frightens one to death. Of course, we sleep very lightly, as it is extremely hot and the perspiration awakens us. The fan helps a little, but the total absence of air vents makes it very close. We put our mattresses on the floor in an attempt to get more air, but it doesn't help a great deal.

January 7, 1943

*W*e are tossing about in a very rough sea. Our convoy is proceeding to some unknown port. It is a beautiful sight to see those big ships on either side of us. We are all puffed up over our Navy. It is marvelous to see such a huge organization working so smoothly. This morning we had another air raid scare, and all hustled up on deck. A plane was detected about 100 miles away, and an alarm was given. We zigzag across the water so the submarines will have difficulty getting us.

January 8, 1943

*T*hanks be to God, we are still safe and coming into cooler waters. We know we are going south. We were able to sleep a little better last night though nearly everyone has a bad case of prickly heat. It started in the submarine, and a fine, red, itchy rash covers our bodies. That, added to a little seasickness, takes away a little from our joy. The first day aboard we received these instructions:

> ### *MEMORAMDUM TO ALL REFUGEES*
> <u>Abandon ship:</u>
> *At abandon ship drill, all refugees take station on officer's veranda with life preservers and be prepared to leave ship in boat designated.*

Darken ship:
The ship is darkened every night from sunset to sunrise for obvious reasons. All refugees are held responsible for no light showing from their rooms. Ports and blackout screens must be closed constantly during these hours.
Signed: E.E.HANH, JR.
Executive Officer

On the submarine, we were classed as guests, on this boat, as refugees, and if we are picked out of the salt water, we'll be survivors.

January 9, 1943

*W*e hear there are about 1,500 people on board this ship, and we think we are heading for New Zealand. We hope to get a boat to California within a short time. It is all so like a dream. Best of all is that feeling of security from a Japanese bayonet. We did fear a knife so much that our last nights on the island were sleepless.

Our dear Lord has sent us a rough sea, which is the best protection against submarines. We are getting into cooler waters. It won't be long before our prickly heat is all cleared up; it can be so annoying.

Last night some of the men got together to form an orchestra. There were a saxophone, a guitar, and a piano accordion. One of the pieces they played was *California, Here I Come,* and it was all Sister Isabelle could do to keep the sisters in the stateroom.

The boys on board noticed that the three little native girls were shivering with the cold. They had each a single, thin, little cotton dress and were barefoot. The afternoon they left, Bobby and his wife had tearfully made up a pathetic little bundle of their treasures and wrapped them in a baby blanket. Sister Henrietta improvised this blanket into a cape for the youngest one. One young sailor started a collection for them and gave them about 100 dollars.

Occasionally, different officers and men stopped at our door to ask questions about the islands. They have many interesting things to tell us about Guadalcanal. They are always sending us nuts, candy bars or ice cream. Captain Jimmie Miles, as he is affectionately called by the crew, saw that we were provided with stamps, stationery and arms full of New York and Boston newspapers. Really, we are becoming very spoiled with all these luxuries after living on the islands. We do enjoy the delicious meals. Fancy, hot dogs and sauerkraut way out here in the South Seas. Yesterday we had corned beef and cabbage—it may be lowbrow to eat such food, but it is mighty good.

January 10, 1943

Today, Sister Isabelle had a visit with Captain Riefschneider to make arrangements for our trip home. Everything looks promising, and we can hardly realize that we may see California again. He has charge of all the Pacific fleet transports, and is a very important official. When he learned that we were going to California, he asked us to write a little note to his wife in La Jolla.

January 11, 1943

Still traveling southward. We haven't had any submarine or air alarms for several days. The weather is much cooler, and we are using our blankets at night. Our thoughts revert sadly to those we left hiding in the bush. We forgot to tell you that the captain on the submarine learned that the Japanese came to the very spot where we left the beach at Teop two hours after we got away. As we get the perspective, we realize that our deliverance is a miracle of God's protection.

January 12, 1943

The sea is calm, and the weather is refreshing. This evening we are having impromptu entertainment on the officer's deck provided by the Seabees. We learned today just who the

Seabees are. They are the specially trained units of the Navy who do all the construction work in a new war zone. They build the powerhouses for the other units who follow. There are several hundred Seabees on board returning to New Zealand for a short rest after many months at Guadalcanal. It is from this group that talent for the entertainment is being supplied.

The master of ceremonies was a born comedian, and it was evident that he was not a mere amateur. He supplied fun for everybody there, even the ship's mascot, a big black cat. Boys sat up in the rigging, in the lifeboats, on coils of rope and everywhere. At the close of the program, all stood to sing *God Bless America.*

Shortly after we headed into Auckland Harbor, we tied up at the wharf at 8:00 P.M. We remained on deck, for we were told that we would very likely stay on board until morning. However, we searched the crowd on the wharf, and saw a very tall priest looking up at us. A wire had been sent to the naval headquarters stating that 29 refugees were on board, including some missionaries. The Navy notified Bishop Liston, and he sent Father McKiffery to meet the boat. Father came on board with several other officials, among them a representative of the American Red Cross. As soon as all the documents were filled out, we were taken in a car to the convent of the Sacred Heart in Remuera. It was wonderful to be in a real convent again and see sisters in black habits. Chairs were placed in a spacious room, and we 14 sisters and three native girls were served hot chocolate and cookies. Then we were assigned to dormitories, and after a visit to their beautiful chapel, we were tucked in for the night.

January 13, 1943

*T*his morning, Bishop Liston came out especially to say Mass for us at 8:00 A.M. The chapel was a picture; we thought we were in heaven. There were tall brass vases filled with exquisite blue hydrangeas against a white marble altar. Then, the Mass. After 12 days without Mass or Communion, you know our joy. At 3:00 P.M., the Marist sisters all left for their house in Wellington. Mother Carmella, S.M.S.M., happened to be in Auckland at the time, and came right out to see her sisters. It is extremely difficult to get transportation to Sydney, as the boats are all in service, and it is very dangerous. Getting across involves a great deal of red tape, so it was decided that they go to their nearest house. We felt very sad at the hour of parting. They had been our companions through so much. We were planning to go on to America.

January 14, 1943

After the Marist Sisters left, we four Sisters of Saint Joseph became the pets of the convent. We were showered with kindness on every side. Mother Morgan was assigned to us as a sort of guardian angel. Whenever we would turn around, there was Mother Morgan to do something for us. We couldn't suggest a thing, as it was always there before we could ask for it. There were books to read, soap and water, and ironing equipment, in fact, everything. Soon we were all starched and ironed and wearing our regular headdress. Mr. Parker from the American Red Cross came to interview us. He gave us a check for 50 pounds and told us to go down to buy what we needed.

January 15, 1943

Today, Mr. Parker called to take us shopping. What a surprise we were to the people on the streets and in the stores. Our tropical clothing attracted attention. One sailor leaning against a doorway said, "Them's Catholics." The rest of the public were not quite certain as to what part of the U.S. force we belonged. In the store, one buyer assisted us to make all of our purchases, then she took us to dinner as her guests. We came home with the Red Cross car full of everything we needed. It was out of the question to attempt to make black habits as we were told to be ready to pack at a moment's notice.

January 18, 1943

*W*e have spent a week in Auckland. During this time, Mr. H. A. Boucher, the American consul, has arranged for our passports and passage to America. In the meantime, we are entertained with car rides around the city. We visited the new hospital and spent the day with the Sisters of Mercy there. In the evening, we received a call from Father McHardy's Uncle Willie, Mr. William McHardy. On one of our visits at naval headquarters we were asked if we knew a Dr. Wood from California. He had been visiting with the executive officer of our transport, who mentioned bringing several missionaries from the islands. Dr. Wood asked to see the passenger list, and there found four Sisters of Saint Joseph from his own hospital in Orange. He came right out to see us; we were so happy to see him and get all of the home news. He invited us to come to visit the naval hospital. He sent a car for us, and we spent a very pleasant two hours of inspection. We visited all of the departments, and even went into the surgery where Dr. Crile from Cleveland was making a skin graft. From there, we visited the kitchen where dozens of American pies were standing around cooling. Dr. Knight, who was making the rounds with us, picked up a choice apple pie and took it with him. We finished the rounds while Dr. Wood procured some much-needed quinine for us. In the officers' quarters, we chatted about the Solomons and the trip down while eating our pie with ice cream.

January 19, 1943

*T*he American consul, Mr. Boucher, telephoned to instruct us to be ready to go on board at 8:00 P.M. At 7:30 A.M., all of the Religious of the Sacred Heart assembled with us on the large porch in front of the convent. A few minutes later Bishop Liston, accompanied by Father McKiffery, arrived. They visited a short time with us and the bishop gave us his blessing. The American consul's car came up the driveway; we made our farewells and were driven to the dock. We gasped when we took a look at our boat. It looked enormous.

Mr. Boucher helped us carry our bags on board, and we were shown to our staterooms. We have a lovely big room and bath on A deck.

January 20, 1943

*W*e have our meals down in the guest officer's dining room at a table by ourselves with a young man to serve us. There are seven or eight nurses traveling on this boat. Some are going to America, and two are going to England. There are about 3,000 servicemen on board, many of whom are Australian airmen going to England. There is a priest with the Australian forces, so we have Mass each morning. How grateful we are, especially when we are at sea and passing through dangerous waters. What a choice find for an enemy submarine. This morning at dawn we had a scare. The ship fired three five-inch guns, and the vibration was terrific. We sat up in our beds and waited for the signal. We are assigned to a certain lifeboat just outside of our cabin. The ship is traveling alone and is going about 22 knots an hour. It is named the SS *West Point*, and is about 38,000 tons.

January 22, 1943

*W*e have just passed the International Date Line, and have had two Wednesdays. The days pass very quickly and we are so happy to be nearing home. So many things have taken place since we left the Solomons. Yesterday, we met a Catholic doctor from Washington, D.C., Commander Don S. Knowlton, and had an enjoyable visit with him. He is on the staff at Georgetown University. For some time, he had been observing us and wondering to what congregation we belonged. Having taught in Washington, he thought he was familiar with every known habit. We explained that the Japanese got our black ones. Everyone seems interested in us, for it is generally known that we are Solomonese "run aways." Doctor Knowlton is with the Marine Corps, has been in Guadalcanal for several months, and is returning home for a rest. Incidentally, he is a good friend of Father Joseph

Sullivan, S.M., through whose kind interest we were invited and persuaded to go to the Solomons.

We spent our time on board very pleasantly. The regularity of our community prayers is comforting, as it has been ever since we boarded the submarine. In our leisure moments we enjoy the newspapers and magazines provided for us by the executive officer, Commander M.J. Malanaphy. We haven't seen any current reading matter in over a year, so we are getting much interesting information about the war, particularly the Solomons. We receive a news bulletin each morning. We have access to a room just across the hall where we can launder our clothing; thus, we are not obligated to wear wrinkled gowns.

January 29, 1943

*W*e are two days from San Francisco, and our hearts are light at the thought of seeing our homeland. The trip has been very pleasant except for the heat through the tropics. There are so many on board that the decks are filled with men sitting about reading or writing, so we have stayed in our cabin. There are about 200 U.S. Marines returning from Guadalcanal. They were the first to go there to take the island, and from the stories they tell, they must have killed a great many Japanese. When we came on board everyone looked at us in wonder. Our white habits puzzled all of the Catholics, as they couldn't recognize our order. When they learned where we were from, it wasn't long till they came to talk to us. Now it is hard to find a minute alone without two or three sailors or Marines coming to talk to us. Dr. Martin from Hollywood introduced himself. His wife is Luella Parsons, the Hearst motion picture reporter. He is a Catholic and a good friend of Father English. Today, everyone is getting ready for the arrival in port. It seems that we are a day ahead of schedule, but cannot go until Sunday morning. We are wondering how the ship uses up the extra time. It zigzags its course to avoid submarines. The coast is a danger zone, but tomorrow we may see some of our planes and possibly a patrol craft. We are told not to feel safe until we put our feet on dry land.

January 30, 1943

*T*he ship is seething with activity. Sailors are running here and there with sheets of typewritten orders. Everyone is intent upon our arrival in San Francisco. The little washroom with the ironing board is in use constantly. First, one excited marine dashes in to press his suit, while two others wait in line. We noticed one poor marine struggling with the electric cord while holding a crease with the other hand. We came to the rescue and pressed his trousers. To repay us he came with a companion to show us his souvenirs. They were both young captains and had a very interesting collection taken from the Japanese. It included rifles, a sword, revolvers, a small Japanese medical kit, some little pellets of opium, and two Japanese flags stained with blood. The boys are all hoping to obtain leave to go home. They deserve it. The waiter who takes care of our table in the dining room is a young marine who does not look over 19 or 20 years old. He has been made a corporal and is very happy about it. During the whole voyage he has been most solicitous; he even sends dainties to our stateroom for our afternoon lunch. Last evening, he sent half of a mince pie because one of the sisters had expressed her pleasure at having it for dinner. The Australian airmen look as homesick as we did in Australia. They sit in every corner on deck writing pages and pages to the folks back home.

This afternoon, we sisters and eight nurses were invited to have tea with the ship's officers. They were gracious hosts. Commander Malanaphy received us and we spent a very pleasant hour.

January 31, 1943

The four Sisters of St. Joseph ring the doorbell of Notre Dame de Victoires convent in San Francisco.

*T*he sound of revile this morning was hardly necessary. Everyone seemed to be up and moving around in the darkness. Lights do not come on until sunrise. After Mass, we came out on deck to look for land. There it was! Our beloved United States was dimly outlined on the horizon. And was it cold! We shivered a moment or two and hurried down to the dining room for breakfast. The place was deserted, and our faithful marine had stayed to serve us, but even he had to set down his tray to climb out the dining room window while we passed under the Golden Gate Bridge. No one could sit down long enough to finish breakfast. We, too, leaned out to look, then hurried up on deck. The skyline of San Francisco gave us a feeling mere words cannot express. Everything we held dear seemed to be wrapped up in that foggy picture. We wanted to fold it all up in our arms and hug it tight. Unless you are a refugee, you cannot know the emotions one experiences on seeing the "stars and stripes" flying gloriously and free from the tops of the highest building.

By 10:00 A.M., we were at the docks, and after passing immigration inspection, we were permitted to go ashore. Commander Malanaphy had arranged for a Red Cross car to meet us and take us to Notre Dame de Victoires convent on Pine Street in San Francisco. We arrived unannounced. By a coincidence, Mother Francis, who accompanied us to the islands, was there to welcome us back. A long distance call put us in touch at once with Reverend Mother Louis at our Motherhouse in Orange, California.

Deo Gratias.

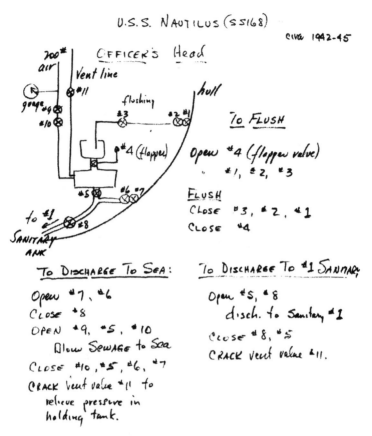

U.S.S. NAUTILUS (SS168)

circa 1942-45

OFFICER'S Head

Flushing the officers' head on the Nautilus *normally required nineteen separate steps, done in exactly the right sequence. The nuns never mastered the art. The proper procedure, sketched by a member of the crew, suggests the complexity of the problem.* (Courtesy Hal M. Winner)

Sketch of how to operate the head on the *Nautilus* [14]

Source: Lord, Walter, 1977, Chapter 8, p. 150.

Thank you letter to the Commander of the *Nautilus*, 1943

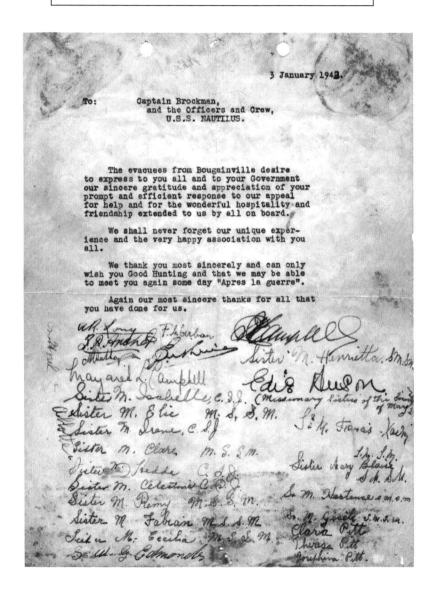

3 January 1943.

To: Captain Brockman,
          and the Officers and Crew,
          U.S.S. NAUTILUS.

The evacuees from Bougainville desire
to express to you all and to your Government
our sincere gratitude and appreciation of your
prompt and efficient response to our appeal
for help and for the wonderful hospitality and
friendship extended to us by all on board.

We shall never forget our unique experience and the very happy association with you
all.

We thank you most sincerely and can only
wish you Good Hunting and that we may be able
to meet you again some day "Apres la guerre".

Again our most sincere thanks for all that
you have done for us.

```
U.S.S. NAUTILUS

MENU

CHICKEN And BARLEY SOUP

BREADED FRIED CHICKEN

CRANBERRY SAUCE

MASHED POTATOES

SAUSAGE DRESSING

GIBLET GRAVY

GREEN PEAS AND BUTTERED ASPARAGUS

BREAD AND BUTTER

PEACH PIE AND FRUIT CAKE

HARD      CANDY

LEMONADE
```

Menu on the *Nautilus*—New Year's Eve. 1943

Unknown Soldiers laid to rest

Archbishop Mitty welcomes the sisters to
San Francisco, February 1943

Father Lamarre
spent 40 months in
a Japanese prison
camp

Reunion of Sisters Celestine, Isabelle, Hedda,
and Irene with Father Lebel, 1972

SEQUEL

War Comes to Buka

"There were dark clouds over Buka after that second visit of Japanese ships. Mr. Percy Good had been executed and Father Hennessey was missing, presumably taken away prisoner. There were four American Sisters of Saint Joseph at Hanahan. Could I risk having them captured?"

Father Joseph Lamarre, March 1942

*A*s their pastor, Father Lamarre assumed responsibility for the sisters' welfare. As word spread of the cruel Japanese treatment of other missionaries, he decided that the sisters must be moved away from the advancing Japanese. He didn't learn until after the war had ended that the sisters were ultimately rescued. In his memoir, he writes, "their evacuation from Buka proved to be their salvation."

The sisters left Buka for the larger island of Bougainville on March 22, 1942. Nine days later the Japanese occupied Buka Passage. On August 26, 1942, Father Lamarre and his missionary companions were captured. He spent the next 3 years as a Japanese prisoner of war, experiencing near starvation, untreated disease, and the ever present risk of death from bombing as the war in the Solomons escalated. On September 13, 1945, his ordeal ended when Australian soldiers arrived at the prison camp at Ramale. His Roll of Honor is a tribute to the Marist priests, brothers and sisters, who gave their lives during World War II while serving the people of the Solomon Islands. Included in this list is a priest from the Archdiocese of Boston, Father James Hennessey who had just completed five years of missionary work. In *War Comes to Buka*, Father Joseph Lamarre, SM, shows us the brutal face of war.

December 8, 1941

*F*or Catholics, it was the feast of the Immaculate Conception. At that very moment the Japanese planes were treacherously bombing Pearl Harbor. Thus began the trouble that brought the Japanese to our peaceful island. Not one of us at that time ever thought our mission would be destroyed by war. We were so far away from the theatre of war. But war did come to Buka and what a war!

On January 11, 1942, we sighted the first Japanese planes. There were six on a reconnaissance tour. Twelve days later they returned and bombed Buka Passage and the small Australian aerodrome. Our 26 Australian soldiers were brave but could do nothing against superior numbers. They took refuge in the mountains of Bougainville and we at Buka were left to the mercy of looting natives until the arrival of the Japanese Navy on March 30th.

March 9, 1942   Father Hennessey's Heroism

*O*n March 9, 1942, Japanese War ships entered the Karola Harbor on the west coast of Buka. Mr. Percy Good of Kessa and Father James Hennessey (Boston) were visited and interrogated. God protected Father Hennessey that day.

One the evening of March 12th, Father Hennessey arrived at my house at Hanahan. He came, as he said, to settle his situation. He related to me all that happened at

Lemanmanu during the terrible two hours of the Japanese visit. He fully realized his precarious situation. "The next few days will tell," he said, "and if they return soon, I'm finished." Someone suggested to him that he leave Buka and seek protection and safety in the mountains of Bougainville. He simply answered, "I am not a coward. By Bishop Wade I was placed in charge of Lemanmanu, and I will remain with my people, cost what may. Yes, even if it means my death. I would rather be killed at my post than live in disgrace. A priest does not run away from his duties to souls. I have seen many years of life; it is better to die as a Good Shepherd than to linger for years in some hospital with cancer or some other illness."

The next morning before sunrise we parted. He wanted to celebrate Mass at Lemanmanu. As I watched him go, I felt I was seeing a hero condemned to death that we would never meet again in this life. According to the catechists, after his return to Lemanmanu he continued his pastoral work with the same zeal and his same smile until his capture the following Sunday morning.

The ships returned to Buka on March 15th. Father Hennessey was immediately captured and kept under guard. On the morning of March 16th, he was allowed to come ashore at Pororan and celebrate Holy Mass in the chapel of the nurses of the Marist Medical Mission. No one was allowed to speak to him. After Mass, he was immediately brought back to the warship and was never seen again in Buka. On the evening of March 16th, Mr. Percy Good, who had been captured, was executed in his house. The following morning the ships left, and as we presumed, with Father Hennessey on board.

From other prisoners who spoke to him later, we know that he was court-martialed, condemned to death and then pardoned. He spent six weeks on the warship, and was then imprisoned for some time in Kaviang, on New Ireland. Missionaries, who were later imprisoned in the same jail, saw written on the wall: *In nomine Domine, speravi, non confundar in aeternum* (My hope is the Lord, I will not be disappointed in eternity)—James Hennessey. From Kaviang,

Father Hennessey was brought to Rabaul. He remained there until the end of June 1942, when with about 300 civilian prisoners and over 900 military prisoners he was put on the *Montevideo Maru* and sent to Japan. The ill-fated ship was torpedoed off the coast of Luzon in the Philippines and all the prisoners went down with the ship.

Thus ended the life of Father James Hennessey, diocesan priest from Boston, who had volunteered for mission work in the North Solomons. He is gone, but his spirit remains. We his fellow missionaries remember him, and the work that he has done still lives. The boys that he trained at the school for catechists are a credit to the mission and proof of the zeal of a self-sacrificing priest who faced death rather than leave his post.

After his capture, I made a visit to the station of Lemanmanu to see to his belongings and the affairs of the station. The whole district was in tears; Catholics, Methodists and pagans all mourned him. His chalice, private papers and some precious belongings I hid in Lemanmanu before my own capture.

March 22, 1942   The Sisters of St. Joseph

There were dark clouds over Buka after that second visit of the Japanese ships. Mr. Percy Good had been executed and Father Hennessey was missing, presumably taken away as a prisoner. Would the ships come again? Would Hanahan be the next station to be visited? There were four American Sisters of St. Joseph at Hanahan. Could I risk having them captured? A decision was reached; the sisters would all go to Gagan in the interior of the island to do some medical work and to temporarily escape the raiding Japanese. That same evening, I reached Buka Passage where the government had decided to immediately evacuate the sisters from Buka. The following evening, the sisters left Buka Passage by launch and reached Tinputz on Bougainville in the early morning of March 22nd. Their evacuation from Buka proved to be their salvation. They were later evacuated from Bougainville by an

American submarine.

March 30, 1942 Japanese Occupation of Buka

*O*n Monday of Holy Week, the Japanese Navy occupied Buka Passage. A large force of Marines landed, but only a small garrison was left on Sohano, a small island at the entrance of the Passage between Buka and Bougainville.

A few days after the occupation, Fathers Servant, Montauban, Caffiaux, Brother Joseph and I presented ourselves to the Japanese authorities. The officer in charge, a rough, rugged warrior who had taken part in the battle of Wake Island, was inclined to distrust us. He was reassured by Mr. Shimabukunaro, his interpreter, who was a Catholic. To this man we owe a debt of gratitude. He explained to the officer that we were missionaries, concerned only with religion and had no part whatsoever in the war.

We were allowed to return to our respective stations and continue our religious work under the following conditions: We were not to keep any firearms, radios or cameras; we were not to communicate with anyone on Bougainville; nor were we to leave the island of Buka. Above all we were not to make any anti-Japanese propaganda or interfere in any way with the military operations of the Japanese Imperial Forces. We were given Imperial persons, safety of life and protector of property. Our mission property was respected until our capture, five months later.

After Father Hennessey's capture, the district of Lemanmanu had fallen upon my shoulders. There were 1,400 Catholics at Lemanmanu, and 2,320 Catholics at Hanahan. Father Servant had come to lend me a hand at Hanahan. For five months, we worked under trying conditions. We were relatively free, but we did not trust the Japanese. We had very good reasons to fear. American planes paid occasional visits to Buka. In May, there was the Battle of the Coral Sea. It was announced to us as a great Japanese victory. News from friends on Bougainville, however, gave us a more accurate account of the battle. The Japanese warships that took refuge in the Karola Harbor showed the scars of battle. Three of them were badly damaged and a large cruiser was scuttled. The natives found parts of planes bearing the mark of the "Rising Sun." To us it was the "Setting Sun"; we knew that the enemy was checked at last.

August 7, 1942 Guadalcanal

*F*ollowing the battle of the Coral Sea things were rather quiet for a while on Buka. We knew that the enemy was checked, and we impatiently waited for the next move. On the afternoon of August 7th, there was a lot of activity in the air; Japanese planes were returning from the Solomons. A large bomber made a forced landing near Lemanmanu. Half a wing had been cut away by machine-guns. Other planes passed over Hanahan, in a hurry, out of formation and seeming to have the devil on their tails. Five Japanese fighters were forced down at Buka Passage. The natives related to us that these were riddled with American bullets. Friends on Bougainville sent us the news of the landing of the American Marines on Guadalcanal. An Allied Victory! Our hopes soared sky-high! They would be in Buka within a few days! Oh, but these few days have been long.

August 15, 1942 The Marist Brothers

*O*n the Feast of the Assumption, natives returning from Buka Passage told us that three Australian Marist Brothers who were stationed at the catechist school in Chabai had been captured. Our hopes came tumbling down. If the three Australians who were stationed at the Catechist School of Chabai were imprisoned, what would happen to the Americans on Buka? After a few days, the Marist Brothers were taken away on a ship. We had no idea of their destination. To the present time we have not heard of them. They are listed as missing, presumed dead.

August 22, 1942 Dark Clouds

*O*rders were issued to us, the five missionaries of Buka to report at the mission station near Buka Passage. We were all to live together at the same station and discontinue our missionary work. Human wisdom reproaches us of not having escaped at that moment. But even at that time, we trusted the Japanese and had hopes of being able to minister to the spiritual needs of our natives. We could not abandon our priestly work in order to seek security in escaping. We followed orders and awaited developments.

August 26, 1942 Capture

*W*e were not long in waiting. On the morning of August 26th, immediately after breakfast, while we were hiding our various belongings and our tinned food, we heard a truck arriving at the house. It was all over. The Japanese Marines armed with rifles and bayonets surrounded us and we were told to gather our clothes and follow. We tried to explain and sought explanation for their actions and their attitudes. The only answer given was that we had to follow. We gathered a few pieces of clothing, but the Japanese (who never steal but take) had already taken the best of what we had.

From the mission station, we were brought to the Headquarters and kept under guard in a copra shed with the promise that we could return to our mission after two days. But when the two days were ended, we found ourselves imprisoned on the small island of Sohano.

On the night of August 29th we received our baptism of fire. Half a dozen American bombers came and dropped their cargo of bombs over the aerodrome. We thought ourselves very miserable and in great danger, but months later we realized that the first bombing had been very light compared with what was reserved for later months.

August 30ᵗʰ, 1942 On a Japanese Warship

*O*n Sunday morning, I was brought alone to one of the destroyers in the harbor and kept there until late in the evening. The other missionaries were also brought there later in the day, and we were all questioned separately. My mental torture lasted for over two hours. The questions concerned only the mission and my own identity. They accepted willingly the fact that I was American, but would not believe that I was a missionary Catholic priest on Buka. In the minds of the Japanese officers, I was a spy in the service of the American Army. The captain of the destroyer was a well-educated man, spoke English perfectly, but dealt with me only through an interpreter. Of all the Japanese that I have met he was the most hateful and sneering. We generally found that educated Japanese were those who had the greatest hate for the white man. A few officers were kind and understanding, but the great majority was as hateful.

August 30ᵗʰ-December 3ʳᵈ, 1942 Three Months of Prison Life

*A*fter the questioning we were all told to remain on Sohano and that we would be kept there for a few weeks, until the war was finished in the Solomons and New Guinea. They may have been sincere, and really believed that they could take back Guadalcanal and capture Port Moresby in a very short while. And from what we saw we were afraid that they would accomplish their purpose.

At Sohano, we were allowed to live in a large Australian government house; we had plenty of room, and we were allowed to roam around parts of the island without guard. Beds, we had none. We were forced to sleep on the hard floor; happily, we had brought a sufficient number of blankets. Our food we had to secure from an abandoned native garden. The Japanese refused to give us rice or any tinned food and prevented the natives from bringing anything to us. The Catholic Chinese who had greater freedom were also forbidden to bring us any vegetables. We had to do our own cooking and that on an open fire. In the beginning we found enough food: taro and pawpaw for breakfast; pawpaw and taro for dinner and the same menu for supper. And so it went on for three months.

Mass – at Last

We had managed to bring a Mass kit into the prison camp. A faithful native secretly brought us Mass wine and altar bread from the nearest mission station at Bougainville. We were able to have one Mass early every morning. They seemed to know that we had religious services, and did not try to interfere or prevent it. The consolation of Holy Mass was granted to us for four and a half months.

Bombing

The Japanese fighter planes were around by the dozens day after day. The American planes came occasionally at night for a raid, but they were never numerous. A few small fires were started, but on the whole there seemed to be very little damage done. The first daylight raid that we witnessed was a cheerful one, at least for us. The Japanese planes had just landed in large numbers on the drome two miles away when we saw a formation of seven Boeings coming over. They lined the drome with bombs. The island shook, fires were started, black smoke was seen for miles around, and the Japanese were in a very bad humor that day. That told a story.

The Visit of Japanese Officers

The Japanese officers connected with Buka Passage never seemed to give us rest; they were daily coming to question us again and again concerning our nationalities, names, occupations. They wanted to know our desires and opinions concerning the war. As often as they came we asked to send letters home through the Red Cross or to send some communication to our Church authorities. The answer was always the same, "It is impossible for the present, but be patient, you will soon be free."

December 3, 1942 Three Fathers Return to Buka

After three months of this life of prison, the three French priests were allowed to return to Buka. They were allowed to live together at the station of Gagan in the interior of the island. They had a certain amount of freedom, and could do spiritual good to the natives. But the time came when they could no more celebrate Mass for lack of Mass wine. By 1944, they were in greater danger than we were: danger from the Japanese, danger from the natives, and still greater danger from the American planes that had then a great air superiority.

The Lonely Life on Sohano

After the three French priests left, Brother Joseph and I had to be satisfied with a small half-destroyed house on the edge of the forest. The treatment that had never been too good became worse. The Japanese authorities still refused to give us food and we found less and less in the abandoned garden. The native food gave out and we had to be satisfied with pawpaw, coconuts and leaves. We saw many really hungry days. We generally found some coconuts, wild fruits and nuts; but the quality was lacking. We were constantly losing weight and our strength was diminishing, from lack of protein and fats.

Our clothes were giving out. For months, we walked about in the bush and around the house without shoes. We had one shirt each and that was worn only on Sundays when we tried to show a bit of vanity. For months and months, we were clad in old khaki trousers—Robinson Crusoe and his man Friday. Soap, we had none, and our only pair of scissors was broken. A few old rusty razors blades were used in shaving and giving one another haircuts.

The American planes continued to pay us visits, bombing and machine-gunning. Even our little corner near the edge of the forest was not respected. By June 1943, it was necessary for us to sleep in caves. It was not safe to be in our little hut at night; very often the first warning of danger was the swish-swish of the bombs coming down upon us. One night we raced to our cave as the planes were overhead dropping bombs; the next morning we counted eighteen bomb holes all within seventy yards of our hiding hole. We could not expect anything different since the "ack" guns were only a hundred yards from our hut.

Malaria

Malaria did not spare us. We had frequent mild attacks that were the only case in which the Japanese helped us. Whenever one of us had a touch of the fever, the other would rush to the officer in charge with a long story and pitifully beg for a bit of quinine. They did show some mercy on that score and gave us a few tablets of quinine. Tobacco was a luxury.

In May 1943, three Buka natives were executed not far from our hut. We were not told anything, but we sensed that something ghastly was happening. Upon investigation, we found out that executions were taking place. So we kept away. We thought that three necks to be cut were enough; we did not feel like increasing the number to five and the best thing to do in that case was to keep away from the orgy. Later we found out that two of the three unfortunates were from my own district in Hanahan.

July 13, 1943 A Welcome Visit

*O*n July 13th, we had a most welcome visitor. Lawrence Chan, one of our Catholic Chinese, was allowed to visit us under guard and bring us a bit of food. How welcome were the tin of butter, the tea and the lard, not to mention the tobacco. In spite of the guards, Laurie managed to give us a bit of news: "T.J.W.'s still free in the heights of the neighboring island. The women missionaries from your station and others were taken away under water by a U boat from your country." That meant enough for me: Bishop Thomas J. Wade was still free in the mountains of Bougainville and the Sisters of St. Joseph together with other missionary sisters had been evacuated by an American submarine. The news later proved to be correct.

Danger Comes Nearer

June and July of 1943 saw more daring attacks from the American planes. The Japanese planes were decreasing in number. When the latter went out on a raid we would count their number and infallibly one third failed to return to their base. The time of the raid was always shorter and shorter; to us that meant that the Yanks were getting nearer and nearer to Buka.

August 27, 1943   Transferred to a Japanese Prison Camp

*W*e had spent a year and a day on our lonely island when we were notified to pack. We were given half an hour to get ready. We were told that for our safety from American planes we were being transferred to Rabaul, and that we would be sent to the Catholic Mission of the Sacred Heart Fathers at Vunapope. We tried to believe them. After running on the reefs, returning to the base, and trying a second and a third time, we finally got into the open sea and in thirty-six hours reached Rabaul, 185 miles away.

The trip was dangerous; any plane could have sent us to the bottom of the sea with a bomb or a bit of strafing. In spite of the danger, we enjoyed the trip; the Japanese were practically all elderly men and they took pity on us; they gave us all the food that we could eat.

August 28, 1943   Rabaul Prison Camp

*W*hen we arrived in Rabaul, we were amazed at the Japanese naval strength. The harbor was full of ships and the air full of planes. It was discouraging! How could Uncle Sam cope with such strength? Little did we dream that in less than six months the American air might would annihilate that Navy, destroy the Japanese planes, and leave Rabaul a stinking hole unfit for human habitation.

On arriving in Rabaul, we were not brought to the Catholic mission as promised. Instead, we soon found ourselves in barbed wire with other prisoners. Immediately, we were strictly forbidden under heavy penalty, to speak to any of them. However, it was not long before we had a few whispering meetings. There were twelve civilians, mostly Australians captured in Rabaul. In the next hut were nine American airmen, four of whom were Catholic. We soon found ways of communicating with one another, and within a week we had exchanged a lot of news. The airmen who had taken part in the defense of Port Moresby and the Battle of the Bismarck Sea had been shot down over New Britain. They gave me all the news of the first eighteen months of the war against Japan. It was from them that we first heard the complete story of the Battle of the Coral Sea, the Battle of the Bismarck Sea and the invasion of Guadalcanal.

The first few days, Brother and I were kept by ourselves, and the only work given to us was the sweeping of the hut and raking the grounds. Soon they found that we were still able to do some useful work and we were required to put in our hours at the building of the trenches and dugouts. The food ration allowed for this hard labor was half a pound of rice a day per person.

October, 1943   Under American Bombs

*U*p to October 1943, none of us Civilians had ever seen more than ten Allied planes together over Japanese territory. The airmen prisoners told us unbelievable stories of the American air power. We only hoped that they were telling the truth. On October 12 1943, it was proved to us. When all the Japanese planes were down on the aerodromes and all the Japanese were sitting down to their bowl of rice at midday, we heard a heavy drone coming up the channel. At that moment I was having a secret talk with one of the Yanks; he turned around, listened, then he pointed to the sky and yelled, "Father, they are ours; there they come!" And come they did, in groups over the aerodromes. We did not wait for the bombs, but like rabbits dove down into our holes. We were shaking with fright and with the trembling of the ground. For half an hour it was hell let loose on Rabaul. Nine Japanese ships were sunk right before our own eyes, others at a distance were also under the bombs; hundreds of small crafts at the beach and the wharves were destroyed. It took the Japanese almost a week to clean the debris and collect their dead. We were jubilant in our hearts, but we did not dare express it outwardly. The Japanese were not so happy. It was not the time to whistle *The Stars and Stripes Forever.*

My Catholic Boys

The battle for Rabaul and New Britain was on. We feared for the worst. Was it not the Japanese custom to execute prisoners in retaliation for losses? I had some secret meetings with Bob Curry, Phil Beck, John Mulligan, George Kurisko and Ed Crocker. These five American airmen were Catholic. They made their confession and were ready for anything. It was my first bit of ministry for more than a year. I will never forget the happiness of those boys at being at peace with their God and ready to face Him. And I was happy to bring the consolation of the Sacrament of Penance to these my new parishioners. Never will I forget these Catholic boys. They were super. Not only were they a credit to their country and the American Air Force, they were an honor and a consolation to their Church. On November 25, 1943, together with a few others, they were taken away from our camp. I have not heard of them since, but I have notified their families and now I am expecting news from their relatives, anxious to know if they have survived the war.

November 1943 American Aircraft Carriers

During October, we had experienced five big raids from the American planes. But October was mild compared to November. From the 2nd to the 12th, we were bombed again; this time the USS *Saratoga* and four other carriers were within striking distance of Rabaul. And heavy bombers came from Port Moresby and other aerodromes in New Guinea; the navy bombers came from the Solomons. Bombs came down like rain over Rabaul and the other military targets of the north end of New Britain.

There seemed to be no end to the American air power. Some of the raids lasted for hours, wave after wave of bombers and fighters came over and unleashed a merciless war on everything Japanese.

Indian Prisoners

The Indian prisoners who had been captured and brought from Singapore were jubilant. They realized for the first time that the tide had turned and they turned to America for liberation. When our party made excursions in the bush in search of timber for the buildings of the tunnels and dugouts, we often met these poor unfortunates who were very badly treated. They had to give from ten to twelve hours of hard labor a day under starvation rations. They were full of sympathy for us. They gave us everything that they could bring. One took off his shoes to give them to us; others stole quinine and brought it to us for the sick airmen.

Japanese Losses

The number of men lost by the Japanese was astounding; thousands went to the bottom of the sea with the ships, and thousands more were killed by the bombing. Sickness also took a heavy toll. As much as we hated the Japanese, we were moved to pity when we saw hundreds of them trudging to the dispensaries. Half of them were tubercular. Men that should never have been in the army were on the front line and receiving practically no medical attention. The wounded were often left to die by the road. Even the natives were shocked by their disregard for human life. "Father, now we understand what you meant by the darkness of paganism," was the frequent comment.

January 1944 Beriberi Gets Us

*W*e, in the prison camp, were made to work harder than most of the coolies, and we did not have half their food and yet most of us could stand it better than they did. However, there is a limit to everything, and the human body is a machine that can wear out very quickly. At the end of the five months in this Rabaul camp, Brother Joseph and I were at the end of our tether. Brother had gone down from 165 to 103 lbs. He had only skin left to cover his bones. His stomach could not keep down any more rice; he was finished. He had become practically blind and could do no more than recite his prayers and say his many rosaries. I was not much better. My weight was down to 132 pounds, and I could no longer digest rice—only stolen food could sustain me. Beriberi had such a hold on me that there did not remain many weeks of life. The legs were gone, no more feeling in my knees and I could stand up only with great difficulty. My hands and parts of my face were paralyzed. Beriberi had attacked my nerves.

January 27, 1944 The Japanese Doctor

*O*n January 27, 1944, the corporal in charge of our camp had pity on us and brought us to one of their hospitals to be examined by the doctor. He examined us from a distance of about twenty yards, and on hearing that we were Americans he chased us away as we would a neighbor's dog. Could we expect anything better when they had wounded and sick by the tens of thousands and paid little attention to the lives of their own men?

It was at that time that a humane Japanese interpreter educated in California and probably a Christian, took pity on us and took upon himself the task of having us transferred to the mission concentration camp twenty-five miles away. He first went to Bishop Scharmach asking permission to accept us. Needless to say the bishop was only too glad to receive us, and he sent us a short letter of welcome through the officer. It was the letter of salvation; we knew that if we reached the Mission Camp we would be safe.

January 29, 1944 The Mission Camp

*O*n the morning of January 29th, we left our American and Australian friends of the prison camp, and went by truck to one of the docks to embark for the mission. It was necessary to pass through one of the aerodromes. We had a glance at the damage done by the American bombing. Wrecked Japanese planes were everywhere. We were just there when the siren announced the coming of the American planes, and we had to seek refuge in one of the Japanese air raid shelters—a miserable rat hole that was no protection at all, not even against a bullet. Dive bombers came down with their cargo of 500 pound bombs only 200 yards from our hole. The earth shook, and shrapnel and bullets flew everywhere. We thought ourselves in the bottom of a mad volcano. After twenty minutes, we realized that we were still alive, and in spite of the detonations of the explosions and the many fires in our surroundings, we were still safe. We embarked on a landing barge and headed for Vunapope. After an hour and a half at sea we were face to face with the military police, with our guards presenting a letter from the high command, indicating that we were American Catholic missionaries, and to be treated accordingly.

The Warmest Welcome

At the gate we were met by His Excellency, the Most Rev. Leo Scharmach, M.S.C., Vicar Apostolic of the Rabaul Mission. Over a hundred and fifty missionary priests, brothers and sisters came to bid welcome us—two human wrecks that were arriving in their midst. We were more like scarecrows than human beings and we were received as only Christians and priests can welcome a fellow priest in misery. Since the time of my ordination, I do not believe that I have experienced greater joy and happiness in meeting fellow priests. We were still prisoners but in a mission camp. There was a chapel, where the Blessed Sacrament was reserved, where Holy Mass could be celebrated and where there was a fellow priest to hear my confession.

Marist Brothers and Sisters

Among the missionaries to meet us were Father George Lepping from Philadelphia, formerly a neighbor on Buka, and Father Maurice Boch, both Marist missionaries who had been captured in Shortland in September 1942, and brought to Rabaul. With them were Fathers Peter Schank and J.B. Poncelet, Brother Bruno and seven Marist missionary sisters. All of these had been captured in Buin, on the southern end of Bougainville, and after lingering in the prison camp of Rabaul for six months, had been brought to the mission camp at the end of February 1943. An eighth sister was Sr. M. Domitilla, who had come to Vunapope in 1941 because of sickness and had been caught there when the Japanese invaded Rabaul. It was a happy Marist reunion, and I was able to reassure them as to the safety of the bishop, some of the priests and of the fourteen sisters who had been evacuated by the American submarine a year previously.

One can, to a certain degree, understand why the Japanese imprisoned the priests and brothers. But we cannot forget the treatment that they gave Mother Wendelina and her sisters in the prison camp of Rabaul. The sisters were kept in the same huts as the men prisoners, had no privacy, were exposed to the bombing even at times when the shelters had not yet been built, were made to work at the most humiliating tasks, and were given the same pagan consideration that the Japanese give their own women. When the sisters were sick they could not obtain any medical assistance.

The other prisoners, including the non-Catholics, were loud in their condemnation of the treatment given to the sisters. Japanese nurses cried when they saw the pitiful state of the sisters; some of them returned to bring the sisters a few sweets, some tins of milk and even offered them some money. The nurses were the only Japanese who showed any kindness towards these suffering sisters.

The Japanese soldiers and officers only laughed at the sisters, even striking some of them in the face and forcing them to wash and repair their clothes. Never did they try to reward the sisters for the work done or show any consideration for the services received. Yet, the sisters bore it all with a smile. Missionary sisters, you have given a lesson of unselfishness, courage and charity towards your persecutors.

News! News!

When we entered the mission camp we were warned against giving any war news to the inmates. Since no new prisoner had arrived in the camp for almost a year, they had received only unreliable news from the Japanese and rumors from the natives. I was able to tell them a lot about the war in Europe and the Pacific. Remembering the warning of the Japanese, it was my intention to be reserved and silent for some days and to communicate the good news bit by bit. They saw at once that I knew much more than I was telling, so in the evening a little welcome party was organized. Over a glass of wine, *in vino veritas*, I told the other prisoners all news that I had about the invasion of Sicily, the landing at Naples, the capitulation of Italy, the Allied advances towards France and the possibility of peace in Europe, the American victories in the Solomons, the destruction of the Navy and Air Force in New Guinea. News! And more news! Many of them did not sleep that night. I tried to sleep, but the excitement was too much.

A New First Mass

The next morning, not being strong enough to celebrate Mass, I was satisfied with sitting down and receiving Holy Communion. After a few days, with the excitement over, I made my first confession in fifteen months and celebrated my first Mass in fifty-one weeks. It was like being ordained a second time, being able to offer the holy mysteries again after being deprived of that consolation for so long. It was like a dream, being able to walk in the chapel and visit the Blessed Sacrament, hearing religious hymns and seeing natives in church. The war, the prison camps and the Japanese had hardened our natures. We had no regard for the finer things of life, we had become hardened and blood-thirsty like the soldiers on the fighting lines; but as we came in contact again with the Divine, the soul within us seemed to revive and brought back a sense of things eternal. Yes, life did matter after all, and there were such things as religion and eternal values. We were in an earthly paradise.

February 11, 1944   War! Bombing! Killing!

*W*e were walking on air; we forgot the war and the planes and the bombs, but not for long! Our "castles in Spain" soon came tumbling down. The happy life was too good to last. On February 11, 1944, the siren went off announcing the coming of the American planes. Most of us went to the shelters, the sisters and the children were safely inside, while most of us watched the hundreds of planes coming up the harbor and over the aerodromes with their message of death. For ten minutes that seemed like ten hours, the planes bombed and machine gunned our camp and the neighboring camps of the Japanese. When the smoke cleared, most of our huts and houses had been burnt, some other houses were half-demolished and seven missionaries were wounded by shrapnel or bullets.

Brother Joseph

In the turmoil no one had thought of Brother Joseph. He had been in the small hospital when the raid started. Children were sent to look for him. He was nowhere to be found. The hospital had been blown away by one of the first bombs that hit about ten yards away. I had no illusion about what had happened to him. Father Lepping organized a searching party. In a few minutes Brother Joseph was found under the debris of the hospital. He was dead, pierced by shrapnel, reduced to pulp. He was immediately put into a box less than three feet long and within an hour was interred in the Cemetery of the Sacred Heart Missionaries at Vunapope. Father M. Boch, S.M., performed the funeral service.

Tribute to a True Marist

For seventeen months Brother Joseph Redman, S.M. was the only white man with whom I could associate. A bond of friendship had sprung up between us that only war can produce. We were companions in misery; we were buddies. And there in a small box, after the terrible bombing, was the mangled body of the man who had been my only companion through fire and water. Now I understand the feelings of our soldiers when they say that they have lost their buddy.

Brother Joseph had been not only a companion to me, he had been an inspiration. When the dark clouds of war were hovering over us and things seemed to have no value except to kill and to maim, Brother Joseph never lost his sense of the spiritual. For weeks and months, he lived his spiritual life as one would wish to have lived it when at the moment of death. He was faithful to his weekly confession, to his meditation, and especially to his many rosaries. We had always seen in him a very special devotion to our Blessed Mother. In those seventeen months I had ample opportunity to witness that strong, yet childlike, devotion to Mary. He was a true Marist, faithful to Mary to the last. Is there any wonder that Mary came for him at the feast of Our Lady Lourdes?

His Sacrifice

Brother Joseph understood the value of the priest in the missions; he fully realized the necessity of priests to minister to the spiritual wants of the natives. In my mind I feel that Brother Joseph offered his life that I might be spared for the sake of the natives. The secret of that sacrifice will never be truly known in this life, but I, for whom it was made, understand and appreciate it. It is not easy to make the sacrifice of one's life in wartime. I had not the courage to do likewise. He had the courage and the heroism. Vale, Brother Joseph! I will live to remember.

Life in the Dug-Outs

We thought that the first bombing of the mission camp was a

mistake. We soon realized that it was not. The end of February brought some more planes bound on the total destruction of our camp and that of the Japanese next to us. For four days, we were the target of every description of bombing plane that the American Forces could muster. The Catholic Mission of Vunapope was bombed during the day; the American destroyers shelled us at night. For four days, it was almost impossible to go out of our tunnels under the mountain. The Yanks seemed to think that victory depended upon their bombing of our dug-outs. They changed the face of the mountainside, and we in the bowels of the mountain expected to be buried alive at any moment. The wounded died; others contracted pneumonia and went to a better world; many were sick; life did not seem worthwhile. Still, we lived to bury our dead and to see Rabaul completely destroyed as a Japanese base and stronghold in the South Pacific.

In the weeks that followed we were forced to live in our tunnels, with only the food that we could gather from the destroyed Japanese stores. It was a miserable life, especially for the sick and the aged. But there was hope ever springing anew in our breasts—*The Yanks Are Coming*. They came but they always returned. They came, bombed, shelled, machine-gunned, destroyed, killed, wounded, and returned to their bases.

All around us was death! Death of our own wounded and aged missionaries, death of the natives, death of the disorganized Japanese. In the town of Rabaul and other quarters, the stench of rotting flesh and blood was so bad that no one could remain there. If the Japanese fathers and mothers had seen their sons killed in Rabaul as we saw them, they would forever curse the Emperor, and Tojo and all the others responsible for the carnage. We saw the grim reality of war. We saw the living gathering the blown off arms, legs and heads of those who were once the love and pride of Japanese mothers. War is War! And in Rabaul and the surroundings, America carried on the war with ruthless brutality; they took revenge for Pearl Harbor and the airmen who were murdered on these shores. Japan, what a price you have paid for your folly!

May, 1944   On to Ramale Camp

*B*y the beginning of May 1944, Rabaul was in ruins and was useless as a base. The Americans had moved on to Japan. We were by-passed and we would have to wait for the end of the war to be delivered. Hence the Japanese commander decided that our camp should be moved on to the interior of the island.

A suitable spot was chosen in the bush of the interior, about six miles from the beach, in an unfrequented spot, deep in a valley called Ramale. There the lay brothers and the natives prepared a new camp. Tunnels were dug under the mountains, some native huts were erected, facilities for camp life were created, a water supply guaranteed. As the work progressed, we moved into the new camp where we spent a comparatively quiet fifteen months.

Over one hundred natives, who remained faithful to the Mission under all adversities, did most of the hard work. Over six hundred yards of tunnel were dug under the mountain for protection in case of bombing; huts were built, and chapels where we could celebrate Holy Mass. Under the towering giants of the Ramale forest we built a camp hidden from view of the planes, and where we lived in expectation.

Religious Services

The Japanese Authorities did not interfere in anyway with our religious practices. Masses were said every morning; being too many priests for the convenient number of altars and in consideration of the limited amount of altar wine, we took turns. Each one of us managed to celebrate about ten Masses each month. The natives that remained with us in the camp were allowed to follow their religious practices.

Always Hungry

Food was a problem for many months in the Ramale camp.

Under such abnormal conditions it was difficult to obtain what was necessary to feed 160 prisoners and as many half-castes and natives. Our farm and gardens would have been sufficient had the Japanese left us free to reap all that was produced, but most of our vegetables and fruits were stolen. Occasionally they would give us a bit of rice in exchange, but the exchange was far from free and fair. The mission had to accept what the Japanese gave in exchange. Meat was not abundant. During the first few weeks the remaining heads of cattle and the few pigs that had escaped the bombing were sacrificed for food. Even the horses were not spared. We found horse meat so lean we resorted to coconut oil for fats. That proved only a fair substitute. We all became meat hungry. Hence no one was surprised when a priest was caught with the natives enjoying a piece of cat or dog meat. It tasted like turkey. I know from experience. Father William O'Connell and I have the envied distinction of having had a good meal of "Irish Snake Stew." We did not know at the time what the meat was, and though we would not like to repeat the experience, I have to admit that it was good—as good as any Christmas or Thanksgiving dinner. Hunger knows no law!

Staying Alive

Health in the camp was fairly satisfactory. An average of one person a month died of sickness. Those who died could have lived in normal times; but considering that we had no medicine and could not get any from the Japanese doctors, the mission doctor and the nursing sisters did some wonderful work in keeping the inmates in the camp healthy. We had little or no quinine, but we managed to escape any serious attacks of malaria. We had many light cases, a few more serious, but not a single mortal case.

Brave Native Sisters

Women seem to show their best qualities when attending

human suffering. The greatest example of heroism in our prison life came from the native sisters. These native women, whose grandparents were murderers and cannibals, aided by their religious life and mission training, taught a lesson to the world. At the risk of their own lives, they secretly brought food to the starving British prisoners captured at Singapore and imprisoned not far from the Catholic mission. In spite of threats and menaces from the Japanese, they buried the American airmen who were killed in crashes around the Gazelle Peninsula. These native sisters ministered to the sick and wounded natives in the various villages; they worked at their gardens, brought us all the food that they could spare and very often secretly obtained medicine for the missionaries. Non-Catholic whites who saw them at work have sung their praises. As our Catholic native men showed true heroism in the battle for freedom and Christianity, so the native sisters gave a lesson of true, heroic, self-sacrificing charity under the most adverse conditions.

Their virtue was put to the test by the immoral Japanese and their native supporters. The sisters proved equal to the test. They endured torture rather than prove unfaithful to their vows. We know the frightful torture they endured and we know also how faithful they remained. Even the Japanese wondered at such constancy! Native sisters of Vunapope, Oblates of Mary Immaculate, we owe you a debt of gratitude and we are proud of you. You have given an example of Christian virtue; even the pagans admired your faithfulness and constancy!

The Death of Sister M. Domitilla, S·M·S·M

Sister M. Domitilla, a Marist sister from Southern Bougainville in the North Solomons, had been sent to Vunapope before the outbreak of the Japanese war for medical treatment. We knew her to be very sick, and all of us Marists were surprised to find her alive when we arrived at the camp. Her health was satisfactory for most of the duration of the war; she stood the bombing and the starvation diet as well as anyone else. She did more work than any other; she never refused any work or any service asked of her; she was known for her willingness to be of service to anyone at any time. At the end of November 1944, she felt sick, took to her bed and lasted only a few days. She was blessed with all the last sacraments and was assisted by her sisters in religion and the five Marist priests in the camp. Her funeral was performed by Father Poncelet, S.M. In losing Sister M. Domitilla, we lost one of our most energetic sisters, admired by everyone for her unselfish devotion to duty and lack of all self-consideration.

A Long Waiting

Waiting in prison is a long and tedious thing; waiting in a Japanese prison camp is beyond description. One needed a supernatural outlook and a good sense of humor not to go mad. To make matters worse the Japanese seemed to take a special delight in annoying us; mental torture is a specialty of the Japanese military police. Those in charge of our camp were experts at that torture. Bishop Scharmach and Father Muller, the mission manager, were daily annoyed by the Japanese. The treatment meted out to our faithful natives was beyond description.

January 6, 1945 Official News

*I*t was against all the principles of the Japanese Authorities to give us any news at any time. But on January 6, 1945, news was sent to us officially from headquarters. The news concerned only the situation of Europe. We were told of the encirclement of Germany, the landing in Normandy, and the advances of the Allied armies. We could read between the lines and suspected that the war in Europe would soon be at an end. Nothing was said of the military operations in the Pacific.

Some of us had secret ways of getting news, but the news was not always reliable. At least we were able to have some idea of the advances of the Americans in the Pacific.

Towards the middle of 1945, we managed to get a few pamphlets that had been dropped from Australian planes. The natives brought them into the camp secretly. Those in pidgin English we understood easily enough. The others that were dropped for the benefit of the Japanese proved to be very informative to us. Two Chinese lads in the camp were able to decipher them and we learned of the invasion of the Philippines and the taking of Okinawa. From this information we felt certain that Christmas 1945, would see us free from the Japanese prison camp. We would not have been far from the truth even if the atomic bombs had not been dropped on Hiroshima and Nagasaki.

Peace at Last

On August 17th, we realized by the conduct of our Japanese guards that something was up. We hardly hoped that the war was at an end; certainly we knew that Japan was getting the worse of some battles or had suffered a major setback. Restrictions for going to our gardens were lifted. We were no more molested by the military police and the natives reported queer happenings outside the camp; the Japanese seemed to be preparing for some evacuation. On Sunday morning, August 19th, Bishop Scharmach was called to the officer in charge and notified that Germany had surrendered some weeks previously. They drew a very gloomy picture of the situation over the whole of Europe. When at last the bishop asked them bluntly how the war stood in the Pacific they found themselves obligated to tell the truth, "The war is finished; of course we Japanese did not surrender as did Germany. But the war is finished and you are free now." That meant enough for us. We were jubilant; our misery had come to an end. We knew that we could expect the Australian troops in the near future.

September 6, 1945 The Aussies Arrive

*O*n the morning of the September 6th, a special formation of planes from the carrier *Glorious* flew over the Gazelle

Peninsula. That was the signal for us. The same day natives arrived at our hidden camp and told us that the ships were in the harbor at Rabaul, and that the Australian soldiers had landed. Our feelings of joy were increasing, and patiently we waited for their coming to liberate us from the hands of our tormenters.

Javanese prisoners captured in the Dutch East Indies and Indians captured at Singapore made many visits to our camp and expressed their joy at the Allied victory. There was music in the air. It seemed too good to be true.

September 13th, 1945 Aussies at Ramale Camp

On the morning of September 13th, four of us had gone to visit the Indian prison camp and were on our way back to Ramale. We heard a truck on the road; we stepped aside in order to let the defeated enemy go by, using words that should not be heard by pious ears. A few seconds later, we heard another sound of a motor coming up the road. We turned around with the intention of expressing the same terms, when we saw an apparition. Two Jeeps driven by Aussies in green uniforms! Shouts of joy! They had arrived! The first one to step out and greet us was Father Maurice Boland, C.S.S.R., chaplain of the Australian Forces. The others were all former residents of Rabaul who had known the missionaries before the war. With joy, shouts, and singing we led them down the steep incline to our prison camp. Any one arriving at the camp and not knowing the situation would have thought that we were all lunatics. Certainly we were mad with joy. After waiting for almost four years we were free again, in the hands of civilized white soldiers.

In spite of their limited space in the two jeeps, our liberators had brought a few cases of much desired goods. We were given all the news of the war in Europe, the Pacific and the atomic bomb. We fought for the magazines, the newspapers and the cigarettes. Yes, indeed the war was over. And the end of the war meant the end of suffering and danger from the hands of an unscrupulous enemy.

The Red Cross

The Australian Red Cross was not long in coming to our help. On September 16th, seven truckloads of food, medicine and clothing were delivered to our camp. It was like a Christmas in September. Again we were able to sit down to a white man's dinner. Our stomachs were not used to good food. We had to take it by degrees; some were not feeling too good after the first meals. And we received clothing. No more were we dressed like gypsies; the song, *Hallelujah, I'm a Bum,* had no more meaning in our camp. Letters were written home. The General allowed each of us to send a telegram to any part of the world. Our people, who had not heard of us for almost four years, received assurance that we were still alive.

Our First Bread

On the day the Red Cross arrived at our camp, Father William O'Connell and I made a trip to the town of Rabaul for the purpose of finding documents regarding the twelve civilians that had disappeared. Our search proved to be in vain. The documents had disappeared and the twelve prisoners were not to be traced. These twelve men were left in the Navy military prison on January 29, 1944, when Brother Joseph and I were transferred to Vunapope. Brother Joseph had been killed by an American bomb. We fear that the other twelve were beheaded by the Japanese, so the fact remains that I am the only one of fourteen civilian prisoners of the prison camp left to tell the tale.

As we arrived at the camp of the civilian administration we sighted freshly baked bread. Bread! After three years and eight months. Bread and butter! Did we eat! "Father O'Connell, you may say what you want but I've gone away with eight good slices!" And he answered: "Is that all? I've put away eleven myself!" That evening, after listening to the radio, the news and good music, we made another attack on the bread. This time, in the form of "Rabaul Hot Dogs"—bananas between slices of bread. And we were not sick!

Bishop Wade Arrives

As soon as we had made contact with the Australians, a telegram had been sent to Bishop Wade to notify him of his missionaries who were still alive. He received the telegram on September 20th, and two days later he arrived at the camp at Ramale. That was a happy reunion for him and for us. He gave us a hearty shake, looked around and then asked: "Where are the others?" Father Hennessey and the three Australian Brothers were not to be found. He still had hopes of finding them, but his hopes vanished on that day. The war had cost him twelve of his missionaries.

After due consideration it was decided that Father Lepping who had not suffered so much and who, having youth in his favor, had remained in good physical condition, should return with him to resume missionary work as soon as possible. All of the others were to go to Sydney for a rest. I pleaded to follow Father Lepping and return to my natives at Buka. But seeing that my nerves were not in the best of condition, the bishop insisted that I take a deserved rest in Australia.

Farewell, Ramale

On October 6th, we left Ramale for the Australian headquarters in Rabaul. There we were under the care of the Red Cross for two days. On October 8th, four priests, one brother, and seven sisters of the Marist Mission, together with eighteen of the Sacred Heart Mission, embarked on the SS *Ormiston* bound for Sydney. The ship was a very comfortable one, and though it was overcrowded with Australian troops returning to Sydney, we were given preference of first class cabins and all due consideration from the captain to the lowest ranking amiable crew member. The Aussies were overjoyed to travel with released P.O.Ws. It was a beautiful, calm trip. Many were the stories of the war related on that trip. And the Aussies supplied us with much appreciated cigarettes and sweets.

Torokina, Bougainville

From Rabaul, the ship went straight to Torokina, the base built by the Americans on Bougainville. In November 1943, the Yanks made a landing on the west coast of Bougainville and there built a town that astonished both whites and natives. Roads were built overnight, and from that base they had carried on their war to Rabaul and to the Carolines. Most of the American troops had been removed long before the surrender of Japan. The base had been left to the Australians and the aerodromes to the New Zealanders.

Meeting Our Missionaries

Arriving at Torokina, we four Marist priests were the only passengers allowed to go ashore. We went straight to Father Richard O'Sullivan, one of our Marist missionaries who had not been taken prisoner by the Japanese, and who had, in time, joined the Australian army as a chaplain and returned to Torokina. He had not only ministered to the spiritual needs of the soldiers, but had also done enormous good to the native population where he was so well known and liked. With Father O'Sullivan, we visited the headquarters of the Australian Army where we were given the kind of warm welcome that only Australians can give. God bless them!

The Buka Fathers

Father O'Sullivan had long stories to tell us of the escape of the sisters by American submarine. After listening to these stories we made a long visit to the Red Cross Hospital where Fathers Montauban, Servant and Caffiaux were being treated and well-cared for by kind and affable doctors. These three priests had left me on December 3, 1942, when they had been allowed to return from Sohano to the station of Gagan on Buka. At Gagan, they had heard varied rumors concerning us from the natives. They had given up hope for us. A few days before our arrival they had heard of the death of Brother Joseph and of my liberation together with the other priests who had been captured in Southern Bougainville and Shortland. It was a happy meeting; we could have talked for days rather than for two short hours. Soon it was time for us to return to our ship and continue our voyage to Australia. They remained in the hands of the medical department, and there they could reassure the natives that the missionaries would soon return to their work.

On to Sydney

From Torokina we headed for Milne Bay on the Eastern tip of New Guinea to take on water, and from there we came straight to Sydney. Freedom! No more Japanese! No more prison life! No more war! On October 18th we passed through the heads of Sydney Harbor in the early hours of the morning and before 10:00 A.M. we were received warmly by Father Bergeron, our Provincial Superior, and by many other confreres of the North Solomons. We were united again after more than three years of prison life. There was no end to the tales that each one had to relate. We had escaped death, but some of our valiant missionaries were no more of this world.

Resting

At the present time we are resting at Villa Maria, the house that has sheltered hundreds of Marist missionaries for more than a century. Here we are getting the medical and dental treatment that was long needed. Most of us are now in good health and anxious to return to our Mission Stations. Arrangements are now being made for our return. Many friends advise us to take a trip home to our people and country. That indeed would do a lot of good to our bodies and to our minds, even to our souls. That trip, however, will have to be delayed because it would be unfair to our Catholic natives of Bougainville and Buka. Our Catholics have suffered very much during the three and half years of pagan Japanese occupation. They have remained faithful to their religion and their priests as far as the conditions permitted. They are clamoring for their former missionaries and for new ones to replace those who have disappeared. We cannot be deaf to their appeals; it is imperative that we return at once to continue the work of the mission.

A Destroyed Mission

We will return soon to our islands; arrangements are now being made between the Church authorities and the government. We expect to be back in Buka and Bougainville in a month or two. But it is to a destroyed mission that we shall return; all of our twenty-two stations have suffered the destruction of the war. What churches, convents, houses, schools and medical centers the Japanese did not tear down, our American planes blew to atoms. There is not left a board upon a board. Our flourishing schools, the medical welfare centers, the "parishes," and the Catholic centers have all been ruined. When we return we shall find a good part of our Catholics but not the familiar landmarks that we loved so well. The churches that housed thousands of worshiping Catholics on Sundays are no more. Our plantations, our gardens, our farms with goats, pigs, fowls, ducks, etc., have all been sacrificed to the passage of Mars.

The natives have suffered a lot. Many have died of sickness, others were forced to labor for the Japanese army and lost their lives in bombing raids. Starvation reigned for months and months in some sections of Bougainville and Buka, and hundreds of children succumbed to malnutrition.

Our Catholic natives have been persecuted and have suffered but they have not been vanquished. They have kept the Faith. There have been irregularities and moral mistakes made, but they have not abandoned their faith; they have remained faithful to the Church of their Baptism. As our Allied armies occupied Bougainville and Buka, our Catholic G.I.'s and the Aussies were astonished to see such a fervent devotion existing among the Catholic natives. Our Catholic chaplains with the American and Australian forces were full of praise for the strong faith of the natives, for their simple yet fervent devotion to Christ. As soon as the chaplains arrived and pitched their chapel-tents, the natives flocked to them by the hundreds and thousands to make their confessions, assist at Mass and receive Holy Communion. Daily they were seen visiting the Blessed Sacrament and they brought their babies to be baptized. At Mass the natives were side by side with the servicemen; natives and whites knelt together at the Communion rail. If our natives were surprised to see so many Catholics in the armed forces, the soldiers were not less astounded to see such a flourishing Catholic faith in the North Solomon Islands.

Our Heroes

The greatest loss of our Mission is not to be counted in the houses destroyed or any other material destruction. Our greatest losses are in the missionaries that have been lost. We have suffered little in comparison to the **Missions of the Divine Word** in New Guinea and the **Sacred Heart Missionaries** on New Britain, yet our losses are considerable and will be felt in our mission for many long years. Two sisters, three lay-brothers, three Australian Marist Teaching Brothers, and four priests have been taken from our ranks.

Those Who Died As a Result of the War in the North Solomons: Our Roll of Honor

Rev. James Hennessey	Captured in Buka, March, 1942. Went down on the *Montevideo Maru* July 1942.
Rev. John Conley, S.M.	Imprisoned in 1943, killed, believed beheaded.
Rev. Florent Wache, S.M.	Died of wounds, January 1944
Rev. William Weer, S.M.	Killed in 1945.
Brothers John, Donatus, and Augustin, Australian Marist Teaching Brothers	Captured August 15, 1942, missing, presumed dead.
Brother Joseph Redman, S.M.	Killed by bombs, Feb. 11, 1944
Brother Karl, S.M., Germany	Died of wounds, May 27, 1944
Sister M. Domitilla, S.M.S.M.	Died of sickness, Nov. 29, 1944
Sister M. Camille, S.M.S.M.	Died of sickness and starvation October 14, 1944

May You Rest in Peace!

Rev. Joseph Lamarre, S.M.,
Catholic Mission,
Hanahan, Buka Passage,
Territory of New Guinea.

Epilogue and Biographies

*E*xcept for Father James Hennessey who died on the *Montevideo Maru* while being shipped to a Japanese prison camp, Bishop Thomas Wade, Fathers Albert Lebel and Joseph Lamarre, as well as Sisters Isabelle, Irene, Hedda and Celestine all returned to missionary work on Buka or Bougainville after the war. Inspired by these first missionaries, between 1946 and 1991, an additional 36 Sisters of St. Joseph have ministered in Papua New Guinea. They formed long and strong bonds with the people of Buka, Bougainville and Nissan islands.

In 1975, nearly eight decades after the Marist priests, brothers and sisters began their work as missionaries in the North Solomon Islands, the nation of Papua New Guinea was formed and is now governed by the people native to those islands.

Developments in the economy, transportation, communication, education and healthcare have impacted the lives of the people of Papua New Guinea. Changes in the Catholic Church after the Second Vatican Council in the early 1960's have resulted in a far less competitive spirit with other Christian faiths as well as a deeper inclusion of the laity in local Church governance and ministry. Native languages, rituals and music have increasingly influenced the practice of faith and worship.

The key figures of this memoir included the following:

Sister Mary Irene

(Born Loretta Rose Alton, 1905-1999)

Sister Irene Alton was born in Huntington Beach, California. As a child, she attended St. Joseph School in Santa Ana and began training to become a Catholic nun when she was 15 years old. Her family owned land in southeast Santa Ana where they ran a dairy. When St. Joseph School opened in 1915, her father bought five bicycles so that the Alton children could bike to and from school each day—a round trip of ten miles. Sister Irene received her nurse's training in Eureka with additional coursework in Oakland and San Francisco. She was 35 years old and the administrator of Trinity Hospital in Arcata, when she volunteered to serve as a missionary nurse in the North Solomon Islands.

On Buka Island, Sister Irene was grateful for her early biking skills because she used them nearly every day. Shortly after her arrival in the Solomon Islands, Sister Irene was afflicted with a severe case of cerebral malaria, a complex form of the disease with a very high mortality rate. A doctor from Australia delivered a badly needed medication by ship and she gradually recovered. Sister Irene served in Buka and Nissan Islands for twenty-three years before she returned to Orange.

Sister Mary Hedda Jaeger

(Born Anna Marie Jaeger, 1901-1973)

Sister Hedda was born in Minot, North Dakota. She received her education at the nursing school attached to the Mayo Clinic. Before World War II, Sister Hedda served in the U.S. Navy Nurse Corps in San Diego. In her late twenties, she re-located to Los Angeles where she continued to work as a nurse and became a convert to Catholicism. She began training to become a Sister of St. Joseph in 1934, and professed her final vows on Buka Island in 1942. Before volunteering for missionary work at the age of 39, Sister Hedda worked at St. Luke's Hospital in Pasadena. After World War II, she returned to Buka and served as a nurse there for eight more years. She died in Orange in 1973 at the age of seventy-two. Sister Hedda served as the chief diarist of these writings and at times hid them behind the statue of St. Joseph to keep them safe from the Japanese.

Sr. M. Celestine

(Born Marie Belanger, 1899-1987)

Born in Ontario, Canada, Sister Celestine moved to Lowell, Massachusetts in her early twenties. For 13 years she worked as a librarian and later was revered as a teacher for boys who were "hard to handle." After joining the Sisters of St. Joseph of Orange in 1930, Sister Celestine taught at Notre Dame de Victoires and Jeanne d'Arc schools in San Francisco. In 1940, when she was 43, she volunteered to be part of the first missionary venture to the South Pacific. After World War II, Sister Celestine taught at St. Mary's Chinese Mission School in San Francisco. She returned to Buka Island in 1950 where she served as a teacher until 1969. She was known for her generous and adventurous spirit and as one who could be most resourceful in almost any crisis.

Sister M. Isabelle Aubin

(Born Beatrice Aubin, 1891-1973)

Sister Isabelle was born in Lowell, Massachusetts in 1891. She began her training to become a Catholic nun in LaGrange, Illinois in 1911 and in 1912 she traveled to Eureka, California as one of the founding members of the Sisters of St. Joseph of Orange. An experienced teacher and a talented musician, Sister Isabelle was the first of the sisters to volunteer as a missionary to the North Solomon Islands. At the age of 50, she was the oldest and most experienced of the new group of missionaries, and for that reason she was appointed as the superior in charge of this endeavor. After the war, in 1946, Sister Isabelle was the first of the sisters to return to Buka where she taught for ten more years.

Sister M Francis Lirette

(Born Mary Lirette, 1887-1969)

Sister Francis (later Mother Francis) Lirette was born in

Quebec, Canada and raised in Lowell, Massachusetts. She entered the Sisters of St. Joseph of LaGrange, Illinois in 1907 and joined Mother Bernard Gosselin in the founding of the Sisters of St. Joseph in Eureka, California in 1912. Sister Francis was elected General Superior of the Sisters of St. Joseph of Orange, and served two terms in this role between 1927-1939. Enthusiastic about missionary work, she accompanied the first four missionary sisters to Buka and returned to California once they were settled. She often acted as their advocate from afar when they were in need. After World War II, Mother Francis founded another branch of the Sisters of St. Joseph in Sydney, Australia. She died in Orange at the age of 82.

Father Albert Lebel (1903-1975)

Father Lebel was born in Maine. After studies in Washington, DC and in Germany, he was ordained a Marist priest at the age of 26. The next year he was sent to Oceania where he served in both the North and South Solomon Islands. He was chiefly responsible for communicating with the U.S. Navy and engineering the rescue of the sisters by submarine on January 1, 1943. Father Lebel served as a missionary in the North Solomon Islands for 45 years. He died while celebrating Mass in 1975.

Bishop Thomas Wade (1893-1969)

Bishop Thomas Wade was born in Providence, Rhode Island, and was ordained as a Marist priest in 1922. Shortly before his ordination, he was assigned to Bougainville in the South Pacific. In 1930, he was ordained as the first bishop for the Vicariate of the North Solomon Islands. After a brief internment by the Japanese during World War II, he escaped and hid with his people in the hills until he was rescued. In 1946, he was named as Military Delegate for the U.S Armed Forces in the South Pacific. While serving in that position, he organized the reconstruction of the mission stations on both Bougainville and Buka, most of which had been completely destroyed or were badly damaged during the war.

Father Joseph Lamarre (1909-1979)

Father Lamarre was a young pastor at the mission station of Hanahan when the first Sisters of St. Joseph served on Buka. During World War II, he was taken prisoner by the Japanese and spent time imprisoned on the small island of Sohano as well as at the prison camps at Rabaul and Ramale. He was a missionary in the North Solomons for 45 years, spending most of his time on Buka. Father Lamarre was the pastor at Hanahan for 18 years. Out of great respect, thousands of people attended his funeral Mass and burial at Hanahan in 1979.

Father James Hennessey (1905-1942)

Father James Hennessey was a diocesan priest from Boston, Massachusetts who was ordained in Rome. In his thirties he felt a call to do missionary work and pleaded with the Archbishop of Boston, Cardinal William O'Connell, three times before the Cardinal released him to serve in the Solomon Islands for a five-year term. He was stationed on the islands of both Bougainville and Buka. Father Hennessey was particularly skilled at training local natives to serve as catechists to outlying villages. He was very much loved by the native people as well as by the Marist priests who served with him. When his five-year term came to an end in 1940, Bishop Wade persuaded him to stay an additional year. Within 90 days after Pearl Harbor, the Japanese landed several war ships near Father Hennessey's mission station at Lemanmanu. The Japanese interrogated him, judged him to be an American spy, and took him aboard their ship as a prisoner. He was imprisoned at Rabaul, and in 1942, he was transported on the *Montevideo Maru* with about 900 other prisoners for internment in Japan. The *Montevideo Maru* was torpedoed by the U.S. Navy off the coast of the Philippines in 1942. Everyone aboard the ship was killed.

Glossary

- **Act of Contrition** – a prayer that expresses sorrow for failing to love God and neighbor.
- **Altar** – a table at which Mass is celebrated.
- **Assumption** – a Catholic belief that at her death, Mary, the mother of Jesus, was assumed into heaven.
- **Betel nut** – a caffeine-like drug from the areca palm used to stave off hunger; can also cause stimulating highs.
- **Bishop** – the spiritual and administrative leader of a Catholic diocese.
- **Blessed Sacrament** – according to Catholic belief, the true presence of Jesus under the appearance of bread (a consecrated host).
- **Bullamacow** – another word for cow.
- **Carondelet** – one of several religious congregations under the patronage of St. Joseph that has roots in 17th Century France.
- **Canonization** – recognition by the Catholic Church that a deceased person is worthy of being named a "saint."
- **Cascara** – bark from this type of tree is used for a cathartic.
- **Catechist** – one who helps others to learn about the Catholic faith
- **Cathedral** – The major church of a Catholic diocese or defined geographical area.
- **Centipede** – a 100 legged insect with a poisonous venom.

- **Chapel** – a dedicated space for private or community prayer—usually attached to a convent, school or large hospital.
- **Chaplain** – a priest who is on a special assignment outside of a parish; may also refer to a Catholic sister who serves in a hospital, a jail or prison.
- **Ciborium** – a container designed to hold consecrated hosts.
- **Cincture** – a rope or cord that circles the waist of a religious habit.
- **Confession (Sacrament of Reconciliation)** – a Catholic sacrament through which one confesses one's sins to God and before a priest, noting one's specific failures to live up to the law of love for God and neighbor, asking for God's forgiveness and pledging to do better.
- **Confirmation** – a sacrament of the Catholic Church in which the power of the Holy Spirit is bestowed in order to strengthen one's faith.
- **Cornette** – the part of a nun's habit that covers the neck and head and to which a veil is attached.
- **Crucifix** – a cross on which the crucified body of Christ is affixed.
- **Discalced Carmelite** – a contemplative Carmelite nun who wears sandals rather than shoes.
- **Divine Providence** – the protective care of God.
- **Epiphany** – the feast of the three Kings, twelve days after Christmas.
- **Extreme Unction** – Latin words for last anointing, a sacrament of the Catholic Church that is now called Anointing of the Sick.
- **Flying Fortresses** – American four-engine heavy

bombers.

- **Grail Ladies** – an association of non-vowed lay women who make a permanent commitment to a particular form of life in the Church. Founded in the Netherlands in 1921 by a Jesuit, they now number 1,000 in 24 countries.
- **Guimpe** – a part of a nun's habit – for Sisters of St. Joseph, the guimpe was a circular flexiline front piece that extended from the neck to cover the chest.
- **Habits** – clothing worn by members of some religious congregations.
- **Half-caste** – a person of mixed racial descent.
- **Head-dress** – part of a religious habit that covers the head and neck.
- **Him/He** – a pronoun, when capitalized can refer to God.
- **Holy Ghost** (Holy Spirit) – the Christian tradition or belief in the third person of the Holy Trinity, the first person being God the Father, the second person being Jesus Christ, the Son of God.
- **Holy Hour** – an hour of prayer.
- **Holy Week** – sacred holy days of the Catholic Church that begin on Palm Sunday and include Holy Thursday, Good Friday, Holy Saturday and Easter Sunday.
- **Host** – bread that has been consecrated by the priest during Mass.
- **Job** – Job 2:8, the lowest moment in the life of the prophet Job.
- **Kieta** – a mission station and the headquarters for the Society of Mary (Marists) in the North

Solomon Islands.

- **Lactogen** – a powdered baby formula.
- **Leprol** – a medication used to treat leprosy.
- **Magnificat** – a canticle or song honoring the Virgin Mary.
- **Mass** (Holy Mass) – the central act of worship in the Catholic Church during which worshippers receive the Holy Eucharist (the body and blood of Christ in the form of bread and wine).
- **Me no savvy** – a response in pidgin English the sisters used when they did not understand the language.
- **Missionary** – one who is dedicated to spread the message of Jesus by word and action throughout the world.
- **Mother General (Superior General)** – the appointed or elected superior of a congregation of Catholic nuns.
- **N.A.B.** – see Salvarsan
- **Nissan** – an atoll 90 miles north west of Buka, historically known as Green Island.
- **Novices** – those who are beginning training in religious life.
- **Novitiate** – a time set aside for training in religious life.
- **Ordo** – a calendar of feast days and readings in the Catholic Church.
- **Pandanus leaves** – waterproof leaves used for roofing and basketry.
- **Parish** – a geographical part of a diocese, a local Catholic community.
- **Paw-paws** – papayas.

- **Perpetual Adoration** – a Catholic devotion in which a sacred host is placed in a visible on the altar and made available for prayer and praise throughout the night and day.
- **Pidgin** – a language formed by one or more existing languages and used to communicate by people in a region without a common language.
- **Pororan** – an island off the west coast of Buka.
- **Prie-dieu** – an armless desk-like kneeling bench for use while praying.
- **Rectory** – a residence for priests and/or brothers who serve in a parish or mission station.
- **Refectory** – a dining area in a convent or monastery.
- **Rosary** – a devotion, in which one prays to Mary, the Mother of God, using beads to count the repetition of prayers.
- **Sac-sac** house – a dwelling made of dried palm fronds.
- **Sacred vessels** – a chalice or ciborium, used during Mass.
- **Sacristan** – one who cares for the priests' vestments and the sacred vessels used for Mass.
- **Salvarsan** – a medication to treat yaws, also known as neoarsephenamine (N.A. B.).
- **Sanctuary lamp** – a lit candle to remind worshippers that Jesus is present in the church as a consecrated host in the tabernacle.
- **Seminary** – an institution of higher education where men prepare for ordination to the priesthood.

- **Shoots** – a native term for injections.
- **Sing-sings** – native celebrations.
- **Sisters-in-Christ** – how Catholic women religious or nuns view one another throughout the world, even though they may belong to different religious congregations.
- **A "splinter of the cross"** – a trial or difficulty that one may suffer, viewed as a very small participation in the sufferings of Jesus on the cross.
- **Sodality** – a Catholic organization devoted to Mary, the mother of Jesus.
- **Sohano** – a small island at the entrance to Buka Passage, used in the past for Australian government headquarters.
- **Superior** – one who serves others as a leader in a religious order or congregation.
- **St. Teresa of Avila** – a Carmelite nun revered for her positive impact on religious life in the 17th Century. The Sisters in Orange celebrate her feast day because their constitutions were approved by the Vatican on this day in 1926.
- **Taro** – a root vegetable, rich in Vitamins A and C.
- **Tabernacle** – a locked container for the Blessed Sacrament. In the 1940's the tabernacle was always kept on the main altar.
- **Triduum** – three days of prayer and contemplation in preparation for a major feast day such as Christmas or Easter.
- **Very Reverend** – a respectful title for a priest.
- **Vestments** – garb worn by a priest as he

administers sacraments and presides at Mass or benediction.

- **Vicariate** – a geographical area of the Catholic Church, not as populous as a diocese, often in mission territory.
- **Vows** – sacred promises made to God.
- **War** – in this journal, refers to the war in Europe that started in 1939.
- **Way of the Cross (Stations of the Cross)** – a Catholic devotion, a walking meditation in which one reflects on the sufferings of Jesus through his arrest, the carrying of the cross, his crucifixion, and burial.
- **White ants** – termites.
- **Zeroes** – Japanese long-range fighter aircraft.

End Notes

[1] **The Sisters of St. Joseph of Orange** is a branch of the Sisters of St. Joseph that was originally founded in 1650 in LePuy, France by Jean Pierre Medaille, S.J., a Jesuit priest, and a group of faith-filled women. From their first days, the sisters were instructed to pay attention to the needs of their neighbors without distinction for race, religion, financial means, education or status in life. Their works of mercy include healthcare, education and a wide variety of social services. They pay particular attention to the needs of those who are impoverished or marginalized. Over many decades, these women have expanded their work first in France, and then to the United States, Canada, India, Italy, South America, Mexico, El Salvador, Australia and Papua New Guinea. As bishops in various dioceses requested the presence and help of Sisters of St. Joseph, many of these groups became independent congregations under the Vatican. *The Sisters of St. Joseph of Orange* were formed in Eureka, California in 1912. Because of close relationships with the Marist priests, they became interested in the missions in the Solomon Islands. In 1939, they made a decision to send some sisters to the missions in the North Solomon Islands in gratitude for God's favors in the first decades of the congregation. Twenty-nine sisters volunteered to go; four were chosen. These four left for the island of Buka in September 1940. The Sisters of St. Joseph of Orange served for fifty-one years on the islands of Buka, Bougainville, and Nissan. When civil war broke out in the northern province of Bougainville in the early 1990's and the missionaries were no longer granted access in or out of this territory, they were compelled to leave.

[2] **Marists Priests (Society of Mary)**, is a congregation of Catholic priests and brothers that was formed in France in the early 19th century and grew rapidly in Europe and the United States. As a congregation devoted to spreading the

gospel throughout the world, the Marists were assigned by the Pope to evangelize mainly Western Oceania—many islands geographically remote and difficult to access. Their earliest efforts to bring Christianity to the people of these remote islands were met with great success and occasional hostility on the part of some of the indigenous people, resulting in tragedy and death. Some of the early Marists in the Pacific were martyred, including a bishop, and others died of debilitating tropical diseases such as cerebral malaria and black water fever. It was difficult in the earlier part of the 19th century to be fully prepared for the hardships of this unknown tropical environment and at times these men lived heroically, even finding it difficult to provide for their own food, safety, and well-being. For various reasons, in the middle of the 19th century, evangelizing efforts were slowed down by the Marist authorities in France. Later in the century, better prepared for the hardships they would face, there was a significant renewed wave of mission which led to an increased number of permanent mission stations throughout the islands. In addition to teaching and preaching Christianity, these valiant missionaries collaborate with both Catholic nuns and lay workers to strengthen education and healthcare in outlying areas. Today, Marist priests and brothers can be found throughout the world with a significant presence in Oceania.

[3]*Marist Sisters (The Missionary Sisters of the Society of Mary, SMSM)* is a world-wide religious congregation that began with 11 French women who traveled to the South Pacific Islands between 1845 and 1860 in response to a call to educate women in these remote areas. Following the vision and spirit of their pioneers, these sisters have always lived close to the people, teaching and nursing. Over the years, the SMSM Congregation has expanded to serve not only in Papua New Guinea, but also in many Pacific countries and in Senegal, Burundi, Rwanda, Madagascar, Tanzania, Jamaica, Peru, Columbia, the Philippines, Bangladesh, Australia, New Zealand and the USA, as well as

countries in Europe. From the beginning, indigenous women from Oceania and Melanesia joined the sisters, and more recently, women from Asia, Africa, South America and the Caribbean have become SMSM. The SMSM Sisters in the South Pacific suffered greatly during World War II. While a number of the SMSM sisters were evacuated, others were imprisoned, two were slain, four died. Two were able to remain in the Solomons throughout the war. Ten SMSM sisters escaped with the Sisters of St. Joseph on the USS *Nautilus* in January 1943.

[4] *St. Therese of Lisieux* was a French Roman Catholic Discalced Carmelite who was born in 1873 and died of tuberculosis at the age of 24 in 1897. In the last year of her life she wrote an autobiography, *Story of a Soul*, in which she called her spirituality "the little way." By that, she meant doing small things and graciously putting up with daily annoyances and inconveniences while asking God to bless missionaries in their work to bring the knowledge of God to those who did not know Him. She was canonized a saint in 1925. Because she was young when she died, she was immensely popular and an inspiration to many young people in the first half of the 20th Century. Although she never spent time as a missionary, because of her constant prayer for them, she was a favorite saint of missionaries and her statue was seen by the sisters in nearly every church and chapel throughout Oceania. Along with St. Francis Xavier, she was named as a Patron of Missionaries by the Catholic Church. Images of her often show her carrying roses and she is sometimes referred to as "The Little Flower."

[5] *Charles Emmet McHardy, SM* was ordained a Marist priest in New Zealand in 1930 at the age of 25. He enthusiastically embraced his first assignment to Tunuru on the island of Bougainville. There, he used his young energy to build relationships with natives in hidden and outlying villages. After his death from tuberculosis in 1933, his family

compiled his letters into a book called *Blazing the Trail*. The four new missionary sisters read this book on board ship as they traveled to Buka in 1940. When they landed in New Zealand, they met Father McHardy's uncle. When they stopped in Bougainville in December 1940, on their way to Buka, they visited Father McHardy's former mission station at Tunuru.

[6] *Vows* are sacred promises made to God. In the Catholic Church, the most common vows made by nuns are poverty, chastity and obedience. For someone new in religious life, these vows are made once a year and renewed annually. When one takes perpetual vows, an individual promises to keep these vows for the rest of her life. Sister Hedda Jaeger made her perpetual vows on Buka Island several weeks after the bombing of Pearl Harbor.

[7] *Three Wishes.* At each port along their way, when the new missionary sisters disembark, they followed a tradition of putting three wishes (or petitions) before God when they visited a new church or cathedral. They most likely asked for the graces of courage and strength for whatever they might face on their journey. It is likely that they also prayed for the native people that they would be soon meeting.

[8] *Yaws* is a tropical disease that permanently disfigures the bones of the legs and arms, also causing deformities of the face and nose. Historically, yaws has been endemic to countries 20 degrees north or south of the equator. In the 1950's, populations in 88 countries were afflicted with yaws. The World Health Organization has a goal of eradicating yaws by 2020. Currently, it is still prevalent in 13 countries, including Papua New Guinea, and the Solomon Islands. It is typically spread by children to each other when there is a lack of water, poor hygiene and little access to healthcare. It is considered a disease of poverty. In the 1940's, Sister Irene

Alton wrote: "The external yaws (sores) look terrible, covering children from head to feet. One morning we counted 100 intravenous injections given for yaws and ulcers. We trained young men to assist us and to keep a saucepan of syringes in boiling water on a kerosene stove. The only water supply for use in the hospital and convent was rain water collected from roofs of buildings into metal water tanks."

[9] *Mission List*. In this journal, the term *mission list* refers to the assignment of Catholic nuns to particular works of mercy done by a religious congregation in its varying geographies. These assignments were made by the Superior General and accepted by each sister in the spirit of her vow of obedience. Assignments could be changed annually, and most typically, these were made without the consultation of the individual who was being assigned. Before being assigned as a missionary to Papua New Guinea, the sisters first had to "volunteer" for such service. After World War II, when more sisters volunteered to serve on Buka, a regional superior was appointed from among the missionary sisters. This regional superior, in consultation with her assistant and the Superior General of the congregation, made decisions about the placement of the sisters to the various mission stations. Sisters assigned to the islands of Buka, Nissan or Bougainville, generally served there for five years before returning to the United States for rest, renewal and a visit with one's family.

[10] *The Cargo Cult* is a decades old Melanesian movement that had a stronghold on the island of Buka. For some natives, it expressed the social unrest related to the perceived affluence of Europeans, including a distrust of missionaries from the outside, who appear to have access to an on-going supply of material goods. This belief holds that white people deliberately prevent the docking of ships with cargo that is meant for the natives, including guns. This inequity is viewed as a European dominance that continues to hold the black people in subjugation and poverty.

[11] ***Marist Martyrs on Guadalcanal*** Two Marist priests and two Marist sisters were killed by the Japanese at the Ruavatu mission station on Guadalcanal on March 9, 1942. They were thrown into a shallow grave. When news of their death spread, Bishop Wade, as well as all the priests, brothers and sisters on Bougainville, knew that the Japanese would spare no effort to hunt them down as well and either kill them or imprison them. When Sister Celestine learned of this killing, she wrote in her notes: *"The Japanese know where we are, it's only a matter of time until they find us."*

[12] ***The USS Nautilus (submarine)*** was one of several vessels built after World War I that was influenced by the German U boats. It was launched in 1935 out of Mare Island in California. The long-term strategy of the United States Navy at that time was to develop submarines that focused more on endurance and efficiency than speed. The role of the *Nautilus* was to navigate through dangerous waters, to identify and drop mines, to torpedo enemy ships and to transport troops if necessary. Japan's strong military strategy in the water as well as in the air, made the waters of the South Pacific among the most dangerous areas to navigate. When the *Nautilus* was called to action at Teop Harbor on Bougainville on January 1, 1943, it had a crew of 90 under the command of Lieutenant Commander William H. Brockman, Jr. In this high-risk venture, the *Nautilus* picked up 29 passengers off the coast of Bougainville—26 adults and 3 children. Sixteen of the passengers were Catholic missionaries—4 Sisters of St. Joseph of Orange, 10 Marist Sisters (Missionary Sisters of the Society of Mary) and 2 elderly Marist priests. After serving in other battles in the South Pacific, the *Nautilus* was decommissioned and scrapped in May 1945. Ten years later the first nuclear powered submarine was launched, also called the *Nautilus*. This nuclear powered submarine was decommissioned from the Naval Vessel Registry in 1980.

[13]*Returning to San Francisco (additional ships)* While the rescue of the refugees from Bougainville by the USS *Nautilus*, was just short of a miracle, they were not yet safe. The waters that surrounded the Solomon Islands were thick with Japanese submarines and warships. After three days on the *Nautilus,* the 29 refugees were quickly transferred to a sub-chaser patrol craft, *PC 486.* Their destination was Guadalcanal, an island that had been nearly cleared of Japanese troops after an intense and deadly battle. At Guadalcanal, they boarded the USS *Hunter Liggett,* a transport ship that carried men into battle and brought the deceased, the wounded, and the survivors out of enemy territory. With the sisters on board, the USS *Hunter Liggett* spent several days zigzagging through the Coral Sea in an effort to lose a Japanese sub chaser that was on its tail. When the USS *Hunter Liggett* finally arrived in Auckland, New Zealand on January 12, 1943, the Marist Sisters moved on to their convent in Wellington, while the four Sisters of St. Joseph graciously accepted the hospitality of the Religious of the Sacred Heart at their convent. Arriving nearly in rags, the sisters spent the week in Auckland making new habits to wear on the final lap of their journey. On January 19, 1943, the four sisters boarded the USS *West Point* with a multitude of Navy personnel. Once out of the most dangerous waters of the Pacific, their trip back to San Francisco was filled with gratitude and joy.

[14]*Head Watch on the Nautilus.* Flushing a toilet on a submerged pre-World War II submarine was a significant challenge. There were 19 separate steps that needed to be taken and those steps had to be made in sequence. All efforts to teach Sister Isabelle these steps so that she could teach the others failed. Since the sisters were on the submarine less than 72 hours before they were moved onto a surface patrol craft, a sub-mariner was assigned "head watch," his principal duty being to flush the toilet for the nuns.

Bibliography

1. Lord, Walter. 1977. *Lonely Vigil: Coastwatchers of the Solomons*. New York: The Viking Press. Lord tells the story of the coast watchers who hid in the jungle, often under the noses of the Japanese forces, and gave advance warnings when Japanese ships and planes came to attack Allied bases. Chapter 8 (pp. 125-153) describes the rescue of civilians, including American and other missionaries, by the submarine *Nautilus* from Bougainville Island on New Year's December 31, 1942.

2. Feuer, A. B. (ed). 1992. *Coast Watching in the Solomon Islands: The Bougainville Reports, December 1941-July 1943* (1st ed). New York: Praeger Publishers.

3. McGee, William L. 2002. *Amphibious Operations in the South Pacific in WWII: Vol II: The Solomons Campaigns, 1942-1943: From Guadalcanal to Bougainville, Pacific War Turning Point.* Santa Barbara, CA: BMC Publications.

4. Gailey, Henry A. 2003. *Bougainville, 1943-1945: The Forgotten Campaign.* Lexington, KY: University Press of Kentucky.

5. Prados, John. 2012. *Islands of Destiny: The Solomons Campaign and the Eclipse of the Rising Sun.* New York: Penguin/New American Library.

6. Greilor, Alois, (ed.) 2009. *Catholic Beginnings in Oceania: Marist Missionary Perspectives.* Hindmarsh, Adelaide, AU: Australasian Theological Forum Ltd. (AFT Press).

7. Sweeney, Mary Therese, and McNerney, Eileen. 2012. *A Bold and Humble Love: Journey of Grace*, Orange,

CA: Sister of St. Joseph of Orange.

8. Agawa, Hiroyuki. 1979. *The Reluctant Admiral.* Tokyo: Kodansha International. This book describes the life of Yamamoto Isoruku, "The architect of Pearl Harbor." After the Japanese defeat at Guadalcanal, he was sent to Rabaul to take charge of action in the South Pacific. On April 18, 1943, while on an inspection trip to Bougainville, his plane was intercepted by American airmen and shot down. (See pp.344-368).

9. Dull, Paul S. 1978. *A Battle History of the Imperial Japanese Navy (1941-1945).* Annapolis: Naval Institute Press. The actions of the Japanese Navy during WWII in the South Pacific are described, based on Japanese records. New Guinea was invaded in March, 1942, and soon after, Japan occupied Buka, Bougainville, and the Shortland Islands. Naval and airbases in the region threatened Australia and blocked Allied forces from the Philippines. (See pp. 106-107).

10. Blair, Clay Jr.1975. *Silent Victory: The U.S. Submarine War against Japan.* Annapolis: Naval Institute Press. This detailed history of the submarine service chronicles details of their successes and failures. Lt. Commander William H. Brockman Jr. of the *Nautilus* had a distinguished service record. He participated in the Battle of Midway (pp. 236-244), the invasion of Attu, and patrols in the South Seas and near Japan. It is also noted that Brockman, "while en route on a mission to evacuate 29 Catholic missionaries from Bougainville, managed to sink a small freighter, damaged a tanker and a freighter, and fired two torpedoes at an attacking Japanese destroyer" (p. 334).

11. Breuer, William 1987. *Devil Boats: The PT War Against Japan.* Novato, CA: Presidio Press. PT boats

were an important weapon in the Solomon Islands, with the objective to stop Japanese reinforcement and supply of their bases. Former President John F. Kennedy was noted for his heroic efforts to save his crew when their boat was rammed by a Japanese destroyer at night (pp. 108-114). PT boats had several bases in the Solomon Islands as the war progressed and moved north as MacArthur's forces leap-frogged towards the Philippines.

12. Waiko, John Dademo, *A Short History of Papua New Guinea*, 1993. Melbourne: Oxford University Press.

13. Garrett, John, *Where Nets Were Cast: Christianity in Oceania Since World War II, 1997.* Institute of Pacific Studies, University of the South Pacific in association with the World Council of Churches, Suva and Geneva.

14. Garrett, John, *Footsteps in the Sea: Christianity in Oceania to World War II, 1992.* Institute of Pacific Studies, University of the South Pacific in association with the World Council of Churches, Suva and Geneva.

15. Laracy, Hugh, *Marists and Melanesians: A History of Catholic Missions in the Solomon Islands*, 1976. Honolulu: The University Press of Hawaii.

16. Feldt, Eric A., R.A.N., *The Coast Watchers: How a Few Daring Men Trapped on Japanese Islands Warned the Allies of Enemy Attacks*, 1979, Garden City, New York: Nelson Doubleday, Inc.

17. Aerts, Theo, Editor, *The Martyrs of Papua New Guinea: 333 Lives Lost During World War II*, 2009, Port Moresby, Papua New Guinea: University of Papua New Guinea Press.

Acknowledgements and Credits

This book has been published with the fidelity, imagination, guidance and support of the following:

- Sister Hedda Jaeger, CSJ, who faithfully kept and protected this journal in good times and bad, and to her sister companions, who between 1940-1943 augmented her first person accounts with their own.
- Father Joseph Lamarre, SM, who wrote the story of his capture, imprisonment and release as a prisoner of war: 1942-1945.
- Leo Catalan and Sisters Adele Marie Korhummel, CSJ, and Patricia Haley, CSJ, staff of the archives of the Sisters of St. Joseph of Orange, for providing documents, photos, and technological assistance.
- The Marist Provincial Council for granting access to their materials and for permission to publish *War Comes to Buka*, with special appreciation to Susan Illis, the Director of the Archives of the Society of Mary, Atlanta, Georgia.
- Daisy Santacruz, who painstakingly transcribed the 1946 Remington version of this journal into current typeface.
- The Sisters at Regina Residence for their feedback through participation in the Jungle Journal Reading Club.
- Stephanie Coats, Sonja Longbotham, Kathy Loretz and Kathy Paradis for invaluable help in editing.
- Sister Louise Ann Micek, CSJ, whose eighteen years in Papua New Guinea made her a credible editor of history, relevance and culture.
- Sister Mary Therese Sweeney, CSJ, a historian of religious life in the 19th and 20th centuries, for providing critical resource material.

- The Communication and Development Departments of the Sisters of St. Joseph of Orange: Rob Cogswell, Stephanie Coats, April Hansen, Sister Ann Marie Steffen and Carol Hunold.
- CDR Thomas M. Duffy, USNR (ret) for providing relevant material from the U.S. Navy archives in Washington, D.C.
- The Nimitz Education and Research Center, National Museum of the Pacific War, Fredericksburg, Texas for permission to print the Captain Brockman letter; Robert Burrell Collection; 1990.519.001.
- Sister Martha Schwertner, CSJ, for artwork used in cover design.
- Mark Neal of BeyondMaps.org for converting our rough sketches into accurate and relevant maps.
- Nancy and Craig Smith of Dockside Sailing Press for their keen interest in this material, their encouragement and their generous donation of time and expertise.

Book Club Discussion Questions

Try to put yourself in the place of the sisters as they left California as new missionaries. What would your feelings be?

If you were in charge of selecting missionaries to go to the South Pacific, what qualities would you look for? What types of interview questions would you ask? How were these qualities expressed in the four sisters?

What aspects of life in the Solomon Islands seemed like paradise?

What were the surprises the sisters encountered when they first arrived in Buka?

In what way did the sisters' view of native culture change over time?

Even in the midst of adversity, Sister Hedda takes time to note the natural beauty of the islands. Which of her descriptions were the most vivid?

The missionaries chose to stay rather than taking the advice of the Australian government to be evacuated. What would your feelings be about choosing to stay?

At what point in the narrative did the sisters first realize the danger they were in? How do you think you would have responded?

What was the relationship between the members of the Marist congregation and the sisters?

How did the sisters' Catholic faith inspire and sustain them?

The four sisters were the newest missionaries on the islands.

How did their inexperience in "knowing the lay of the land" influence their decision-making?

There are frequent references to retreats and conferences. What was the purpose of these gatherings and how did they affect those who participated in them?

Describe some of the humorous parts in the journal.

Often, the journal reflects an optimistic view about a distressing situation. For example, while the sisters are a step ahead of the Japanese on Bougainville, Sister Hedda reflects on African missionaries, saying: "Those poor missionaries must have a hard time of it." How do you explain the sisters' ability to reframe their situation in a positive way throughout their ordeal?

How do you account for the decision that the sisters made to return to the Solomon Islands after the war?

If you had the chance to have dinner with the four sisters, what questions would you want to ask them? What do you think you would serve them?

Index

A

B

C

D

F

K

L

M

N

P

T

U

V

W

Y

Made in the USA
Charleston, SC
14 December 2016